*Learning to Be
an Individual*

Joseph L. DeVitis & Linda Irwin-DeVitis
GENERAL EDITORS

Vol. 41

PETER LANG
New York • Washington, D.C./Baltimore • Bern
Frankfurt am Main • Berlin • Brussels • Vienna • Oxford

Hyang Jin Jung

Learning to Be
an Individual

Emotion and Person in an
American Junior High School

PETER LANG
New York • Washington, D.C./Baltimore • Bern
Frankfurt am Main • Berlin • Brussels • Vienna • Oxford

Library of Congress Cataloging-in-Publication Data

Jung, Hyang Jin.
Learning to be an individual: emotion and person in an American
junior high school / Hyang Jin Jung.
p. cm. — (Adolescent cultures, school and society; vol. 41)
Includes bibliographical references and index.
1. Junior high school students—United States—Case studies.
2. Adolescent psychology—United States—Case studies.
3. Teenagers—United States—Social conditions—Case studies. I. Title.
LB1623.5.J86   373.1801'9—dc22   2006022872
ISBN 978-0-8204-8655-0
ISSN 1091-1464

Bibliographic information published by **Die Deutsche Bibliothek**.
Die Deutsche Bibliothek lists this publication in the "Deutsche
Nationalbibliografie"; detailed bibliographic data is available
on the Internet at http://dnb.ddb.de/.

Cover design by Joni Holst

The paper in this book meets the guidelines for permanence and durability
of the Committee on Production Guidelines for Book Longevity
of the Council of Library Resources.

Printed in the United States of America

For my teachers

CONTENTS

LIST OF TABLES

ACKNOWLEDGMENTS

This book has been made possible by support and gifts of many kinds across the Pacific. Above all, I thank the participants in my field research—teachers and other staff members, students, and parents at Lincoln Junior High School. Without their understanding and generosity, I could not have gained the insights into the American culture and educational process that I now have. Thanks to their support, my fieldwork could become a learning experience, deeply cultural and personal, simultaneously.

The P.E.O. International Scholarship Fund and the Department of Anthropology at the University of Minnesota partially funded the field research in 1998–2000, and the Spencer Foundation generously supported dissertation writing through its fellowship in 2000–2001. The Center for American Studies at Dongeui University assisted in revising the dissertation through a postdoctoral fellowship in 2002. The Faculty Development Grant from Seoul National University enabled me to return to the field site and revise and rewrite parts of the draft in the summer of 2004.

As this book is based on my dissertation, I wish to thank the members of the dissertation committee: Ayers Bagley, Kathleen Barlow, John Ingham, Marion Lundy-Dobbert, and Dick Nunneley. I was truly fortunate to have a committee working as a team in which each member had a keen interest in my work and exceptionally nurturing spirit. The committee members, individually and collectively, helped shape my interests in the intersection of culture, emotion, and education. In particular, my two advisors, Kathleen Barlow and Marion Lundy-Dobbert, made my graduate study deeply fulfilling. Marion Lundy-Dobbert directed my attention to the issues of cultural acquisition and transmission, which would form an area of long-term theoretical interest in my research. Her guidance in the field of anthropology and, above all, her friendship were priceless. Kathleen Barlow encouraged me to undertake this research project and guided my learning about American culture with patience and enthusiasm. She, together with John Ingham, spurred my interest in the anthropological study of emotion. She set an example of being a teacher as well. My experience as her student illuminated the fact that education, in its best sense, necessarily involves a whole person.

I thank my colleagues in the Department of Anthropology at Seoul National University for their support and encouragement: Moon-Woong Lee, Kwang-Ok Kim, Kyung-Soo Chun, Hahn-Sok Wang, Myung-Seok Oh, Ik-Joo Hwang, Jeong-Won Kang, and Sun-Young Pak. Some of them are my former teachers and guided me during the years of my first encounter with anthropology.

Both inside and outside of institutional boundaries, numerous individuals helped me complete this project. Bea Dehler took the job of transcribing the interview tapes. Elaine Dunbar, Dana Lundell, Cindy Rudolph, and Susan Schalge read and gave me their comments on parts of this book in its various stages. Mary Buckley and Howard Kranz read the whole manuscript and shared with me their own views about American culture and education. Among my students, Sudok Han helped preparing the index and some of the bibliography, and Junko Goya helped trace the dates of the quotes from the field data.

I am grateful to the series editors, Joseph Devitis and Linda Irwin-Devitis, for their interest in my work and helpful critiques. Christopher Myers and Sophie Appel at Peter Lang kindly assisted me throughout the publishing process, and Rohini Radhakrishnan meticulously copyedited the manuscript. Important final details were made possible with the help from Joseph Devitis and Christopher Myers.

Some of my friends are to be mentioned here. Dianne O'Donnell and Conrad DeFiebre offered a place to stay during my revisit to the field site in 2004, and enriched my knowledge of American culture by inviting me into their own social world. Becky Hanson, Michelle Sonyoung Lee, and Hyanghee Sunim are the friends who have made the field not just an academic research site but also a place of personal meaning. They gave me emotional shelter during the years away from home. Hyunmi Lee has witnessed the life history of this book project from its inception to the final form, with wit and warmth.

Finally, I thank my family. The love and support of my parents, Shi-Ho Jung and Yoon-Jo Kim, have sustained me through different phases of my professional career, while my brother and two sisters, their spouses, my niece, and two nephews have supplied ample tokens of their affection and humor. Deepest thanks to them.

I humbly offer this book to my spiritual teacher, Dharma Master Jae Woong Kim.

PROLOGUE

Mr. Gibson,* introducing the concept of a map in his geography class, picked up an apple and asked students what would happen if they were to flatten the surface of the apple onto a sheet of paper. Several students said that it would have to be torn to pieces. Mr. Gibson continued, "Yes. A representation is inevitably a distortion." At that moment, I felt despair. I instantly imagined the apple skin cut and flattened, fixed on a two-dimensional surface. I could not but think that what I was doing as an ethnographer was not unlike cutting and flattening down an apple skin. I had had a graduate course solely devoted to the issue of representation, but none of the scholarly discussions affected me as much as Mr. Gibson's apple. I was then sitting in the geography class as a "student." It was not only that being in the field greatly increased my sensibility to the question of representation, but also that assuming the role of a junior high school student and being a cultural learner together, I think, made me very receptive to the teacher's statement.

Mr. Gibson's apple has become a parable for me. I have come to accept that a representation is a distortion in some ways. I do not feel hopeless, nor do I pretend that the apple skin is intact. I admit that my apple skin will have cuts and wrinkles; that I still do not know where or how many cuts and wrinkles it has; and that I do not even present the whole skin. But I attempt to show the kind of tool I used to carve out the apple skin, and what wrinkles might have been caused by that. Many of my fieldnote quotations throughout this book point to the ways

---

*To ensure confidentiality, pseudonyms are used for all the names derived from the fieldwork data, including the ones of participants and the research site. Other identifying features are omitted or altered as well.

in which my understanding of an American school was shaped. In the quoted notes, I often ask myself questions regarding what I was observing in the school. Instead of editing and taming the notes, I let those quotations show that I was at times amused, puzzled, or embarrassed. I agree with Roger Sanjek (1990: 398) when he said, "Ethnographic research is an intensely personal experience for the fieldworker." The following pages will show how this was the case with me.

Many anthropologists with a psychodynamic perspective have pointed out that cultural conceptions of the self may not completely accord with subjectivities of the self (e.g., Bateson 1965; Levy 1984; Spiro 1993; Wellenkamp 1988). The emotional development and expression of the individual are directed by the culturally standardized system of organization of emotions, that is, the ethos of a society. The ethos encourages certain aspects of the personality of an individual by providing cultural categories with which to name and talk about the experiences of the self, while discouraging other aspects by providing minimal or no means to conceptualize them. The aspects of the self that are not, or only poorly, accounted for by the dominant cultural model are suppressed, but they also become sources of creativity, transcultural understanding, or adaptive capacity in the wake of social change (Hollan 2000; Levy 1984).

I feel that the aspect of myself that was marked as "different" by many of my peers in Korea has become a strong tool in my intra- and inter-cultural learning. As my "search" for the self grew more pressing during my college years in South Korea, I was increasingly viewed as "unique," which was not always a compliment. Being "different" could be taken as a sign that I was more concerned about my "self" than about social cohesion. For my part, I felt an acute sense of conflict between the needs of myself as an individual and the norms and expectations of family, friends, and ultimately, society. I seemed to demand more personal space than others and to act upon the notion that "everyone is different." I withdrew myself at any slight hint of social conformity. As my inner conflict was accentuated, I considered a graduate program in anthropology, which had fascinated me since childhood. It seemed that with anthropology I would be able to tackle the question that preoccupied me: to what extent am I Korean?

Through graduate study, I became familiar with theories about the relationship between culture and mind. No profound learning experience about "being Korean," however, came until I took a full-time teaching position as an English teacher at a public junior high school in Busan, a metropolitan city. Despite having grown up Korean, I experienced "culture shock," as a novice teacher in the school. My conviction about "individual difference" and "independence" was sharply challenged by many colleagues and senior educators. Although I attempted to apply my conviction in my teaching, I became more and more aware of cultural values that Korean educators nurtured in their students. I came to realize that it was not the case that individual difference was not recognized or that independence was not encouraged. Rather, independence was pursued through different ways, and other domains of humanity, such as commonality and sociality, were given more prominent cultural value. I perceived that Korean educators applied the same goals—academic and otherwise—to practically all students and encouraged students to view themselves in relation to others, more than just as "individuals."

During my five-and-a-half years of teaching, I was a learner as much as, or perhaps more than, a teacher. As I was expected to help students become "persons" in Korean society, I too was learning about Korean personhood. Most importantly, I learned that the Korean cultural belief in strong egalitarianism, in terms of ability and its outcomes ("everybody can make it"), played a large part in promoting common goals for all students. For common goals, coordination with peers was as important as direct instruction from the teacher, so that fostering good peer relationships was a critical educational task. My personal orientation toward individualism, I believe, rendered me more reflective about Korean schooling practices aimed at peer coordination and social development.

Upon coming to the United States for a doctoral program of study, I again experienced culture shock, this time in a much fuller sense. At the beginning of my stay, it seemed plainly apparent that I came from a different place, namely, Korea. Many times, I was startled to realize how Korean I was. What was especially baffling was American friendliness, which I sometimes confused with emotional closeness. In the meantime, however, I was rapidly socialized into American culture. Instances of culture shock notwithstanding, I perceived that the American cultural conception of the self provided ample means to account for the part of myself that I felt was suppressed by the dominant Korean cultural models. In a sense, I felt easier with the firmer boundary between the self and others conceived in the American cultural model of self, which emphasized self-discipline and independence. It appeared that some of my subjective experiences of the self more readily coincided with the normative model of the self in American individualism. This is not to say that I felt liberated by the discourses of individualism. I rather felt that I was betwixt and between. While I strove and thrived on the American notion of independence, the emotional distance it seemed to presume among people was, at times, difficult to bear.

When I began my field research at Lincoln Junior High in fall 1998, I had been in the United States for three years. The school scenes at Lincoln were not altogether unfamiliar. Korean and American schools shared many features after all, such as age grade and departmentalized subject teaching. And educators in both countries had many common concerns and challenges. Yet the American school was profoundly different from the Korean school, most importantly in its cultural curriculum of personhood. Needless to say, the two-year fieldwork at Lincoln intensified my learning of American culture. During the fieldwork, I naturally came to compare what I was observing at Lincoln with what I knew about the Korean school. One of the most salient differences was that in the American school, the dyadic relationship between the adult and student was given a primary importance, the underlying principle for myriads of educational practices at Lincoln. Compared with the Korean school, however, peer relationships among students themselves were fostered only minimally at an institutional level in the school and largely left to the personal sphere. Rather, many educators openly worried about peer pressure among junior high students, for it was conceived as antithetical to the development of individuality.

It seemed as if I was hearing from many Lincoln educators my own anxiety about social conformity when they expressed concerns about peer pressure. As I deeply valued individuality, I truly appreciated their effort to nurture it in their students. Sometimes I even fantasized, "What if I had received the kind of education Lincoln teachers designed for creativity development?" Again I felt in between. As a "student" at Lincoln, I did not like moving from room to room every hour. I missed being in my own classroom with the same classmates throughout the school day. Through observations of Lincoln students, I sensed that more organized and active involvement by the school in fostering students' peer relationships would benefit many students, especially those who were less social yet needed peer interactions as much. Further, I came to suspect that peer interaction may have strong positive emotional effects on cognitive tasks as well.

I started this prologue with Mr. Gibson's apple. I used the metaphor to point out that representation necessitates a point of view, which may produce some distortion. In my case, as in any ethnographic enterprise, my own subjective experience of the self was a major tool for elucidating cultural premises and highlighting educational practices based on them in an American school. The strength of this tool came from the fact that it did not exactly coincide with the cultural models of the self in either society I experienced—Korean or U.S. My worry now is that my portrayal of Americans in this book may not convey their subjectivities well, which may point to different conceptions of the self than they appeared to subscribe to. I make it clear, however, that this book treats mainly cultural conceptions of the self, not subjective experiences of it. The subjectivity of the self is a complex phenomenon that goes beyond the scope of the present inquiry.

· 1 ·
INTRODUCTION

This book looks into a social world of early adolescents—the junior high school—and attempts to understand how American educators socialize adolescents to become "persons." It is, essentially, a study of American personhood pursued by American educators for their adolescent students. It addresses a set of interrelated questions: How is adolescence conceptualized and how does the concept affect adolescent socialization in an American school? What are the American cultural ideas of person? How does individualism, a powerful ideology of U.S. society, inform the American cultural model of self, emotion, and person in relation to adolescent education? In what ways is learning to become a person also learning to become American? What are the features of the social world of an American school, where adults and adolescents are directly engaged in shaping American personhood?

In U.S. society, adolescence is typically viewed as a period of crisis, which bears promise or peril. Popular titles on adolescence, such as *Reviving Ophelia: Saving the Selves of Adolescent Girls*,[1] articulate the societal preoccupation with adolescence as a precarious time of passage. In research, much effort is directed toward adolescents at risk to understand the socially destructive potentials of this life stage. Adjustment problems related to alcohol and drug abuse, teenage pregnancy, juvenile delinquency, and violence have been focal points in studies of adolescence. Consequently, less attention is paid to what kinds of cultural forces are working in the developmental process of adolescence.

The disproportionate interest in negative "symptoms" of adolescence results, in large part, from a predominating view that emphasizes bio-psychological aspects of adolescent development, summed up as "storm and stress." Yet bio-psychological processes do not occur in a vacuum. Adolescents' lives are situated within specific social and cultural conditions that influence bio-psychological developments. This book focuses on the way adolescent development is affected by the broader cultural process of society at large, choosing the school as a key social context.

Emotion and Person

A major topic in this book is what it means to be a person in America, with particular reference to emotion. An important foundation of this topic is that emotions underlie much of our moral behavior. The moral capacities of humans are based on emotions such as sympathy, guilt, and pride (Evans 2001: 67). Being able to recognize one's own and others' emotions and properly respond to them is essential to a successful life, as a growing body of research on "emotional intelligence" suggests. According to Daniel Goleman (1997), emotional intelligence includes awareness of one's emotions, emotional control, the ability to motivate oneself, and being tuned to emotion in others. The concept of emotional intelligence recognizes the importance of the role of emotions in the social environment. It is at this juncture of emotion and human sociality that personhood involves emotion as a central issue.

Personhood focuses on the human being situated in the socially constructed field of interpersonal relations.[2] It is concerned with the problem of how individual and society are interconnected (Fortes 1973, cited in La Fontaine 1985: 125–126). Emotion plays a pivotal role in personhood, in that emotion conveys information about the relations of a person to his or her social world. Expressed emotion is not only a symptom of one's feeling state but a communication to social others (Levy 1984: 221–222). It is a statement to others about one's relationship to the physical and social environment. To be able to communicate through emotion is crucial to one's interpersonal relations and functioning as an adult member of society, that is, as a person. Thus an important parental goal is that children be integrated into a socially constituted emotional meaning system (Lutz 1983, 1988). Parents and other adults look to cultural models of emotion and person to guide children through the process of emotional development.

This book focuses on adult guidance in the emotional development of early adolescents in the United States. It explores the organizing role of the American cultural conception of emotion in the socialization of personhood. Major concerns are how American educators define, interpret, or conceptualize situations and feelings for adolescents in helping them mature emotionally and socially, that is, how they nurture "emotional intelligence" in their adolescent students, and what are the strengths and possible weaknesses in the American approach to emotional education in a public school.

Early Adolescence

This book attends to the period of early adolescence by looking into a junior high school. The pubescent years are quite different from the late teen years in tempo and tone of physical and physiological changes, witnessing the most observable and dramatic events of sexual maturation. In many traditional or small-scale societies, cultural learning of personhood was formally promoted and organized upon puberty, as pubertal events were considered a signal of a departure from childhood and entry into adulthood. The adults' attempt to prepare the young for the adult life was often epitomized by initiation rites. Educational experiences during this period, compared with pre-puberty, more directly concerned the idea of personhood endorsed by the society and were therefore more subject to the pressure of public opinion (Hart 1987: 369; see Bateson 1958; Herdt 1982; Schlegel 1973).

Puberty has formed an important topical area in classical anthropology, as this liminal stage betwixt and between childhood and adulthood not only reveals the cultural core of the community but also hints at the nature of cultural transmission in human society. However, it seems that when anthropologists study modern complex societies, they do not pay as much attention to this period. In many contemporary societies, puberty rites are given a minimal significance or do not exist altogether. Instead adolescence is much prolonged with the institution of schooling, with late teen years being thought of as "adolescence proper." One unfortunate consequence is that puberty has remained rather marginal in the literature on adolescence of the modern world.

Whether there is an initiation rite or not, puberty is the time when the transitional nature of adolescence is most acutely felt by all those concerned.

American parents and educators are quick to state that it is the "most difficult" time for both the young and adults. What makes this period difficult is, I argue, partly the very force of socialization adults exercise. That is, it is conceived as difficult because at this stage adults attempt to set the tone for the social and emotional development of adolescents, while adolescents themselves try to affirm their own autonomy. I posit that even when a unitary system of schooling is applied, the degree of socialization pressure markedly increases during the pubescent years. This book illustrates the fact that educational effort for personhood in this period is as remarkable as pubertal events themselves.

Why Emotion in School?

A study on affective education in school necessarily challenges a widely held view that narrowly defines schooling in terms of its function for the cognitive development of the student. In the common view, schooling is conceptualized in contrast to, rather than in relation to, informal education or socialization. The view can be traced to the fact that although education is a universal human phenomenon, formalization of the educational process has been very varied in degree. In the past, small, close-knit societies usually relied on informal means of education, utilizing extended family members. In more complex societies, often only a small segment of the population had access to specialized knowledge and formally organized educational institutions (e.g., schools in ancient Greece and traditional China). Modern schooling is unique in that it is not only one of the most formalized educational systems, but also virtually universal in its membership.

The contrast between schooling and socialization, however, tends to overstate the formality of schooling and isolate it from other educational processes. Despite its historical uniqueness, modern schooling still needs to be considered as part of the more inclusive educational endeavor of society. Problematically, the distinction based on the degree of formality has been confounded with the dichotomy of affect and cognition, rooted in the Western folk and academic discourses of emotionality and rationality as separate domains. The dichotomy rather exclusively associates schooling with cognition and socialization with affect (for critiques of the dichotomy, see Diamond 1971; Greenfield and Lave 1982; Strauss 1984). A serious shortcoming of the dichotomy is that affective aspects of formal education, as well as cognitive dimensions of informal learning, are neglected. The assumption that schooling has a positive influence on cognitive development is well accepted by the public and within academia. In contrast, the effect of schooling on emotional development is left little examined or understood, and the "informal" role of the school is rarely viewed in connection with socialization in a broader cultural context. It is an apparent irony that school, in which children spend many hours daily for many years, is not recognized for its role in socialization or affective education.

Schooling involves affect in an encompassing way. On a deeply psychological level, only emotion-laden symbolic processing of percepts brings some kind of integrated unity to the infinite number of pieces of the perceived world, as George Devereux argued (1979, cited in Levy 1984: 218). For cognitive learning to be effective, it draws on the affective capacity of the learner. Gregory Bateson (1976) similarly pointed out that learning is mediated by emotional patterns of the relationship the learner has with the environment, including other individuals. Many studies have shown that cognitive development largely depends on interpersonal relationships of which the learner is a constituting member (e.g., Doise and Mugny 1984; Hinde et al. 1985; Vygotsky 1962).

The school provides a social context in which the learner develops interpersonal relationships with adults and peers. In their daily interactions with students, educators guide students in learning the emotional meanings of various social situations. Further, schools have developed institutionalized means of affective education and have actively participated in emotional socialization. Supportive programs, such as advisory programs, guidance counseling, and school social work, have increasingly become regular features of public schools in the United States. Some professionals in schools are working specifically for "emotional and behavioral" issues. Aside from the establishment of support professions in school, administrators have long been doing the emotion work called "disciplining." Teachers constantly engage students in affective learning, directly and indirectly. For example, they carefully design their instructional activities to develop certain emotional characters in students. The dichotomy between schooling and socialization obscures more than it discloses about the educational process. Schooling is, at least, as much about affect as about cognition.

This book discusses how the school concerns itself with developing the person. It explores affective dimensions of schooling in terms of two different, yet related, features of it: affective aspects of pedagogical practices and affective education directly aimed at emotional socialization of the person. The intention is to investigate cultural assumptions and values underlying the institution of school, while at the same time looking at educational routines that are purposefully designed for affective education, such as "group counseling" and "disciplining." The two, affective aspects of schooling and affective education per se, are deeply interconnected in everyday school life.

Adolescent Emotionality

Perhaps the most enduring question in the study of adolescence is whether or not the supposed emotional turbulence is a universal feature of the period, a question that pertains to the Western folk dichotomy between biology and culture. Since G. Stanley Hall's conceptualization of adolescence as a time of storm and stress, theoretical writings about adolescence in psychology have typically identified adolescence as a period of emotional liability, pointing to "hormones" as its ultimate source. Hall (1916 [1904]) assumed that the age-specific features of the period are behavioral consequences of physiological drives, prioritizing biology in theorizing adolescent development. Incorporating Hall's idea into a psychodynamic perspective, Anna Freud (1946) characterized adolescence by an influx of libido caused by physical and sexual maturity and accompanying stimulation of the instinctual process, and thus by the culminating struggle between ego and id. In adolescence, "aggressive impulses are intensified to the point of complete unruliness, hunger becomes voracity and the naughtiness of the latency-period turns into the criminal behavior of adolescence," she wrote (p. 158; see also Blos 1962, 1967; Erikson 1993 [1950]).

Bio-psychological determinism has been sharply criticized, however. In her famous anthropological work on adolescence, Margaret Mead (1928) reported that Samoan girls did not experience adolescence as a turbulent time. By finding an explanation for the ease of growing up in the cultural context of Samoan society, Mead highlighted a culturally mediated dimension of adolescent development and provided an alternative view to biological universalism. The psychologist Daniel Offer and his colleagues, delving into adolescents' own views of themselves, suggested that adolescence is a relatively calm period for the vast majority of American teenagers (Offer and Offer 1975; Offer, Ostrov, and Howard 1981; Offer and Sabshin 1984). They further argued that many psychoanalytic theorists have overgeneralized the conflicts of disturbed adolescents seen in psychotherapy to the case of normal adolescents, and thus theorized adolescence on the basis of psychopathology. Recently, Janet Finn (2001) made a pointed critique of the turmoil theory, in its relation to human service intervention targeted at adolescents. In her analysis, a history of constructions of adolescence as pathology was located along a trajectory of twentieth-century capitalism in the United States. She asserted that the youth treatment industry, backed up by the turmoil theory, might not be preparing adolescents for healthy adulthood but rather for their place in a continuum of care, control, and containment.

These critiques notwithstanding, Hall's idea was enthusiastically accepted by the public at the time and has exerted a lasting influence on the popular conception of adolescence. A century after the original publication of Hall's book, the public discourse about adolescence still resonates with its main idea. It has provided a scientific rationale for numerous youth activities (Sommer 1978: 20; see also Kett 1977) and, increasingly, treatment programs for adolescents (Finn 2001). It seems, however, that Hall's thesis has enjoyed enormous popularity not because it provided a novel perspective, but rather because it reframed the existing folk model of adolescence into a scientific theory. The folk model of adolescence characterizes the period as one of the highest emotionality (see chapter 3). Hall gave the public a vindication of the folk model with his scholarly language.

The discussions in this book show that the very view of biological determinism on adolescent turbulence forms part of the cultural environment in which American adolescents grow up. Most interestingly, biological determinism itself, which implies that emotional instability during adolescence is inevitable, provides a powerful rationale for socialization efforts to instill emotional control in adolescents. In arguing this, it is important to take into account the influence of individualism on constructing the cultural model of adolescence and emotion in the United States. It will be seen that the American emphasis on the rational self renders adolescent emotionality markedly problematic, emotion becoming something to be managed, controlled, and disciplined.

Individualism, Middle Class, and the American Personhood

A central concern in this book is the influence of individualism on adolescent socialization of personhood in America. Originally a political and economic ideology grown out of the liberalism of the Enlightenment period, individualism has profoundly influenced the cultural conception of personhood in the West.

Marcel Mauss (1985 [1950]), in his seminal essay on the notion of person, viewed the idea of the individual as a cultural category of person, developed out of the social and historical contexts of Western society. Louis Dumont (1985, 1986), building on Mauss's work, further traced the historical development of individualism and emphasized that the idea of the individual constitutes the modern concept of person in the West. In American society, where individualism forms "habits of the heart," its influence has been felt most strongly.[3] As the "first language in which Americans tend to think about their lives" (Bellah et al. 1996: p. viii), the ideology provides a dominant cultural model of personhood in America. In this regard, "individual" becomes a quintessentially American category of person.

In terms of social class orientation, individualism has been most closely linked to middle-class status, for the middle class is distinctive in its alliance to the core American values derived from the ideology (Wolfe 1998). The middle class is "a group that seeks to embody in its own continuous progress and advancement the very meaning of the American project" (Bellah et al. 1996: 151). In the middle-class conception, the individual is unfettered by family or other group affiliations, and one is afforded equality of opportunity to make the best of oneself (ibid.: 148). Rationality is the basis for decision making and a major guide for behavior. David Schneider and Raymond Smith (1978: 107) observed that the middle class applies universal and rationalized rules in comprehending individual and social behavior, whereas the lower and upper classes tend to attribute more importance to a particular history of the relationships in which behavior is embedded. The stress on reason as the ultimate authority leads to special attention to impulse control or self-discipline in child rearing (ibid.: 49). An important task of middle-class socialization is to train the child to be an independent person capable of making rational choices. For middle-class parents, the child's future success in the occupational sphere (i.e., upward mobility) is strongly dependent upon his or her sense of competence and ability to exert rational control over impulses.

The middle class has led the American project, not only by aligning itself with the norms of individualism and living up to them, but also by having a hegemonic influence on the educational process, most notably in public schools. An important task of public education in the United States involves Americanization, a project that gains impetus from middle-class values (Cremin 1964: 66–75). The "hidden curriculum" of the public school is designed to develop the independent and self-reliant person, the model of person of the middle class. Child-rearing practices of the middle-class family are routinely adopted by educators in school. Partly this is so because most educators themselves are from a middle-class background. It is only natural for them to employ familiar practices in interacting with students. However, when there is a diverse body of students in terms of class, race, and ethnicity, the middle-class, mostly Euro-American, notion of personhood and the corresponding interaction pattern may put students with different backgrounds at a serious disadvantage. To use Bourdieu's term, they lack the kind of cultural capital that is closely linked to success in school and beyond (for cultural capital, see Bourdieu 1977; Bourdieu and Passeron 1977). This book carefully analyzes the workings of the middle-class hegemony in the public school, at the same time asking what it means to be an "individual" and how American educators socialize adolescent students to grow into American persons. An important part of the analysis consists of the social class, race, and ethnicity politics of emotion in school.[4]

The Research Site

When I took preliminary steps to decide on a field research site, I looked for an urban and public junior high school for two reasons. A major purpose of my study was to examine the American middle-class ideology, individualism, in the educational context. For that, a public school, rather than a parochial or other private school, was considered more appropriate, as public schools have historically been a major agent of Americanization for the middle-class norms in U.S. society. Regarding parochial schools, I feared that my research findings would be confounded by religious education. Non-parochial private schools of which the main clientele are middle-middle to upper-middle class, predominantly European American, might manifest the ideology of individualism even more strongly in many aspects of schooling. Yet I wanted to have a diversity of social class, race, and ethnicity in the student population, so that I could examine how the middle-class ideology would affect educational practices when heterogeneous and possibly conflicting values coexisted. My prior experience of urban, public junior high schools in South Korea, as a teacher and researcher, was another factor in choosing a public school in an urban setting. I thought that my cross-cultural perspective would be better utilized if at least some conditions of the Korean and American schools were similar.

Among several possible sites, Lincoln Junior High seemed best qualified for my research purposes. It was a public school located in a metropolitan area in Midwest America, the region "regarded as the most nearly representative of the national average."[5] Being an urban school, it had a diverse student body in terms of racial and ethnic composition (see the section on Demographic Features of the School in chapter 2). An important reason for my final decision was that it had more students from middle- to upper-middle-class backgrounds than other candidates. The school had a large number of students with the socioeconomic background to which individualism was most strongly attributed, while at the same time serving a diverse population. I expected that the school would have a strong ideological orientation toward middle-class values for the education of early adolescents. In fact, in the process of initial inquiry, I was told that Lincoln was a "traditional junior high." I did not then understand what the labeling exactly meant, but I suspected that being "traditional" was related to the school's ideological and cultural features.

The Fieldwork

The fieldwork at Lincoln was conducted over two academic years from 1998 to 2000, four months in the first year and eight months in the second. Participants were mainly the educators at the school. Forty-six out of fifty-three staff members of the school participated in overall aspects of the research to varying degrees, some of them becoming key informants. I participated in and observed many different aspects of everyday life in school, including classroom instruction, field trips, after-school activities, and parent–teacher conferences. For several classes, I assumed the role of a student for a certain period, ranging from four to eight weeks, and could experience what being a seventh or eighth grader might mean. Interviewing was used to elicit the educators' views on personhood and adolescent development, their philosophy of education, pedagogical approaches, and other cultural knowledge related to education. Students were extensively observed during their school day, in their interaction with the school personnel and among themselves. Later in the second year, some students and parents were recruited for interviews and became more active participants in my research. Twenty-six students and nine parents were interviewed.

From the very beginning of and throughout the fieldwork, I was an "adjunct staff" member of the school. I was given a staff name tag with my title as "researcher," a shared office, and a mail box in the main office. The administrators were very supportive of my research and helped me gain access to various inside meetings or any other situations of which they were in charge. They well understood that I needed their sponsorship, especially at the beginning stage. They consented to participate in my project themselves and provided official support for my research, at times explicitly but most of the time inconspicuously, throughout the research period. The rest of the staff members were very open and many of them invited me to their classes or offices early on in the research period.

In the beginning of the fieldwork, my attention was drawn to the "emotion work" performed by the support staff, administrators, and special education teachers, while I was familiarizing myself with different aspects of school life. I spent a good deal of time participating in the specialized domain of emotion work. I sat in on preventive or disciplinary meetings and meetings related to special education, and observed EBD (Emotional and Behavioral Disorder) program classes and adult–student interactions in affective contexts (e.g., disciplining).

As I was concentrating on activities in the "emotion domain" at the school, I came to realize that I had more or less taken for granted the dichotomous establishment in the school between "academics" and "behavior," which was ultimately rooted in the dualistic view of cognition and emotion, the very dualism I had wanted to challenge. This reflection led me to examine more carefully what the teachers did in or outside their classrooms. I wanted to look at the affective dimensions of the class and emotion work by teachers. An emerging research goal was to understand how the relationship between cognition and emotion was perceived by the educators, both teachers and other professionals. While I intensified my research about the emotion domain, I spent more time with regular classroom teachers. I became a "student" in more classes, volunteered more often for events organized by teachers, and talked with more teachers about their work. As I was working closely with teachers, I found myself identifying with teachers, perhaps more so than with other educators, largely because of my past experiences as a teacher. I deeply sympathized with their sense of accomplishment in teaching as well as strains from constant, often unrealistic if not impossible, demands put on their shoulders. Time spent in classroom settings brought insight into affective dimensions of everyday pedagogical practices as well as emotion work by teachers. During the last phase of the field research, I was increasingly interested in the cultural ideas of creativity and the educational practices for developing it. I found that the educators at the school saw creativity development as an important educational goal for the students, considering creativity critical to American personhood.

This process of researching the American school—from emotion work to creativity—was not just a chronological development of the fieldwork.

In itself, it was the process of my own learning about American personhood. As I learned, the American educators assumed that emotion work, to which training for self-discipline was central, was the groundwork for creativity development. The course of my cultural learning about the American "person" is reflected in the organization of this book.

A Study-Up

My field research was a study-up in terms of both the international political context, where the United States is a superpower, and the domestic race and ethnicity politics of American society. In the school, I was regarded primarily as a "researcher," which would usually convey a rather prestigious social status. But my being a foreigner, more specifically Korean, seemed marked and countered my prestige as researcher. South Korea was still little known to the American public, except for the Korean War, a civil war that involved major superpowers. Otherwise, I was a "person of color" or a "minority person," belonging to the racial category of "Asian/Pacific Islanders," according to the domestic classification of race and ethnicity.

As a Korean or "person of color" anthropologist working among predominantly Euro-American and middle-class professionals, I did not have the powerful backing of being associated with my country of origin, unlike a Western scholar researching in a non-Western society. Moreover, my status as a student, though doctoral, also seemed readily noticed. When my affiliation with a research university in the United States was recognized, it was usually to refer to me as a "student." That my field setting was a school and most participants were teachers or other professionals (i.e., power holders in the school), I think, made my being a "student" more noticeable than other field situations would have. Being a foreign, Asian, Korean, person of color, female student, I struggled to be considered a professional, while I certainly did not want to be regarded as someone who came from "up" to "study" them. I dressed carefully to possibly cover up my low status, but not to look too formal at the same time.

My status as a foreigner or person of color brought certain advantages to the research, however. I felt that my low status helped the staff members of the school to more willingly accept me as a cultural learner. Middle-aged participants, women in particular, let me follow them around or included me in their social interaction with ease. It seemed that their self-confidence as respected members of the school community allowed them to be less conscious of being "studied" by me, and to be more generous teaching me about their profession (they were there to teach, after all!). From my part, I felt easier being a "learner" with participants older than myself. That the staff of the school was predominantly middle-aged was an advantage in this respect. Most of my key participants were middle-aged senior members. With younger participants, it seemed that my researcher status stood more in the foreground, but it did not prevent me from having a few junior members on the school staff as key participants.

My "minority" status was also helpful in interactions with students of color and their parents. For example, when there was a disciplinary meeting about a minority student, I was often one of the few minority persons (sometimes the only one) in attendance, except the student and her/his parent. I could sit in those meetings if the parent and student would allow me to. When I was introduced, they usually allowed me to sit in. Because I was presented as a school person, like other staff members at the meeting, parents would most likely not disapprove of my attending the meeting. But I also think that my minority status at least made it easier for the teachers or administrators to ask parents on my behalf, as they openly worried about the racial imbalance of such meetings.

While I had multiple statuses that were not necessarily concordant with one another, I was regarded, above all, as a researcher by the members of the school. I felt that many staff members were conscious of being observed or "studied" by me. As I developed rapport with them, the tension eased away gradually, but not completely. The strain of implicit tension between me and the adult participants in the school was not simply the one generated by a researcher studying human subjects. Two other factors, in my view, further contributed to making my presence seem intrusive at times. One was that educators in public schools, teachers in particular, were already in a vulnerable position, with the too-often-heard criticisms of the public school in the media and press coverage of educational issues. Amid all the pressures for the "improvement" of public education, a researcher could easily be regarded as judgmental of their work. The other factor was the issue of confidentiality when information on individual students was involved. Teachers and other staff members were rightly concerned about confidentiality when discussing student cases in my presence. I not only explained the terms of confidentiality to each participant upon his or her agreeing to participate in my research, but also asked for permission each time the issue of confidentiality might arise. Many times I was allowed to be present, but sometimes not. There were a few occasions when I was most obviously viewed as a "researcher," thus as an "outsider."

Whereas I was trying to cover up my low status with adult participants, with students I tried to downplay the prestige of being an "adult." I generally avoided acting as one of the adults in the building, except when adult help was needed from me. Most of all, I did not quite know how to act "adult" to American students, especially when authoritative roles were expected. More importantly, I wanted to develop rapport with a possible pool of student participants through a more egalitarian relationship. Having an egalitarian relationship with students was, in fact, closer to the reality, in the sense that I was also a learner. I introduced myself to students as a researcher, but many students called me by my first name, as I asked them to (all the adults in the building were called by their last name following Mr. or Ms.). They treated me as a learner, if not as someone of their age, when I sat in their class and worked just as they did. Sometimes they were confused about me (I fondly recall a student asking me, "What grade are you in?"). Other times it was a little hard for me not to assume an adult authority, for instance, when my "classmates" did not trust my answer. I became acquainted well with some thirty students, most of whom were interviewed later. The student participants shared with me what it was like being an American adolescent, with great articulation and lucid self-reflection, characteristic of the liminal stage called adolescence.

The Organization of This Book

Chapter 2 introduces the school, Lincoln Junior High, its student population, staff, reputation, and neighborhood. It looks at the school as a community, as well as the socioeconomic dimensions of the school's recent history. The schedule of a typical school day is also provided. Chapter 3 lays out the cultural construction of early adolescence, on which further discussions of adolescent education of this book are based. It paves the way for the following chapters to examine how the American conception of this life stage intersects with the American idea of person and influences the socialization practices of personhood in a junior high school.

Chapters 4, 5, and 6 contain the main thesis of this book. Chapter 4 singles out self-discipline as a major theme in the socialization of personhood in the school, and a key aspect of self-discipline, emotional control, is further examined in chapter 5. Along with emotion management training, ability grouping and the practice of medication for "psychophysiological" symptoms (most notably the use of psycho-stimulants and antidepressants) are viewed in relation to the emphasis on emotional control. A significant portion of this chapter is devoted to the politics of emotion in terms of social class, race, and ethnicity, for which a case is presented in rich detail. Chapter 6 focuses on creativity, which the educators at Lincoln regarded as an affirmative sign of personhood embodying core American values, such as "choice," "self-motivation," and "intrinsic rewards." These chapters (4, 5, and 6) show that self-discipline was perceived as the basis on which to cultivate creativity, so that self-discipline and creativity formed one set of pedagogical goals for personhood. In chapter 7, I provide a cultural critique of American schooling by highlighting the most salient features of affective education observed at Lincoln Junior High. This final chapter is a match to the Prologue in further elaborating my cross-cultural perspective, which was more implicit in the Prologue. My critique touches on the issues of adolescent emotionality, peer group, and multicultural education in American schools.

· 2 ·

LINCOLN JUNIOR HIGH SCHOOL

"We are always a competitor," said Marjorie Olson, the long-time principal of Lincoln Junior High, capturing the confidence of the school and its expectation of itself. In the accounts of many educators and parents in the area, Lincoln was exceptionally "upbeat" and "positive" for an urban public school. The school was known for its rigorous curriculum and a high level of academic performance by the student body. It was one of the most desired public schools in the school district, especially by middle- to upper-middle-class families. Publicly the school had the reputation of being "the best junior high" in the city, and inwardly its staff members had a strong sense of community.

The City, School District, and Attendance Area

The school is in a city in the Midwest United States. The city is one of the five largest cities in the state, and part of a metropolitan area, including its suburban environs. The city witnessed renewed economic growth in the 1990s. The majority of the city population had been European American, but the city is becoming more and more diverse in its racial and ethnic composition. It had been a home to many African Americans, and in the late 1980s and early 1990s had an influx of Southeast Asian refugee immigrants. Its Hispanic population was growing and the newest immigrant groups include people from East Africa.

Lincoln Junior High belonged to the city school district, which consisted of fifty-two elementary schools, nine middle/junior high schools, seven high schools, and other special schools and learning sites. As part of the school district's voluntary desegregation efforts, secondary schools ran specialty programs that drew students from across the city, apart from their own attendance area. The admission policy of the district was that students who lived within a school's attendance area had first preference for acceptance into that school. Once accepted, students could choose to register for the specialty programs offered at the school. Under this rubric, Lincoln had two specialty programs, Gifted and Talented (GT) and Humanities, in addition to its comprehensive program called Regular.[1] Students were recommended or assigned to the specialty programs on the basis of their previous teacher's recommendation, their standardized test scores, and/or their own choice. With the specialty programs, Lincoln drew students both from its attendance area and from across the city. About half of the student population in Lincoln came from outside its attendance area.

Lincoln's attendance area included a neighborhood known as Hilltop Avenue. Hilltop Avenue, on which the school building stood, was noted in the city for many old mansion houses associated with "seven-figure" incomes. In the vicinity of Hilltop Avenue lived a large number of upper-middle-class and professional families. It was said that the area had the highest rate of private school attendance in the city. Yet within the attendance area there were many "poor sections" as well. When describing the attendance area, the principal Marjorie Olson said, "Some go to Europe for a ski vacation, and some can't afford a field trip."

The School Building and the Community Within

The school occupied a block between two streets, Hilltop Avenue and Glory Avenue. On the Hilltop Avenue side, the school faced a residential street of affluent homes, while on Glory Avenue, it was close to many small businesses, including bookstores and coffee shops frequented by students of a nearby college. The school site included a main building and its annex, together shaped like the letter L, a soccer field, a yard, and two parking lots. The exterior of the building, with its brownish red brick surface, angular shape, and thick windows, gave a sturdy and somewhat conservative look.

Originally founded in 1887, the school became a junior high school in 1927, with the construction of a new building, which has functioned as the main building of the school since then. Several additions have been constructed, and presently the main building has four stories, including a basement floor. The main building houses most classrooms and staff offices. The library, cafeteria-cum-auditorium, and two gyms are in the annex building.

The interior space of the building was functionally divided and individualized for specific purposes. There were many small offices used by teachers or the support staff. Not only were there special classrooms (e.g., art studio, music room, science labs), but practically every classroom was specified for a certain subject. Classrooms were separated from each other and hallways by permanent walls (they did not have windows on the hallway-side wall). Unlike many newer school buildings, the Lincoln building was composed of straight lines and did not have any undesignated extra spaces. The following fieldnote recorded my impression of the building:

> It feels "typical" with the straight hallways with lockers, classrooms filled with individual desks, lattice framed windows, and no open space. There are heavy doors on the hallways connecting to stairways or the annex wing. Overall there are many doors that can separate one space from the other completely. Virtually there is no space that can be left seen from outside. Every space can be closed down. It may be very functional, but certainly it is not postmodern. (Jan. 18, 2000)*

I once had occasion to visit an elementary school, Parkview Elementary, which was the other work place of Sarah Cooper, Lincoln's school nurse. The school building was only one year old, and I was surprised by its features in comparison to the Lincoln building. When I talked to Sarah Cooper about my comparison of the two buildings, she responded by making another comparison in favor of Lincoln. She contrasted the two schools in terms of social atmosphere, and relationship among the staff members in particular. Here is an excerpt from my fieldnote after the visit:

> The interior of the Parkview building was very spacious, brightly colored, and rather fashionably designed. It had a courtyard, and sun came through the ceiling of the central open area of the building. . . . I was being amazed by the building, and naturally came to realize how old-fashioned the Lincoln building was. No room for indoor plants, crowded hallways, old carpets, stuffy staff lounge, packed office, etc. Sarah and I agreed how poor various conditions of the Lincoln building were. Then interestingly, Sarah said nevertheless Lincoln was "more fun." "The staff are friendlier. They interact with

---

* The date at the end of each quotation from the fieldnote or interview transcript indicates the date when the incident, situation, or interview happened.

each other more. For instance, they have lots of parties. There's a sense of team at
Lincoln," said Sarah. It is so crowded that after a day at Lincoln, she feels "like getting
a headache and going nuts." But then she enjoys the intimacy that Lincoln has. At
Parkview, it feels there's a lot more distance between people, physically and psycho-
logically. . . . When Sarah told her colleagues and friends that she began working at
Lincoln, everyone said, "It's such a good school. You will like it." Sarah said, "Whether
it was 10 years ago or 2 years ago, they all said they had a great experience with
Lincoln." (May 26, 2000)

The sense of community among the Lincoln staff was almost always mentioned
when a remark on the school was made by a staff member. Even when I was
inquiring about the possibility of doing a field research project at Lincoln, the
retiring principal said, "These people stay together," comparing Lincoln with
other schools she had worked in. On the first day of my fieldwork, a teacher
said to me, "This is a good place to observe. People get along well here." Many
of the staff members who had worked in other schools before made similar
comments about the Lincoln staff being a "team." During the fieldwork I had
many opportunities to observe how Lincoln staff built and maintained a community. For example, through various social events, such as "choir practice"
(a nickname for the weekly Friday social), the Christmas party, and the end-
of-year river cruise, to name a few, the staff members fostered their sense of
belonging to the school community and developed their identity as professional
educators.

A high level of open communication among the Lincoln staff and their
professionalism as a whole were remarkable aspects of the school community.
During his class visit, when a student asked what he liked about Lincoln,
Tom Morris, then an administrative intern, pointed out that teachers "talked to
each other" at Lincoln. Susan Loring, a chemical health counselor, mentioned
that, compared with the staff of other schools she was working in, teachers and
administrators at Lincoln were very supportive of her work and willing to talk
to her about issues regarding students. Professionalism was especially notable
among teachers. The principal Bill Meyer, then newly appointed to the school,
said to guests from another school:

> I am impressed with the school. It is quite academic. Teachers are highly motivated.
> They put in a lot of extra time to prepare classes. (Oct. 9, 1998)

Teachers had high expectations of students, with heavy emphasis on academic achievement, and themselves worked hard to realize their expectations.
Their strong sense of community and professional identity as teachers at "the

best school in town" were important underlying forces that made the school "upbeat," "positive," or "fun."

Demographic Features of the School

In 1999–2000, there were fifty-three licensed staff, six paraprofessionals, five civil service personnel, and five food service personnel on the staff. Licensed staff consisted of three administrators, six support professionals, and forty-four teachers. In terms of race/ethnicity, the vast majority of the licensed staff were Euro-American (see table 2.1).

On the administrative staff, the school had a principal, an assistant principal, and an administrative intern. The administrative intern performed tasks expected of an assistant principal.[2] The support personnel included the school social worker, guidance counselors, chemical health counselor, nurse, and librarian. It was said that Lincoln had more senior teachers than other public schools and a very low turnover of staff. Most of the tenured teachers had been at Lincoln for more than ten years, several having taught at Lincoln for more than twenty years. The average number of years at Lincoln among teachers was approximately twelve.[3]

The student body, its enrollment numbering close to 800, was more diverse than the staff in its racial and ethnic background mix (see table 2.2).

Table 2.1. Racial/ethnic and gender composition of the licensed staff (in 1999–2000)

	Afro	Asian	Euro	Hispanic	Total	Percentage
Female	1	2	28	1	32	60.4
Male	0	1	20	0	21	39.6
Total	1	3	48	1	53	
Percentage	1.89	5.66	90.57	1.89		100

Table 2.2. Racial/ethnic composition of the student body (as of April 10, 2000)

	Afro	Asian	Euro	Hispanic	Native	Total
Number	181	183	365	36	7	772
Percentage	23.4	23.7	47.3	4.7	0.9	100

About half of the student population were Euro-American and the remaining half were minority students. Among the minority population, African and Asian American students were the two biggest groups, almost equal in size. Other minority groups included Native American and Hispanic students. In the school year 1999–2000, 11 percent of the student population were receiving ELL (English Language Learner) service, most of whom were Asian Americans from recent immigrant families from Southeast Asia. The same year, 46 percent were eligible for free or reduced-price lunch. The proportion of students eligible for the free or reduced-price lunch program, mostly minority students, was the most often used measure of the socioeconomic level of a student body. In comparison with other middle/junior high schools in the district, Lincoln had the lowest score in the number of students on the free or reduced-price lunch program, and the highest in the number of Euro-American students. This shows that Lincoln had fewer students from low-income families, and conversely more students from middle-class families, than other schools.

"The Best Junior High in Town"

Throughout and even before my fieldwork, I constantly encountered statements regarding the reputation of Lincoln Junior High, made by both Lincoln members and outsiders. At the beginning of a school year, adult members of the school, administrators in particular, repeatedly assured students that Lincoln was "the best junior high in town" and they were to continue to build on this reputation. At showcases, open houses, or other school meetings, parents were likewise assured and presented Lincoln's scores in standardized exams in comparison to scores of other public schools in the city, as a fine testimony of its being "the best." Indeed, in the years of my fieldwork, Lincoln performed better than any other public junior high/middle schools in the school district in the two standardized exams, the Metropolitan Achievement Test Seventh Edition (MAT7) and a statewide standards test. Along with "test scores," a high attendance rate and having few "gang"-related problems were other important measures of Lincoln's success. Gloria Simpson, a guidance counselor, remarked on the school as follows:

> This school is very different from other city schools. Kids are more mature and stay focused. And teachers are determined to maintain a high quality. (Oct. 26, 1999)

It seemed that the reputation of the school was well circulated among parents in the school district. Lincoln was enrolled to the maximum of the building's physical capacity (and beyond an optimal level in the estimation of many staff members), and still had a long waiting list of some 200 students. Once at a teacher–parent conference, a father, thinking that I was on the school staff, anxiously asked me about the probability of admission to Lincoln from outside the attendance area. A comment by a college professor in the area exemplified the public recognition of the school:

> Some friends of mine have kids in school. They consider Emerald for elementary, Lincoln for junior high, and Sheffield [for high] as the best choices among public schools. Otherwise, they'd send their kids to private schools. (May 7, 1999)

The reputation of Lincoln as "the best junior high" was, however, a rather dramatic accomplishment of the school since the mid-1980s. Lincoln was once considered a very poor school, making the national news as an example of bad urban schools in 1983. Regarded as "the worst" in the city, the school did not draw students from the wealthy neighborhood it was in. In an effort to improve the school, the district designated the school as a gifted and talented education specialty school, bringing in new teachers. The GT program started with nineteen students in 1983–1984 and built a reputation as an excellent learning opportunity over the years. As there was then no other public or private school in the city with a GT program for the middle/junior high level, academically advanced students slowly began to migrate to Lincoln from across the city, and families in the neighborhood started to send their children to the school.

The GT program flourished and Lincoln continued to rebuild itself. But from the mid-1990s, several factors affected Lincoln's recruitment of GT students. Above all, Lincoln now had to compete with other schools for GT students. The GT elementary school in the district extended its GT program to include the seventh and eighth grades, and several parochial schools created their own GT programs for junior high years. Subsequently, the size of the GT program at Lincoln began to decrease. This coincided with a citywide demographic change. The influx of Southeast Asian refugee immigrants brought about a rapid increase in the number of students with ELL and other academic needs to Lincoln and other public schools in the district.

During my fieldwork, especially in the second year, there was a growing concern about Lincoln "going downhill." In terms of test scores, Lincoln still scored best in the district and above the national average. But the district office, with a school improvement project, put Lincoln on its "watch list" for the school's decrease in the test scores in the past several years. Internally, there was a change in the administration, as in the summer of 1998, Marjorie Olson retired after ten years' strong leadership at Lincoln. And shockingly, in the fall of 1999, the school experienced a racial conflict between African and Asian American students that involved shooting. Although no one was hurt in the incident, it profoundly affected the school community. Lincoln had prided itself on being a safe school, at a time when public concerns about safety in urban schools were deepening. This incident brought for the staff members a stark realization that Lincoln could not be an exception. The shooting seemed to testify that the academic strength of the school and reputation largely based on it were giving way to behavioral issues. Many staff members were deeply concerned about the future of the school.

My fieldwork was conducted during what many considered was a time of transition for the school. Lincoln was by no means alone in facing numerous challenges on a daily basis among urban public schools in the contemporary United States. When I mentioned the worries about Lincoln's reputation being tainted, the assistant principal Gwen Lundy did not sympathize with what she referred to as "nostalgia." She plainly stated that the school should face the recent challenge from the demographic change of the student population:

> We now have more children with academic needs. A large population of students is in poverty and second language users. It requires different teaching, a different starting point. The product should be the same. (Nov. 16, 1999)

The emphasis on "academics" and concerns about "diversity" together rendered educational tasks very challenging. In the time of my field research, the rhetoric of academic excellence was strongly supported in Lincoln by a large number of middle-class families, while increasingly more students from minority and low-income families were attending the school. Academics per se is not my focus, but this book is concerned with, though indirectly, the "rhetoric" of academics as it imparts the hegemonic status of the middle class enacted in public education.

The Organization of a School Day

In both years of my fieldwork, a school day at Lincoln consisted of a homeroom, lunch, and six class periods from 8:10 am to 2:40 pm. The homeroom period, running for seven minutes, was mainly for checking attendance, making announcements, and other official matters. Each class was a fifty-five minute period, and in between classes, four minutes were allowed as a "passing time" for students to move to the next classroom. The fourth period was extended to combine lunch time, which for twenty-six minutes came either at the beginning, in the middle, or at the end of the fourth period, depending on one's schedule. In addition, breakfast and the open gym session started at 7:30 am as before-school programs, and after school there were routinely extracurricular activities, such as sports and band.

In the first year of my fieldwork, Lincoln had a regular six-period schedule, in which students had six classes a day, and the six classes repeated every school day. During that year, the district office demanded that middle/junior high schools accommodate eight classes in their schedule from the next year. A major force behind the demand were the state-implemented standards, for which more classes were deemed necessary. The district recommended the "Eight-Over-Two" schedule, where two sets of four classes would alternate in two days, each class period being eighty-five minutes. It was claimed that in addition to allowing eight choices of classes, it was simple to follow and allowed a calmer school day, by making moves between different classrooms less frequent. However, Lincoln teachers opposed it because the class periods were too long, and adopted a "Rotate Eight" schedule. With the Rotate Eight schedule, there were still six fifty-five-minute periods during a day, but students took eight classes. Each of the eight classes came three times within a four-day frame, which repeated as a time unit. The schedule of each day was different within the four days, as the three morning periods rotated a set of four classes and the three afternoon periods did the other set of four classes. With Rotate Eight, each school day was designated as Day 1, 2, 3, or 4.

While many other schools accepted the district-recommended schedule, Lincoln started its chosen schedule in 1999–2000. Students were given a class schedule organizer sheet as well as a sheet showing all the school days of the year numbered according to the schedule (as Days 1 to 4). Keeping track of class periods in this new schedule could be a daunting task, especially at the beginning, as it required more organizational skills from students as well as teachers than other kinds of class schedule. In my view, Lincoln teachers' adoption of a Rotate Eight schedule is an example that showed their expectation from students of "responsibility" and "independence" as important aspects of self-discipline (see chapter 4), a central American value that they tried to instill.

· 3 ·

THE ETHNOPSYCHOLOGY OF EARLY ADOLESCENCE

"The Brain on Vacation"

In the first month of my fieldwork, Philip Kasper, an English teacher, asked me:

> "Are junior highs hyper there too?" (I said yes, smiling.) "I'm glad to hear that. I thought kids overseas were more disciplined, and then if you look at American kids, they are wild." (Sept. 24, 1998)

I wondered why he would think "kids overseas" were more disciplined, when I was thinking otherwise, at least from my comparison between American and Korean junior high students in class. I was observing that American students overall remained quiet in class, continued working when the teacher was not present, or waited patiently to be called, with their hand raised. I rarely saw noisy and feverish competition for the teacher's approval or heard loud laughter among students. American students seemed to be disciplined to the point that classes generally looked very low-key.[1] During passing times and lunch, I could see that American students were "wild," but not more so than Korean students in similar situations. Yet I was asked several times, by different people, basically the same question Mr. Kasper asked.

As my fieldwork proceeded, I found that the educators in the school characterized early adolescence as an emotional period, drastically different from other life stages and different still from adolescence proper. When describing junior high students, educators used expressions such as "weird," "nuts," "crazy," "flaky," "goofy," "volatile," "unsettled," and "boisterous," whereas they viewed senior high students as more "settled," "responsible," and "under control." On the other hand, the emotionality of early adolescence was also part of "fun." Junior highs were "optimistic," "energetic," "honest and open," "enthusiastic," "kept you young," and liked to "relate to their teachers," compared with senior highs, who were "less energetic" and "more on their own." Junior highs were always "in flux and change." Because of their "emotional ups and downs," early adolescence was a difficult time for both the adolescents and educators.[2] Gloria Simpson, a guidance counselor, commented:

> This is a neat but hard age. It's hard to be and to do parenting. I don't want to be 13 or 14 again. There are some ages that you want to be again, but I never want to be this age again. (Dec. 1, 1999)

Susan Loring, who rotated among one senior high and two junior high schools as a chemical health counselor, pointed out that the emotionality of junior high students, coupled with the lack of proper curriculum, made her job challenging:

> Nobody likes to work in junior high. They are icky, hard, goofy, squally. It's hard. It's HARD. I don't dislike them. It's very hard. There's no curriculum for junior high. It's either for grade school or for senior high. Part of it is because personal developments vary so much. There are 7th grade kids who are like 18 and there are kids who are like 8. In a senior high, you can have a sane conversation. It gives me a little break. . . . It [working in junior high] is a personal challenge. (Oct. 20, 1998)

To me, the portrayal of early adolescents as being extremely emotional, both positively and negatively, was a novel one. My colleagues in South Korea did acknowledge that junior high students presented rewards and challenges particular to that age, but they did not relate them to the "emotionality" of that age in such a pointed manner as American teachers did. The principal features of adolescence were thought to be heightened sensitivity and self-reflection, which were attributed more to the senior high school years.[3] Further, Korean college students, finally free of the pressure of college entrance exams, seemed to act (and were granted to be) more emotional, in pursuit of various self-expressive activities in the personal realm and student activism in the political sphere. In fact, junior high students were perceived as childlike or immature rather than emotional, which made the junior high teacher's job easier in a sense. The teacher's authority was still very strong for junior high students.

At Lincoln, however, both teachers and other educational professionals consistently stressed that seventh and eighth graders were the most difficult grades to teach, although they were "fun" as well. One day, while listening to the assistant principal, Gwen Lundy, in her class visit to eighth graders, I came across a metaphor that allegedly "explained" why early adolescents were emotional and, therefore, why the junior high school educator's job was so challenging. It was because junior high students did not have a "brain," metaphorically speaking. In her words:

> People's perception of junior high students is about half true. They say junior high students can move their arms and legs, but their brain's on vacation. It may be true. Some maybe don't think. This is what really happened. (She tells an incident that was caused by a "fashion judge."[4]) The only thing I can think of is a vacation for the brain. No one can be so deliberately bad. (Sept. 11, 1998)

"The brain on vacation" metaphor was striking to me, albeit humorous. This metaphor of the brain suggests that early adolescents do not have a functioning brain, conceived exclusively as the organ of rationality, so that they are left only with emotions; consequently, their behaviors are irrational. Further, being emotional is not something that can be controlled in itself ("No one can be so deliberately bad"). In a conversation after the classroom visit, when I specifically asked about the metaphor, the assistant principal added, "You don't know why they are angry with us other than their brains are on vacation." It was remarkable that emotions, for example anger, were not considered to be a result of an assessment of a given situation. The assumption seemed to be that emotions are incomprehensible in rational terms, that they are produced by organic disturbance insulated from rationality, while the brain is "dead or at least on vacation."

Note that Gwen Lundy made it clear that she did not entirely subscribe to the popular view. Interestingly, the view that she believed was "about half true" was nevertheless openly communicated to students. At the beginning of the academic year especially, when adults in the school were most active in efforts to establish a proper school climate, students were frequently exposed to the popular view of their life stage. This would occur most often in assemblies or during class visits by administrators, who came to talk about school rules and conduct codes. It may be noted at this point that the emotionality of early adolescents highlighted by educators serves to exalt rationality. The metaphor of "no brain," moreover, attests to the folk dichotomy between emotionality and rationality, which, in turn, strongly associates early adolescence with emotionality. It associates the brain with rationality, severing it from emotions. This familiar and tenacious dualism is challenged by studies of emotion (e.g., Damasio 1994; Schachter and Singer 1962). Emotions are fundamentally involved in reasoning about social circumstances. However, the belief that emotions are not related to rational assessment of reality was so strong at Lincoln that it affected the socialization of personhood in the school in a profound way.

Early Adolescence as a "Stage"

Sara Harkness et al. (1992) discovered that in the American cultural model of human development, the notion of developmental stage is central. In their study of the American cultural model of parenting, they found that parents employ the idea of stage to organize the flow of daily events and behavior into a larger meaningful framework, presuming that a child goes through a series of distinctive stages as he or she matures. Likewise, educators and parents at Lincoln utilized the stage model to conceptualize early adolescence as a unique life phase. The model provided them with an apt framework for characterizing the period when the most observable and dramatic events of sexual maturation occur.

In the view of educators and parents, early adolescence as a life stage was associated with a remarkable emotional vulnerability, and the high emotionality was explained in psychophysiological terms ("hormones"). Their view was strikingly similar to that of G. Stanley Hall, who in 1904 characterized adolescence as a period of *Sturm und Drang*. For example, "They are just crazy," said Elaine Ferguson, a science teacher, when I asked her to describe the characteristics of early adolescence. She went on to compare early adolescence to pregnancy for the marked emotionality and bodily changes of the period:

> In junior high we are dealing with hormones. Their whole body is changing where a girl used to be flat chested. I have this one girl who sits in my class and it is so funny. She is really big busted and she just lays them right on the table. I think, lady, I hope you get over that soon. But she probably didn't have them 2 years ago, what do you do with these things? I think preadolescence and adolescence, the only possible comparison is pregnancy. When you become pregnant, your hormones go crazy, your body is changing, the way you feel about the world is changing, so adolescence and

pregnancy have a lot in common. (I: By that metaphor, you mean that adolescents do not have control over their body?) No, they really don't. Their hormones are coming in and they are doing things to these kids that have never been done before, and the kids have to learn how to control that. (Feb. 25, 2000)

Ms. Ferguson presumed high emotionality to be the nature of early adolescence and found its cause in the physiological process accompanying sexual maturation and physical growth. According to her, like pregnancy, the body changes and "hormones go crazy" during early adolescence, a process over which an adolescent has no more control than a pregnant woman has over her bodily processes.

G. Stanley Hall's conception of adolescence as a time of emotional turmoil has had a particular appeal to the public, and it has been followed by many other similar theories. The following statement by Susan Loring shows the very way in which an expert theory about early adolescence is transferred to the practitioner in the educational institution:[5]

> I went to a seminar for chemical dependency counselors, and the professor said junior high kids are in *developmental insanity*. It's a very difficult time in their life. (Oct. 9, 1998, emphasis added)

The notion of "developmental insanity," which provided Ms. Loring with a framework for understanding the junior high years, strongly resonates with the classical psychoanalytic view that "the upholding of a steady equilibrium during the adolescent process is in itself abnormal" (A. Freud 1958: 275). The assumption is that "insanity" or extreme emotionality is expected as part of the normal developmental process in adolescence, and early adolescence is particularly an abnormal period because of the dramatic pubertal changes. According to the psychoanalytic theory, psychic disequilibrium and its manifestations, such as rebellious behaviors, are almost obligatory during the period as a direct result of the ego being overwhelmed by an onslaught of hormones and the concomitant upsurge of sexual and aggressive drives (Blos 1962, 1967, 1979; A. Freud 1958, 1965; Rabichow and Sklansky 1980). The psychoanalytic conception of adolescence was amply found in the discourses of early adolescence in the school. For example, the assistant principal Gwen Lundy said:

> It's a period that has pretty dangerous experimentations with inappropriate behavior or with drugs or whatever. They are likely to try to stab off the feeling that I'm changing and things are out of control. (Apr. 13, 2000)

At another time she assured me that emotional outbursts are not only obligatory, but could also be desirable for healthy maturation:

> Sometimes they experiment a failing, to see what's going to happen. They try on a lot of attitudes, behaviors that are not accepted by family. It's relatively safe for them to rebel at this age. They are still in the family. If they don't pass, they may have to do it eventually, with more dangerous consequences. A 13-year-old can say I want to go to boy scouts camp and spend a week in the bush, but a 20-year-old wants to go to Alaska. If we solve the problem now, they can go and do everything. They may not have to go through it again in the long run. (Oct. 27, 1998)

The popularized psychoanalytic view was combined with the cultural model of stage, resulting in an interesting parallel between early adolescence and the age of two. Early adolescence was compared to the stage of "terrible two" for the child's sense of independence and accompanying defiance. The following quotes are from a teacher and a parent, respectively.

> I can compare them to 2-year-old babies, when they are first starting to have language and suddenly, I think, for the child, I am becoming real because I can communicate, you understand me. It is sort of entering into being a person and not just a baby and the helplessness. And I think that the adolescence is the other, more significant threshold where physically I am becoming more real. I am bigger, I am more adult and I know so much and I have to make some decisions and I am looking at the time when I am going to drive a car. But I am not quite there yet. I think that sometimes the defiance and the arrogance are real similar to the two. (Mar. 28, 2000)

> When they get about 12, it is 11, 12, 13, right in there. I call it the terrible 13s. It is like going through the terrible 2s all over again, but it is a different sort of tantrum that they have. . . . Well, a 2-year-old, if they decide that they are going to do something they are going to do it, regardless. I felt like Mike could move the refrigerator if he set his mind to do it. I mean he was that stubborn. And then in a minute they could be over it and be on to something else. (May 4, 2000)

By comparing the two "stages," they stressed that both two-year-old kids and early adolescents experience a developmental leap, most notably a linguistic and cognitive leap by the two-year-old and a physical and sexual leap by the early adolescent. These developmental leaps are characterized by the "desire to do it yourself" and "defiance." It is the sense of empowerment that both the toddler and the early adolescent share.

In short, in the American ethnopsychology, early adolescence is viewed as a very, perhaps the most, emotional life stage, brought on by hormonal effects of the pubertal body. It was claimed that the "emotionality" of this stage posed serious challenges for education. The difficulty was real, but not so much because American students were more difficult. There is reason to conclude, however, that the difficulty reported by the American educators came, in large part, from their emphasis on self-discipline and emotional control grounded in the cultural idea of the rational self, which made "emotionality" at once marked and problematic. In the subsequent chapters, I examine how the ethnopsychology of early adolescence intersects the American idea of person and influences the socialization practices of personhood in a junior high school.

· 4 ·

SELF-DISCIPLINE

"Freedom Is Constrained"

Throughout my fieldwork at Lincoln, I was much puzzled by the extensive behavior control over students, or more precisely, by the coexistence of high degrees of freedom allowed in some areas of behavior and strong constraints imposed in others. Initially, behavior control, routine supervision over the student body in particular, arrested my attention more than anything else in the school. Below is my journal entry after the first day of fieldwork.

> I am so tired and sick from today. I got a terrible headache by noon, and I wanted to get home. . . . It seems so bizarre that they do not have any actual break during the school day. I mean a recess period. Teachers have their empty periods, but students don't. The time between classes is four or five minutes, which is to travel to another classroom, and they have only twenty minutes for lunch. Even then, they have to stay in the cafeteria, supervised and having announcements from microphone, which seemed to speak all the time. If I were a student, I would get stomachache from such a lunch period. Crowdedness is totally understandable, partly because it is familiar to me. But I can't understand "how come" of having no recess, not even after lunch. How can they think students can study right after lunch? The schedule might be thought as "efficient" in terms of time allocation. But I can't think of a worse schedule in terms of "human" efficiency. The message I get from the schedule is: the school is a place

where you are expected only to study, nothing else. . . . [T]oday was the first day of the
entire year. It is natural to feel confused and nervous. However, if the school had had
a recess time, so that I could see teachers and students more relaxed during the time,
I would have felt a bit better than now. My anxiety also comes from watching administrators and paraprofessionals walking in the hallway with wireless radios. It looks to
me like their main concern is in controlling every single move of the students. Since
it is students who move around from room to room, there is literally a heavy traffic
going on the hallways [during] every in between; they need people to control and direct
the traffic; since there seem a lot more opportunities for a student to wander out of a
place, her/his moves need to be in careful control. The French teacher said [to her
homeroom students], "Here at Lincoln, you need a pass to go out of a classroom." The
idea of pass doesn't feel very sound to me. It might be necessary with this kind of traffic, but then I suspect it has a background belief about disciplining the young as well.
It seems to me that Americans control the behaviors Koreans do not, and vice versa.
The stereotype says that Americans enjoy more freedom, whereas East Asians are
discipline-lovers. It just seems to me that what Asians impose upon a group is imposed
upon an individual in the United States. . . . Well, the strongest impression of the first
school day is that they, students and teachers alike, don't seem to have much freedom.
(Sept. 8, 1998)

I was overwhelmingly noticing that from the moment they arrived at the
school, students were under constant adult supervision. Most surprisingly, students had no recess or break, not even after lunch, but only "passing times" of
four minutes to move to the next classroom. I wondered when students could
go to the bathroom, for the passing times seemed too short for even going to
another classroom, often on a different floor, amid the heavy traffic. Lunch time
of only twenty-six minutes, including the traveling time to and from the cafeteria, was squeezed in between classes. Even then, many students had to spend
considerable time waiting in line to buy a school lunch. I felt very uneasy that
lunch time was very short, and during that time students remained seated and
monitored in one place, with continuous directions announced over the micro-
phone by the adult monitors. (It was most difficult to adjust myself to the lunch
schedule during my fieldwork.) Because there was no recess, there was no time
that students could spend among themselves. They were either in class, traveling in the hallway for a short passing time, or in the cafeteria, and monitored
at all times. Moreover, they needed a "pass" to go anywhere other than where
they were supposed to be at the time, including the bathroom. When returning home, still under supervision, they walked out of the building and were
bused.

My astonishment derived in large part from my previous experiences in
Korean schools both as student and as teacher. In Korean junior high schools,

students stayed most of the time in a single classroom, which was visited by different teachers. Still, they had a ten-minute break every forty-five minutes, and fifty minutes for lunch, during which times they were not much supervised by adults. Lunch time served as a major recess, as after their meal students relaxed in their room or played in the playground. In contrast, the schedule at Lincoln, which allowed students no free time, seemed heavily regulatory and even inhumane. That play time was not set in the schedule was most troubling to me, as I could not even imagine a school without it. It seemed that American students were deprived of something dear and precious about school.

In addition to the contrast with the Korean school, the extensive supervision at Lincoln also contrasted on the one hand with a certain freedom explicitly enjoyed by students themselves and on the other with a public myth of "American freedom." It was apparent that students had a great deal of liberty in personal matters such as clothing and adornment. I could easily find girls with make-up, dyed hair, or jewelry. Many boys also dyed their hair or wore jewelry. Such liberty seemed overwhelming at times when I saw, for instance, a girl in a shirt with too deep a cut or a boy in too loose trousers. Nonetheless, I enjoyed American teenagers' confidence expressed in their tone of voice, facial expression, and body posture. The following journal entry shows the contrast that caught my attention. I was observing a student council meeting, and my attention was drawn to a particular student,

> [who] was taking notes of the meeting. Later I found she was one of the two presidents of the council. She talked assertively but calmly. She was wearing decorative rings on the fingers, including the thumb. Her finger nails were painted a little dark green. She was wearing a sleeveless top with two strings on the shoulder [string top]. Her freedom to wear a sleeveless top, rings, or cosmetics was contrasted with her reserved manner of talking and her note taking (a responsible job at the meeting). Such dress would be regarded as an expression of uninterestedness in study or other school-related works in Korean schools. (Sept. 18, 1998)

It seemed that this student embodied the two opposing elements at once in herself, freedom and constraints, the former by expressive adornment and the latter by taking responsibility for the meeting and her reserved way of addressing others. She spoke confidently but remained composed. As my fieldwork advanced, I would see the girl in many contexts where students from the GT program were more likely to actively participate. She was one of the students who went to the History Day national competition in Washington, D.C., when she was a seventh grader. By any standard measure, she was a very successful, indeed excellent, student. But I noticed her first partly for her "unscholarly" outward presentation of herself. I realized that not only in the school routine but also in the individual, elements of freedom and constraint were juxtaposed.

Equally remarkable was the fact that interpersonal interactions between students and adults were highly egalitarian. Students were not required to display a stylized bodily deference code toward teachers (e.g., bowing in Korean schools). Instead, it looked as if they were more or less taking an equal part with an adult in conversational contexts, although the hierarchy between students and adults in school existed intrinsically. Their verbal interaction with adults was not distinguishable in its informality from that between adults, including joking. Some students put their hand on the adult's shoulder to get attention or to express their intimacy. There were times when I wished that American students would show more respect for their teachers, but it was still very assuring of the value of such freedom to see a student able to openly oppose what a teacher had said. For example, one day in a social studies class, the teacher made a passing comment about World War I that if Germany had won the war Americans now might be speaking German. A boy then raised his hand and said in a clear and confident voice, "It doesn't make sense, because . . . ," which sounded rather impolite to me. The teacher replied in a plain tone, "Yes. That's a good point. (He points to the Atlantic on the map.) The water is a good barrier." It was not so much that the student was "challenging" the teacher as that he was taking a stance equal to the teacher's over an argument.

However, many marked instances of freedom did not prevent me from observing situations in which the hierarchy between the adult and the student was unmistakable and direct, and the student's attempt to take an equal stance would be regarded and consequently dealt with as a "challenge to authority." The following interaction between a boy and his teacher occurred in a seventh grade math class, where I was sitting in as a "student."

> For the first half of the class, we solved the homework again and did a quiz for the second half. When we were doing the homework problem, Peter was sent out. At first he got a warning from DA [Dawn Anderson]. While still working on the homework solving over the overhead, without looking at him, DA quietly said, "Peter. If I have to tell you once more, you have to leave the room." She continued solving the problems, but after a short while, she told Peter to leave the room: "Peter, you have to leave now. You can't stay focused." Peter said, "I don't have the worksheet." "You could raise your hand. Instead, you were just talking to Cindy." DA didn't spend much time talking to him. I wasn't having a worksheet for the assignment either and I got a little uneasy. I didn't dare to ask DA for a sheet, but I realized I should have. Peter didn't

seem to show resentment over being sent out. He half raised his hand, looking aside at DA, as if to read DA's face. I thought at first that Peter wasn't going out of the room, taking DA's saying as a second warning. As DA finished a problem, she handed out several hand-outs to him, saying "These are today's assignments." I think DA gave him worksheets for yesterday's assignment and today's. Upon receiving the hand-outs, Peter packed his bag and left. . . . I was again surprised at DA's sending a student out for not paying attention. I didn't even notice or hear him talking. I guess it was a very quiet and short talking. The tolerance level from DA's part seems to be very low, especially when she is demonstrating problem solving. (Oct. 27, 1999)

To me, Peter's misbehavior, not staying focused and talking to someone (quietly) was unlikely to be bad enough to send him out of the classroom. Dawn Anderson was a strict teacher, but not atypically so compared with other teachers. Rather, she was typical in that she showed great kindness and patience in helping ready students, but a very low level of tolerance to those who did not meet her expectation of inner discipline. As a "student," I felt warned by Anderson to stay focused as much as she wanted me to, by watching Peter being sent out for such distractions that were not so serious to me. The class proceeded and we had a quiz after the teacher's demonstration of homework problems.

For the quiz, we had to work by ourselves with "no talking." It was quiet and most students were working hard. Many either raised their hand or went to DA to ask about some questions. DA wouldn't give them the answers, but helped them to find textbook pages for glossaries or gave some further explanation of the problem. DA walked around to help individually or sat at her desk working on something. I got bored, but finished the quiz quickly and spent the rest of my time in observing other students. One girl looked puzzled and seemed to be having a hard time on the quiz. Another girl looked like she was enjoying the quiz very much. I didn't enjoy the quiz. More accurately, I didn't enjoy the low-key air of the class. I felt like I was being forced to be shut for good. The feeling of being controlled was quite strong in me. I may feel that way, because I never raise my hand to present my answers. Unless I do that, I usually don't have any chance to open my mouth, except for group work. But there are some students who are like me. Students who raise their hand are usually the ones who do so all the time. (Oct. 27, 1999)

By the time we took the quiz, I was keenly aware that I was unmotivated ("bored"), all the while feeling "controlled." It was not precisely because I could not talk during the quiz, but rather because my general feeling toward the class became accentuated during the quiz, by having seen Peter sent out, subsequently feeling myself warned, and the class afterward proceeding in such a reserved atmosphere that I had no chance to release my tension. There was nothing unusual about the particular hour in terms of the proceeding and atmosphere of the class. Sending a student out was not uncommon in Anderson's class, or in other classes. The teacher never seemed to cause fear in students and rarely showed her frustration overtly. But the pressures to be focused on a given task and to work independently were ever present, so that I was often anxious about sitting quietly all the time without an intermission. I missed, for instance, the communal laughter triggered by someone, be it a student or the teacher, during class, which was often experienced in Korean classrooms. I do not know whether other students shared my feeling of being controlled and to what extent they did, · if at all. My peculiar circumstances, I think, magnified my sense of constraints or pressure in the class. I was in fact an adult, that is, a social equal with the teacher, and I was usually perceived by myself as highly self-disciplined and self-motivated. I did not like to be told what to do by the teacher. Yet in this class, I was a "student" and indeed felt subject to the teacher's authority. It is notable that when Peter was told he could have asked for a worksheet, I became uneasy because I felt I was also, though indirectly, being told by the teacher what I should have done. At the same time, I was not interested in the subject taught and was not motivated to succeed in the class (my grade would not matter to me or anyone else). Uninterested as I was, I still needed to be at least an "average" student to remain in the class. Being just an average student, however, still cost me, in terms of feeling "bored" and "controlled." As I further observed and experienced many facets of daily school life, I found that the seeming contradiction of freedom and constraints ever interested me. I wrote:

> As I experience students' life more, I get to think more about freedom and constraints of school life at Lincoln. It feels like a fine sieve is being imposed on the young souls. Why is it a sieve? Because here constraints are all around. I mean there isn't any area of behavior left untouched by the sieve of constraints. Yet freedom is also all around. It is believed that the being has to be free. There isn't any area that one is completely free in/about, but at the same time there isn't any area that one is not free in/about. The point is: the freedom of the individual is taken for granted, but a fine sieve of constraints silently but firmly and always coexists with it, to the extent that the sieve is unnoticed by the very mind that creates it. (Sept. 17, 1999)

The image of a sieve, a fine net on a frame, was conjured up by close guidance and constant attention to behavioral details I observed. Metaphorically speaking, behaviors, and feelings to some extent, were sieved in or out. It seemed that the ethnopsychological blueprint of American personhood functioned as a "sieve," through which affective educational goals were enacted, as well as negotiated and contested. The goals to be accomplished through sieving involved many different levels and contents, but there was one general theme to which the multitude of behavioral goals could be condensed: self-discipline.

The contrast between constraints and freedom observed at Lincoln informed me about two of the most important aspects of American education, education for self-discipline and for creativity. The two were interrelated as one set of educational goals, both closely tied to the ethnopsychology of the self in the United States. In this chapter, I examine why self-discipline was such an important educational goal and how the educators in Lincoln Junior High attempted to develop self-discipline in their students. These questions necessarily pertain to the cultural model of personhood and child-rearing practices applied to the formal educational setting.

The Locus of Control: Inside

In the ethnopsychological frame of American individualism, the self is viewed as an independent, autonomous entity that comprises a unique configuration of internal attributes (e.g., traits, abilities, motives, and values), and an individual is thought to behave primarily as a consequence of these internal attributes (Markus and Kitayama 1991: 224). The nature of the self–non-self boundary is conceived as firm rather than fluid, and thus it is believed that there exists a psychological region intrinsic to the person (Geertz 1975; Heelas and Lock 1981; Lukes 1973; Sampson 1988; Shweder and Bourne 1984). As Edward Sampson (1988: 16) points out, the assumption of a firm self–non-self boundary has significant implications for the locus of control over a person's acts and feelings. When the self is construed as a separate entity, the agency of power and control is understood as personal rather than relational. Power and control are thought to reside within the firmly bounded self. In other words, the locus of power and control is presumably inside the self.

Needless to say, the agency exclusively belonging to and residing inside the self is a critical part of what defines personhood in American individualism. That is, mature persons "own" their acts and feelings and are governed "internally" rather than externally. Personal agency was a common theme that many educators at Lincoln elaborated upon in their views of personhood when I asked what kind of person they hoped their students would become. They stated, for example:

> I want them to be an independent, self-reliant person who takes responsibility for their own actions. (Donna Jensen, Apr. 14, 2000)

I hope that they become a person who is capable of thinking on their own, taking information and actually thinking it through on their own, and I think science is a good place to do that. (Elaine Ferguson, Feb. 25, 2000)

I want them to have a sense of justice, like a sense of what is right and wrong, from the inside, not the outside, not from rules imposed on them, but from their own sense. (Emily Robbins, June 6, 2000)

All three educators quoted above, and many others, attended to the issue of self, control, and individual agency, conceived in contrast to other people or external agency. To restate what they said, people should take responsibility for their actions, for they are their own; think things through on their own, instead of simply taking information; or have a sense of justice from inside, compared with having outside rules imposed on them. The self was put in the forefront as the source of power and locus of control in dealing with the external world. The boundary between the internal and external worlds was firm and explicit, and the vantage point was from the internal over to the external.

Internal Agency and the Hierarchy of Personhood

It is the issue of power and control that grounds the hierarchy of personhood in American individualism. Those who have their own agency and thus are "independent" of others (e.g., peers) are placed higher in the ethnopsychological rank of personhood, relative to those who are more "dependent" on others and controlled by external rules or agents. In reality, most individuals are dependent on some other people, and the degree of their dependence or independence is predicated on specific circumstances. Notwithstanding the complexity of the reality, in the folk theory of American personhood, internal agency is categorically superior to external agency. An interesting parallel is found in an analysis of the social hierarchy of Jane Austen's world by Richard Handler and Daniel Segal (1985). Handler and Segal point out that the concept of independence underlay organizing principles of macro-sociological hierarchies of class and interpersonal hierarchies of gender, generation, and birth order in early nineteenth-century England, as represented in the novels of Jane Austen. One who was "independent," that is, one who had the power to make "choices" and was not governed by the will of others, was fully a person in his/her own right, in contrast to those who must depend upon or defer to others (e.g., patrons, customers, parents). The male head of a family, owning landed wealth, epitomized independence and personhood among the gentry of early nineteenth-century English society.

While in Jane Austen's social world, the concept of independence was closely associated with the economic power to make choices, in the ethnopsychology of American individualism it is more linked with the internal power of the self to be independent of external influences. Those who are their own agents are truly "individuals" and thus fully persons. In the hierarchy of personhood defined in terms of self-agency, children are a prime example of low-ranked persons for their dependency upon adults. They have yet to develop "ownership" for their acts. At Lincoln, the issue of agency and control provided a pivotal concern for the socialization of personhood in early adolescence, particularly as the junior high school years were considered a departure from childhood, represented by the elementary school. The junior high school years were thought of as the beginning of a transitional time during which a child learns to become a "person," that is, an "independent" person. A teacher at Lincoln, Ms. Jensen, stated:

> They do want to be independent but they are not quite there yet, so I feel like I want to help them. And I think junior high is a breaking-out point, and I notice it in my dealings with parents, that I want them to understand that now is the time to let their children start accepting responsibility for their work, their actions. They break out of being totally dependent on their parents and family. They think of themselves as so grown up and they have this quest for independence, you know, I am grown up, when they are not really, but here is the time where they have the incentive to be grown up. . . . So this is like a big life raft in here and so let them face the little consequences, be independent in some ways and let go of them a little bit, so that it is gradual. (Apr. 14, 2000)

Ms. Jensen's concept of growing up centered around the notion of independence. In her view, the growing-up process from childhood to adulthood is a directional move from a point of dependence to a point of independence. Adults provide adolescents with a "big life raft," so that they can safely try out independence on their "quest" for it. Independence is an ultimate goal for everyone to reach, for "basically we are all on that road to responsibility," as she said during the same interview.

While educators encouraged adolescents to move away from their parents as a sign of their growing up, they were wary of their simultaneous move toward their peer group. The development of peer relations during adolescence was ·viewed separately from, rather than in relation to, the individuation process from parents. Typically, the peer group was conceived of as a source of conformity, and therefore as antithetical to self-agency and independence. Ms. Jensen listed peer conformity as characteristic of early adolescence and attributed it to "insecurity" about oneself:

> They are a bundle of insecurities, because they look around and everybody seems, I even remember it, everybody seems like they have everything the way it should be, the way it is on TV or the way you see it in magazines. They see themselves as always striving to measure up to that image that they have. (Apr. 14, 2000)

Ms. Jensen perceived that adolescents strove to conform to external standards embodied in their peers, because they had not fully developed self-agency and confidence in themselves. Another teacher, Ms. Ferguson, asserted that one of the most important things during the early adolescent years, therefore, was

> to figure out who they are. In junior high they have to come to terms with who they are and what they want *as opposed to what their peers think* they ought to have. (Feb. 25, 2000, emphasis added)

Ms. Ferguson sharply contrasted "what they want" with "what their peers think they ought to have" to underscore the importance of self-agency over peer influence.

The development of self during adolescence is, however, much influenced by peer interaction (Erikson 1993 [1950]: 263). The adolescent branching out in a broader social context concurs with the separation process from the parent–child dyad. Peer relationships provide adolescents with a sense of belonging and security, while they labor to grow independent of the world of family to which they have been tightly attached. Further, peer groups can function as a positive learning environment. Jake, a seventh-grade boy, talked of his peers:

> I go over to their houses, we have parties and it is pretty much the same. We call, I call and we talk for an hour about nothing. That is what teens do, talk about nothing for an hour, two hours. Tie up the phone line. . . . One is James I look up to, sort of. He is more athletic than me so I sort of look up to him for that. Then Albert, I, looking up to my friends, and Albert I look up to, because he is really good on the piano and so we do that. And Jody is someone I can talk to and Kevin, he has been really nice to me here at Lincoln and he is in eighth grade, he is cool. (May 11, 2000)

Jake was excelling in school, particularly in math (taking eighth-grade math, the most advanced course offered in Lincoln), and involved in many extracurricular activities, including the school play, math team, and website management. At any rate, he was one of the most successful students, and during interviews, I felt that he was very confident about himself. This was suggested by his posture, tone of voice, and how articulate he was about himself. It did not seem that his "looking up" to his friends was undermining his sense of agency and self-confidence. Rather Jake and his close friends seemed to motivate each other to do well, while they enjoyed relating to each other. It can be argued that Jake was an exceptional student with strong self-confidence, so that his relationship with peers was not one of "conformity." Conformity, in my view, does not have a clear-cut distinction from other kinds of peer influence, however, and it is only one aspect of peer relationship.

The deeply held ambivalence about peer groups comes largely from the cultural construction of personhood grounded in the conception of internal agency. It also expresses the ethnopsychological hierarchy of personhood in American individualism, in which an individual with internal power and control is ranked higher. The educators worried that adolescents tended to depend upon non-self-agency, personified by the peer group, when it was a critical time for them to learn to be self-reliant. In their view, the peer group represented a locus of power and control, not inside the self but outside. The perception was that the peer group negated educators' efforts to develop independence and self-reliance in adolescents. The peer group may contribute to this very goal, but the concern about self-agency generally overshadowed recognition of positive peer influence. In a sense, the reservation about the adolescent peer group is a telling sign of the accentuated socialization for self-reliance during adolescence.

Learning Style and Personhood

In Lincoln Junior High, the issue of self-agency was also applied to cognitive learning, which is viewed as the mission of schooling. The categorical superiority of internal agency was a criterion by which a learning style that relied on internal agency was placed higher than one relying on external agency. Another important and related criterion was whether, or to what extent, a learning style involved "emotion," learning being perceived as a "cognitive" process. It was conceived that the less "emotion" and more "rationality" were involved, the more learning occurred, and thus the better a learning style was. The folk hierarchy of learning styles, as constructed by these criteria, was closely related to the hierarchy of personhood in its underlying assumption. And the hierarchy of learning styles implicitly reflected the hierarchy of social classes, in that each learning style was attributed to a certain social class.

The assistant principal Gwen Lundy asserted that provided there were good nutrition and emotional support, anyone could rise to a high level of cognitive development, though some might take more time than others. But in reality, "To some children, the level of anxiety is so crippling that they can't rise up to pay any attention to what-so-ever," she said. She went on to claim that to those who grow up in adverse conditions, often because of poverty, their learning success tends to depend more on their relationship with the teacher or peers. In so arguing, she described two different learning styles, compared them, and related differences between the two to class differences in socialization within the family:

> Relational-oriented kids think, "The teachers don't like me, I am not gonna work." Idea-oriented kids are more independent of other people. Where they get angry, how to handle stresses are different. Introverted people would withdraw and read books. Extroverted people find other people. An intuitive person would seek internal understanding, and information comes from inside. In an extreme case, they may not be aware of the external world. Sensing persons feel. They always get information from the outer world. (She drew a table of four sets of ideal personality types presented by Myers-Briggs: Introverted–Extroverted, Intuitive–Sensing, Thinking–Feeling, Judging–Procrastinating [Perceiving].) There are sixteen possible types. Extroverted, sensing, feeling, and procrastinating are a more likely combination, from the socialization of poor/low-class families. Introverted, intuitive, thinking, judging persons may not be affected by how the teacher does as much as the person at the other extreme may. Extroverted, sensing, feeling, procrastinating persons need more hands-on activities because they have no stimulus, living in poverty. They learn from their friends but not by themselves, and may be affected much by who teaches and how one teaches. . . . As a group, they tend to do most learning through sense. They are tactile, not theoretical. (Feb. 7, 2000)

Gwen Lundy employed the Myers-Briggs Type Indicators (MBTI) to explain different learning styles, but interpreted the typology quite differently from its Jungian implication for universalism. Isabel Myers and Katharine Briggs developed the Type Indicators to identify the "inborn preferences" for use of perception and judgment, based on Carl Jung's psychological type theory (Myers and McCaulley 1985 [1962]: 18). In the manual of MBTI, Myers and McCaulley stated that "type differences can be expected to occur across a very broad range of life events" (ibid.: 223), and made no correlation between type distribu-tions and social class background. At the time of the interview, I was not familiar with MBTI. While listening to Gwen Lundy's description of them, I understood that they were about innate personality orientation, but soon became confused, as she explicitly related them to social backgrounds.

Gwen Lundy did not recall the fourth set of indicators correctly, but at least it is clear that she grouped Extroversion, Sensing, and Feeling together to refer to a "relational" learning style, and compared it with "idea-oriented" learning style, which was represented by Introversion, Intuition, and Thinking.[1] Her comparison of the two learning styles can be summarized as in table 4.1.

It is obvious that her dichotomous classification of learning styles was grounded on the issue of internal agency. According to Gwen Lundy, "idea-oriented" students are "independent" of what happens outside the self, so that they are not much affected by their relationship with teachers. They seek "internal understanding," and for them, "information comes from inside." They learn "by themselves" rather than from their peers, and are theoretical, not needing as many hands-on activities. In short, they have their own agency in learning. On the other hand, "relational" students are affected more readily by what happens out-side the self. It is more important for them to have a good relationship with teachers to be able to learn, and they tend to learn "from their friends but not by themselves." They get information "from the outer world" rather than from inside. They are "tactile" rather than theoretical. Therefore, they need more external stimuli, like hands-on activities. "Relational" students depend more on external agency than their own. Gwen Lundy did not explicitly prioritize one over the other, but hinted that it was desirable not to be easily affected by either the teacher or peers. Once again, the issue concerns the locus of power and control. The self is to exercise its own agency to be "independent" and "rational."

Gwen Lundy stated that students from poor/low-class families were more likely to be "relational" learners (extroverted, sensing, and feeling), largely because of their socialization process affected by "living in poverty." Conversely, it was implied that students with a middle-class background were

Table 4.1 Cultural conception of learning style

	"Idea-oriented" learning style	"Relational" learning style
Relationship with teacher	Independent of	Affected much by
Stress handling	Withdraw	Find other people
Source of information	Inside	Outer world
Effective method	[Abstraction]	Hands-on activities
Strength	Theoretical	Tactile
Preferred setting	By themselves	With friends
Family background	[Middle-class families]	Poor/low-class families

more likely "idea-oriented" (introverted, intuitive, and thinking). In her view, the personality-type indicators functioned roughly as social class indicators. What is remarkable is not so much that she confounded the type indicators with differential socialization along the ladder of social classes, as that in so doing she revealed the middle class emphasis on self-agency and rationality and the hegemonic status of the middle class in the construction of personhood. In her conception, it seems that preference for introversion and intuition was equated with having internal agency, whereas preference for extroversion and sensing was equated with seeking and relying on external sources of power and control. Preference for thinking was likened to a rational response to surroundings, and preference for feeling to an emotional response. The dichotomy between "idea-oriented" learning and "relational" learning is a subset of the dichotomy between cognition and emotion or rationality and emotionality. However, in these dichotomies the two poles are not given equal status: "idea-oriented" style and rationality are conceived as more advantageous than and superior to "relational" style and emotionality.

It was in terms of this contrast between "idea"-orientedness and "relation"-orientedness that differences in cognitive process between students in the GT program and students in other programs were articulated by the educators and expressed through differentiated curricular designs and pedagogical approaches in the school. For example, one of the differences in course requirements between the GT and two other academic programs (Humanities and Regular) was that a beginning-level joint course of Home Economics and Industrial Arts (alternating after nine weeks during a semester) was required for students in Humanities and Regular programs, but not for GT students, "Because GT kids are considered more academic, and this one is more hands-on," explained the Home Economics teacher.

Another example of curricular design differentiated according to the differences between "idea-oriented" and "relational" students involved the History Day events sponsored by the English Department. Because GT students were thought to be "theoretical," "independent," and "self-motivated," they were exclusively given opportunities to participate in the History Day events. All the four divisions of the events (research paper, poster, drama, and media) required a high level of academic endeavor over a long period of time (for more on the History Day events, see chapter 6). The yearly calendar of the GT English course in fact revolved around the History Day events, from school level, through city and state levels, to national competition. But students in either the Humanities or Regular programs were not solicited to participate in the events. When I asked why students in other programs were not doing a History Day project, Philip Kasper, an English teacher, said, "It is so self-directed, so it is hard to have them do it, when they are less motivated."

Math classes were illustrative of how the conceived difference in cognitive process was reflected in pedagogical approaches.[2] Dawn Anderson designed her low-ability classes to be more "cooperative," so that students routinely worked with their peers. When I was participating as a seventh grader in Math 7, one of her low-ability classes, I was assigned partners to keep for the semester. By comparison, I observed that her highest-level course, Geometry, was much different. In the class, students either interacted individually with the teacher during a demonstration session or worked alone on their problems. One day, according to my notes:

> I sat in both classes, which came one after the other, to see if there are any differences in teacher–students and students–students interactions. Math 7 had only about 1/3 of Euro students, whereas they were the majority in Geometry. . . . Apparently Geometry class students were more focused on the ongoing lesson (Dawn didn't have to say, like "Roger, write this down," which she did in Math 7 class). While Math 7 students were told to work on their problem with their partner during the last phase of the class, Geometry students worked individually throughout their class. I asked one boy if they have a partner for the math class, and the answer was no. When I asked about group work, Dawn said probably next year, Geometry students would work more in group, as the new textbook requires more cooperative learning. (Mar. 17, 2000)

Not only were students in low-ability classes given more opportunities for interacting with peers; they were also provided generally with more hands-on activities, compared with students in high-level classes. My comparison of the two math classes continued:

> I felt that problems in Math 7 were more concrete. A textbook problem described an island where wild ponies were living, and Dawn asked them to guess what might have happened. In Geometry class, she used various shapes of polyhedron, but the class felt much abstract. Both Dawn and the students heavily relied on formulas or theorems to solve problems. (Mar. 17, 2000)

Among the reasons why I felt the Geometry class was more abstract may have been the design of the textbook itself and content of the course. However, the class could have been more concrete, if students themselves had used poly-hedron shapes as well as watched their teacher's demonstration. While Dawn Anderson had boxes of small objects in her classroom, she didn't seem to use them as often for her higher-level classes. Although she was very innovative in utilizing manipulatives, she still reasoned that higher-ability students didn't need tangible objects to help their abstraction as often as lower-ability students. She said she became interested in manipulatives because "the students [in low level classes] could do a better job if they can use their hands and manipulate objects." But she said of high-ability students:

> They can see it once. They can see somebody else do it as opposed to even doing it themselves and they would understand it better. (June 12, 2000)

Whether or not there were two different learning styles influenced by family backgrounds, Gwen Lundy showed that the nature and process of learning were defined and conceived largely in terms of the middle-class conception of personhood as applied to education. According to the folk model of cognitive process, which was expressed through pedagogical approaches and curricular designs in the school, the stance of self toward non-self was crucial to how learning occurred. In the middle-class conception, the self is the exclusive agency of learning. The self as such may also need external stimuli, teachers, and peers, but it is ultimately the self that has the power and control to process external information, independent of outer influences and one's own emotions, to reach a higher level of cognitive development. The self as the locus of power and control was best exemplified and fostered by "idea-oriented" learning, compared with "relational" learning. It was not a coincidence that the majority of students in the GT program, who were thought to be "idea-oriented," were from Euro-American, middle- to upper-middle-class families, while students from poor/low-class families, who were thought to be less idea-oriented but more "relational," were likely to be in the Regular program. That emotional control, according to the middle-class norm, was regarded as a critical indication of the intellectual ability of the student shows the hegemonic influence of the Euro-American middle class on key aspects of schooling. Testifying to the point was the fact that ability grouping was strongly supported by the middle-class parents, despite great imbalance in terms of social class, race, and ethnicity.

Developing Self-Discipline: From External to Internal Discipline

As discussed earlier, in the ethnopsychology of individualism, internal agency is viewed as categorically superior to external agency and functions as a major criterion on the basis of which the hierarchy of personhood is constructed: the more someone has self-agency, the less he or she needs external agency and the more fully he or she is a person. The categorical superiority of internal agency was not simply a criterion to judge one's personhood. Still more significantly in the context of schooling, it actively mobilized educators by positing the development of self-agency as a major educational goal. To achieve the goal, the educators employed the ethno-theory of education that asserted that external agency could eventually lead to inner agency. That is, educators attempted to foster internal discipline by utilizing external means.

Self-discipline was an urgent educational goal, particularly because in the educators' view, early adolescents were in a sort of imbalance of self-agency. Early adolescents, the adults contended, had an emerging sense of power, but had yet to learn how to direct and control their own power. Their freedom had to be constrained, lest it lead to self-indulgence. The self being the ultimate agency, the balance between power and control was, most desirably, to be made by the self. Self-discipline constituted the core of American personhood that adolescents must learn.

How then did the educators develop self-discipline in early adolescents? Elaine Ferguson, a science teacher, argued that "external discipline" necessarily preceded "internal discipline" and the educator's task was to provide the young with external discipline:

> In my class I tend to be quite strict as far as behavior is concerned and I do that for two reasons. First, I believe that *students need to have external discipline before they can learn internal discipline.* Unless you know what a disciplined situation is like, how can you do that within yourself? And so, I set up that circumstance, so that it is orderly and I think that makes it a safe place for them too. If there is discipline and if it is orderly, it makes it safe and it gives them an opportunity to learn that you can do this and this out here. Maybe I can do it inside as well. (Feb. 25, 2000, emphasis added)

Two assumptions can be inferred from the above statement by Elaine Ferguson about self-discipline. First, self-discipline is learned. It is not intrinsically given. Second, it is learned through external discipline. An orderly environment models internal discipline. These are the reasons that students "need to have external discipline before they can learn internal discipline." Because self-discipline is not an innate trait, unlike "ability," but integral to personhood, it becomes an important educational goal. And because self-discipline is modeled on external discipline, the adult should design the external environment so that it generates the emotional effect of self-discipline for the learner. She claimed that students would learn what having internal discipline is like by experiencing an "orderly" environment in which they feel "safe." I will repeatedly refer back to what Elaine Ferguson said, for she captured the essence of the American ethnopedagogy for developing self-discipline.

Ferguson hinted at behaviorism in that she argued that a psychological state, self-discipline in this case, was conditioned through external behavioral training. Many other educators shared this behaviorist stance in their discourses about self-discipline and educational practices for cultivating inner discipline in their students. From the adult's perspective, self-discipline was not self-taught. Rather, the formation of self-discipline needed an orchestration of rules, careful supervision, rewards and sanctions, and ready intervention. The adult needed to "walk them through." As a pertinent aside, it may be noted here that this behaviorism, however, did not permeate all the practices regarding developing self-discipline. It curiously intermingled with the psychophysiological view, according to which psychological states were determined by physiological process and, by corollary, behavioral learning was of little use. The psychophysiological view was a dominant social discourse regarding the practice of medication for psychological symptoms such as ADHD and depression (see chapter 5). Here I examine several important aspects of the folk behaviorism applied in the development of self-discipline in early adolescents. My guiding question is: What did Lincoln educators actually do to create and maintain external discipline on which students would model their inner discipline?

Setting Up Boundaries

A major groundwork for creating an "orderly" environment was to set up rules and communicate the rules to students. Adults in the school often talked about "setting up boundaries," "defining boundaries," or some students being "unable to understand the boundaries." Usually adults set the rules, although on some occasions they might have a "discussion" with their students as to what rules to have in a given setting. Many teachers started the semester by "going over the rules" in their first class. Their course introduction sheets most likely included "Behavior" or "Rules of the Class." For example, "Guidelines and Expectations" for Math 7, co-prepared by Donna Jensen and Dawn Anderson, had a section for behavior, which read:

> Behavior—Regular attendance, readiness to work, and willingness to try are essential for student success. Classroom rules include:
>
> 1. Be on time—in your seat when the bell rings
> 2. Be prepared—with pencil and three ringed binder every day

3. Be respectful—to the classroom, the teacher, and your classmates

Detention will be assigned for misbehavior or missing work. The student will serve this before or after school the following day.

Students were asked to bring the bottom portion of this sheet back to the teacher with their and their parent's signatures. It is notable that the behavior guide included not only what was expected of students, but also possible disciplinary actions to be taken, should the expectations not be met. Rules posted on the wall were an inconspicuous but regular feature in classrooms, offices of support professionals, and even the ISD (In School Detention) room. The first of the following two examples is from the front blackboard in an LD (Learning Disorder) classroom. In the rule, "Ms. Davis" meant that for the second failure to follow directions, the student was to be sent to Ms. Davis, who was the EBD (Emotional and Behavioral Disorder) teacher and known to special education students for her strictness. The second example gives the group counseling rules posted in the office of the chemical health counselor, Tamara Farris:

1. Follow Directions: 1) One verbal warning 2) Ms. Davis
2. Show up on time! 3 tardies = Detention
3. Worry about YOURSELF

Confidentiality

Practice Respect

Listen to What Others Are Saying

Participate But Pass If You Need To

By making their rules explicit, adults clearly communicated to students where the behavioral "boundaries" were in a particular place. The boundaries set up by rules functioned as a basis for specifying reinforcements and consequences for certain behaviors. For example, Tamara Farris one day had a special activity in her Girls' Group session, when she felt one of her rules, "Listen to What Others Are Saying," had not been well observed. She had all the participants, including me, worked in pairs on an "interruption game," in which each of us, taking turns, had to constantly interrupt the other person while she was talking. We all experienced what it was like being interrupted and not listened to, in the midst of our laughter. Ms. Farris concluded the game by asking us what messages were being given to us when we were not heard.

With boundaries set, stepping out of the boundaries meant being far short of self-discipline and thus the necessity of more direct external disciplines, namely, "consequences." Valerie Hagel, a Home Economics teacher, asserted that keeping firm boundaries was essential for ensuring disciplined behavior in students. When I asked what she would do if students were disrespectful to other students or to her, she responded:

> I do not have a problem with them being disrespectful to me, because when they come in class the very first week I take a class period. I give them a sheet that has most of my classroom expectations written on. They have to carry that sheet home, parents sign it and bring it back to me for the point on the book. And I just talk to them. I tell them what will be and what will not be in this particular space. And there is an adage that the classroom is the student's classroom, you know. I beg to differ with that. When I give the classroom to the students, things begin to happen that I don't particularly care for in my space with me. So I do not tell them, I do not discuss whether or not the classroom is their classroom or whatever. I tell them these are the rules for this room. I don't care who the teacher is in here with them. The rules remain the same always, no matter what day of the week it is, no matter who the teacher is, no matter how they are feeling that day, etc. There are rules in place and they are not to break those rules. If they do, there are consequences. (Mar. 13, 2000)

She went on to tell me about a boy who had had such a "consequence."

> He was going to come in ruling me, ruling my room. It just so happened that day, the assistant principal was outside the door, ok, and after I said a couple of things to him and it was like, oh no, I am going to do this in here and I am going to do that and what have you. I walked out there and told her that there was a student that was not welcome in my classroom until he decided that he wanted to come in and be a student like all the other students. And I said to her I do not want him back in my room until he is ready. If he is never ready, will you please find another class for him? . . . He was out of my room for 3 weeks, and he and the hall monitor came back one day and the hall monitor was talking for him, telling me that he was going to do this and he was going to do that, etc., if I would let him back in my room. So I asked the monitor why was he talking for the student? I said, he is a big boy now, he can speak for himself and if he would like to talk to me and if he would like to say any of these things to me, I am willing to listen to him. So they left. The student came back the next day alone and apologized to me and asked me if he could come back into my class and we made a verbal contract. That student came back into this room and I never had another moment's problem from him. Not one. He ended up getting a "B+" out of the class. (Mar. 13, 2000)

Ms. Hagel told the student not to come back to the class "until he was ready." He was banned from coming to the class until he "decided [to be] a student like all the other students," during which time he stayed in the ISD room for the class period. Interestingly, Ms. Hagel phrased the situation in such a way that seemingly implied it was the student who was the decision maker who decided as to whether to come back to her class. All the while she was conveying her message otherwise; as she said in the same interview, "I let them know that they are the students, I am the adult and there is only place for one adult in my room." The student could "decide" whether or not he "wanted" to be in her class. He was viewed as having self-agency and asked to act upon it, while he was being punished by authority. The message was very clear: there were defined roles to respect and rules to follow, and these were not subject to negotiation. In a sense, the student was asked to exercise his self-agency to conform to the rules and stay within the set boundary. In other words, he was expected to gain a balance between power and control, that is, self-discipline.

In the above case, Ms. Hagel let three weeks pass without initiating any attempt to have the student return. And when the student first came back to her with a hall monitor, she demanded that he show willingness to be back in her class by speaking for himself, instead of having the hall monitor speak for him. For he was "a big boy now," not a child any more. It is not that learning to observe rules begins only at the onset of puberty. But during adolescence, the expectation of observing rules accompanies more rigorous training, and the ramifications of failure to meet expectations are more serious and far reaching. At Lincoln, following rules and staying within boundaries were viewed as imperatives that adolescents must acquire for adulthood. Diane Nash underscored the importance of learning "rules" during the adolescent period, using a metaphor of chess:

> I thought of chess as a kind of metaphor. They have to learn different strategies to get through life. If you think of an adolescent as like chess and maybe they would be like the pawns. Well, I don't know, the pawns are powerful in their own way but they really aren't. They can't do that much except kill diagonally. . . . If you are learning how to play versus having learned, adolescence is kind of the beginning and you might get killed a lot until you learn the rules. Because I know when I started playing, at the beginning when I didn't know how to play, someone had to say to me you do this, you do that. . . . Chess is kind of like life and they are the beginning stages. They are learning, what the queen does, what can the bishop do, he can move diagonally, this and that. (Feb. 24, 2000)

Diane Nash illuminated several important features of adolescence through this metaphor of chess. First, as in chess, rules are given and adolescents are expected to learn the rules. Novice chess players might "get killed a lot," and novices in adulthood might face many consequences until they learn the rules. Second, just as beginning chess players need guidance from someone who knows how to play, adolescents need adult guidance to learn strategies for adult life. Third, in terms of power, adolescents are more like pawns than the bishop or queen. They are on their way to reaching adulthood, and in the meantime they need to accept and play by the rules set by adults. From the adult's point of view, therefore, it was very important to make explicit what the rules were and to follow through to help novices behave according to the rules. The idea was that adolescents needed externally given discipline from which to foster their inner discipline, and it was the adult's task to provide such discipline and guidance for them. Donna Jensen, a math teacher, explained that such tasks were a crucial part of her role as a teacher:

> You spend a lot of time with some of these children if they are in your class all year and you care about them an awful lot and sometimes that means being firm and setting limits, and setting up rules, things like that. . . . There are certain things that they have to learn at this stage in their life and I have to set the limits. I have to say these are the rules, this is what we have to follow and then have consequences for those. There are certain things you have to teach them. And they have to follow the rules and standards and everything else in order for them to be learning, and for the setting to be conducive to learning. (Apr. 14, 2000)

Setting up boundaries was not all about "rules" per se. It also meant that adults should be role models by being disciplined persons themselves and a boundary within which students could stay safe. Emily Robbins, the school social worker, described her role in the emotional development of students at risk in these terms:[3]

> Of being a very steady person and being very predictable, because nothing around them is predictable and even if it is predictable, they don't know how they are going to feel. Kids say that to you actually. "Every day I wake up I don't know how I am going to feel today." So what they need from me is to be very predictable and very steady. So that is what I think I provide for them. That they can count on me being here at a certain time in the morning and me behaving a certain way with them. Me having particular rules with them and guidelines and boundaries with them, that they can count on that, I think, is my role. (June 6, 2000)

According to Emily Robbins, many students she worked with did not have well-established guidelines and rules at home, nor did they have role models for disciplined behavior. Her role, she articulated, was to set up boundaries, by herself being a model as a consistent and steady person who "they can count on," as well as providing them with specific rules to follow. Students would experience through the role model that being steady and predictable feels "safe," and they would want to cultivate these traits in themselves.

Rewards and Sanctions

Educators at Lincoln used rewards and sanctions frequently and regularly, particularly for those who were thought to be lacking self-agency. The use of rewards and sanctions in classrooms was a prime example of the middle-class child-rearing practice adopted into the school context. In middle-class homes, it is assumed that children, being "dependent" and lacking "self-agency," need incentives for staying within boundaries. Margaret Keith, the mother of an eighth-grade boy in the GT program at Lincoln, explained to me how she had used incentives to reinforce good behaviors when all three of her sons were young:

> When they were all in grade school together, they are very close in age, so yeah, we had rules set up and incentives. I forget how it worked, but we had this deal one summer. Summers can get really long. I think they got points against them for doing certain things. If they were involved in major fights or something like that, there were so many points, but if they had few enough points against them each week, then we would do some event, like we would go to Fun Fair or somewhere, so that there would be a positive reinforcement. And that worked pretty well. (May 4, 2000)

With the point system, certain behaviors were itemized, graded, and their consequences materialized into rewards. In the above statement, the three boys were supposedly induced to behave well, because good behavior would bring fun activities.

I rarely observed a GT class relying on incentives or rewards. Students in the GT program were mostly regarded as self-motivated and disciplined enough not to need reinforcement through immediate rewards. Maggie Ingold, a teacher in the GT program, commented once, "Some of the kids are so self-motivated for no one's sake." Being motivated "for no one's sake" was most desirable, for it would mean that the self was the agency of motivation, not needing external rewards. In contrast, ELL, EBD, and LD programs frequently used rewards and sanctions. It was generally thought that students in these programs were less mature (or less Americanized in the case of ELL) and needed more concrete and immediate rewards for their behavior, just as younger children would. Among various groups of students in the school, they occupied the bottom rung of the ladder of personhood hierarchy, for they were considered least "independent" socially and emotionally. Of these three programs, classes in the EBD program were most structured, centering around rewards and sanctions. As EBD students were thought to be on the bottom of the self-agency scale, they were individually monitored by an adult, and given directions constantly, and faced firmly enforced rules. The ground rule, "Stay within boundaries, and get rewarded, or get sanctioned," was made most explicit and direct, and applied most promptly in the EBD classroom. In other words, EBD students were most subject to external direction.

Ms. Davis, the EBD teacher, attempted to maintain a sense of structuredness in her routine class procedure by being formal and holding firmly onto her rules. For example, students could initiate an interaction with her only by raising their hand and waiting to be called on by her. When responding to the raised hand, she usually said, "Thank you for raising your hand, Mr./Ms. [last name]." Most of all, she had high expectations for her students' academic undertaking and kept track of their performances in both her class and mainstream classes. In her view, academic success would boost students' self-esteem and they would be less likely to "act out." She used a point system for rewards and sanctions to ensure their efforts, academic and otherwise. On the wall of the EBD classroom were posted rewards and sanctions:

MENU
Today's Special

Soda	100 points	Pencil	100
Candy Bar	75	Notebook	250
Chips	100	Out of Classroom	100
Pretzels	100		

The left column was for rewards and the right for sanctions. Students earned and accumulated their points by following directions and working on their task, and they could "buy" treats of their choice with their earned points. On the other hand, they would lose or owe points if they didn't bring a pencil or notebook with them and had to "buy" one from Ms. Davis, or if they were sent out of their regular classes to Ms. Davis's room. Ms. Davis frequently reminded her students of their current points, especially when there was either a decrease or increase in their overall points. The following is an observation note of an EBD class.

S. Davis's class:
Three boys, 1 Euro (Adam) and 2 Afro boys (Ben, Chris), were waiting outside on the hallway. . . . Soon Davis came. As soon as the three entered the room, Davis told each of them what to work on or where to sit. . . . Ben moved to an individualized desk, next to Chris (I wondered why he moved there. Maybe because he didn't want to face Davis and the desk with a side wall seemed to be a shelter from her controlling gaze).

Ben sat and put out his social studies textbook on the desk. But I could see that he was not doing his work, since he was sitting slightly sideways toward me, sort of blocking the right side space between the chair and the wall with his flank. During the hour, he never turned his face or body toward Davis while sitting at the desk. Soon after Ben moved to the desk, Davis got a visitor (I guess she was a special education person from the district office—she had a name tag of the school district). Davis and the visitor talked to each other in quiet voices. Davis asked me if I would stay with the students [while she would go out with the visitor to take care of something], and I said yes. She was out for about 7 minutes. Meantime, Adam and Ben enjoyed the liberty given by the absence of Davis. Adam went to Davis's desk and checked their points. He asked me to tell Davis that they were doing good so that they could earn points for pops. I told them to work on their assignment so that I could tell Ms. Davis favorably of their behavior. I went over to Ben. Ben was supposed to do his social studies assignment, but he was not doing it. Chris was writing something. I asked him what he was writing. He said it was a letter to Bill Meyer [the principal]. I asked if that was what Ms. Davis told him to do. He said no. I was back to my seat, and everybody else was on his seat. Davis came back with the visitor. Adam asked me about a question that he was trying to work on (he was doing Health). He read it to me. I didn't quite understand the question. I went over to his side, read it, and went through the book together with him. It was a short answer question, for which the answer was supposed to be somewhere in the chapter in exact words. As I tried some answers, Adam said they were not, because they didn't match the criteria put in the question. But I finally found the answer and Adam was glad to find it. He wrote it down. Then instead of returning to my seat directly, I went over to Ben (I simply assumed it was all right to go and help him). Ben was doing nothing about his social studies task. As I stood beside him and asked what was the assignment, he explained it. It was to read some sections and find answers to the questions at the end of each section. I was going to solve the problem together, like I did with Adam. Looked like he was interested in doing so. I asked him if he had read the section, and he said he'd read the section already. He grabbed his pencil to get ready to write answers down, but he found the pencil was broken. He went to the pencil sharpener, which was on the wall, right side of Davis. Then Davis looked at him and said in a stern voice, "Ben, you are using the visitor (me). You've been working on the chapter for 3 weeks, doing nothing. Now it's time for you to work by yourself. You are losing 50 points for that." I came back to my seat. Still at the pencil sharpener, Ben looked surprised and disappointed. "Am I gonna lose 50 points?" said he. He shambled back to his seat, uttering "Oh, my gosh." Sounded like he was very disappointed at losing his points. Afterwards, he didn't work, but made noise by tapping the desk with the pencil or knocking it with his hand. He looked very frustrated. I felt so sorry and uneasy for causing such a situation. I moved to an armchair by the door, because I felt I was being a distraction to the boys. . . . For the rest of the class hour [after an episode involving Chris's medication], Ben seemed to work a little and showed what he did to Davis at the end of the hour. Upon the bell for the lunch hour, as all of us were leaving, Davis told Ben to apologize to me for asking help. Ben looked resisting. He didn't say anything, but didn't apologize right away. I didn't know what to say. I just thought Davis was disciplining him and I shouldn't step in. After a pause, Ben said, "Sorry." I said, "OK." My voice was small and my words were quick, in embarrassment for Ben. I left the room and caught up Ben outside on the hallway. I said "Sorry" and he said "All right," but he still looked pretty offended.

I stopped by the office to find out about Chris's pills. But both the APs were not there. There I realized I had left my water bottle in Davis's room. . . . As I was getting my water bottle from the floor, Davis apologized to me for Ben's asking me help. Then I realized that Davis mistakenly thought Ben had asked me to help. I corrected that Ben didn't ask for help and that I voluntarily went to him and offered help, and I apologized to her for doing it. "Oh, he didn't ask you help," said Davis. I added I realized I was distracting them so that I moved to a corner chair. Davis just smiled. Later after lunch, I saw Ben again. I said now Davis knew that he didn't ask my help. I didn't know if Davis was going to give him his lost points back. But he did look relieved. He smiled in talking to another student, who was walking with him, but I don't know if he smiled just because of something with him or because of Davis's learning of his innocence in the case. (Dec. 13, 1999)

In the above class, two of three students (Adam and Ben) showed great concern about their points. In particular, the situation that I unknowingly caused for Ben was telling of the effect the reward system could have on the students. Ben's disappointment at losing points was so clear and vivid that I felt immensely sorry for him and embarrassed for causing such a situation. His disappointment was probably more acute because he did not exactly intend to be "using the visitor"; all the while he did intend to work on his task, which would have meant more points instead of losing them. After losing points, he did not work at all but appeared frustrated and distracted for quite a while. When he had to apologize to me at the end of the class, the resentment he had over the situation was again obvious. Not only had he lost his points, but now he was asked to apologize for something he didn't do.

Yet at the moment and until the end of the class, I was unaware of the reason for Ms. Davis's discipline. In fact, I had not exactly comprehended the situation, except that Ben lost his points because of me. When I returned to the room, I was surprised first that Ms. Davis assumed that Ben had asked me for help; second that "asking for help" had been an offense; and third that Ms. Davis herself apologized to me again for Ben's supposed wrongdoing. To me, "asking for help" could not be such a big offense. In fact, I had taken it as a sign of willingness to work on the given task. I do not know why Adam was allowed to receive help from me, while Ben was being sanctioned for the mistaken sign of asking for help. That Ben had spent three weeks on the task, "doing nothing," as Ms. Davis said, could be a reason. Or it could be that whereas Adam had tried to find the answers by himself but couldn't, Ben didn't even try to work by himself, in which case the goal of the sanction was to increase his self-directed action. In any case, this episode revealed several aspects of affective education. First, students were to learn to be "independent," that is, to develop self-agency, rather than "asking for help." Second, external discipline was used to foster inner discipline. In Ben's case, he was sanctioned for the supposed lack of "independence," by losing his points. Third, it may be plausible to assume that the use of points, a means of external discipline, had the intended emotional effect, at least to the extent that some students were much concerned about their points, which would motivate them to behave for more points, to a certain degree. That is, rewards and sanctions were considered to be a way to motivate students whose motivation was thought to be low otherwise.

Self-motivation was regarded as a crucial aspect of self-discipline, especially because in the context of schooling, motivation weighed strongly for academic achievement and school success. Teachers reasoned that if students were self- or intrinsically motivated, they chose to do a task, instead of being told to do it, and sought "intrinsic reward." If less self-motivated, they would need externally given rewards to get motivated. That is, when self-motivation was low, incentives as external motivator were needed, as shown in the case of the EBD class. But the use of incentives or rewards was to be limited and directed to lead eventually to intrinsic motivation. Diane Nash, an LD teacher, stated how she would try to cultivate self-motivation in her students by using incentives:

> Sometimes it is a tangible thing like candy that motivates them. Just to get them going. That is part of the fun. It just gets them to do what you want them to do. . . . How does that happen? Well I think, it is to hold up, kind of, something that makes them want to be more [motivated] and makes them want to learn. And then you are going to get a motivation. They want to know, they want to learn, they want to read well. Like I can sometimes hear them read and they say "I can do that, I can do that." They want that. So, that is already instilled in them, I think, just human nature. And then I think for that to be nurtured and fostered in the environment, *that becomes intrinsic*. They want to do it for themselves. They are not doing it for candy. They are not doing it for whatever. They have some idea in their head of what they want and they go after it. That to me is intrinsic motivation. . . . I don't believe in candy that much, but I find we use it at times when we really feel like zero: these kids are just dead and we just zap them up a little bit, we use candy so it isn't always. Because they have to learn to want to do it for themselves. (Feb. 24, 2000, emphasis added)

Ms. Nash argued that motivation externally induced by incentives could ultimately lead to intrinsic motivation. According to her, if students' motivation is fostered well enough by external means, it "becomes intrinsic." That is, once students are given an opportunity to feel what it is like to be motivated, they can motivate themselves internally.

Intervention

Repeated failure to follow rules and stay within boundaries resulted in intensive adult-directed emotion work, "intervention," usually involving special education teachers, support professionals, and administrators. "Intervention" referred to a variety of support work, including crisis intervention, but the term was generally used for the support work aimed at certain students who were identified as lagging considerably behind the age-appropriate social and emotional development. Intervention in this sense meant focused attention and more direct guidance from the adult. The "individual needs" of the student under discussion had to be assessed by a team of professionals, including the psychologist, social worker, guidance counselor, and special education teacher, and the needs would be best satisfied by "individual attention." A "step-by-step" approach via a "one-on-one" relationship was the main pedagogical means employed to enhance the social and emotional development of the student at risk. When this systematic and full-blown emotion work was enacted, the adult–student dyad was adamantly and faithfully practiced. It is notable that at-risk students most fully activated the ethnophilosophy of education based on conceiving of the individual as the ultimate goal of education and accordingly the ethnopedagogy featuring the adult–student dyad.[4]

I illustrate intervention work through the case of Peter. He was a seventh-grade boy in the Humanities, the intermediate ability level program. I came to know Peter through a math class I was visiting as a "student." My first encounter with him was rather amusing, as he posed a question of my identity.

> We had our lunch during the math class. When we were going out for lunch, a boy (Peter, African American) asked if I was a student teacher. I said, "No. I am a student." The boy nodded without hiding his suspicion. I laughed and his suspicion seemed to be reaffirmed. At the end of the class, as I was leaving, he looked at me again. I think he was curious about me. I better explain what I was doing and why I was in his class. (Sept. 17, 1999)

The above note was taken very early in the first semester. Ms. Anderson, our math teacher, was still busy helping us get organized and familiar with the routine procedure of her class. But the curiosity about me expressed by Peter and a few other students in the class prompted me to suggest to her that I use some class time to introduce myself and my research to fellow classmates, which I did.

As the school year proceeded, however, I found that Peter was often told to focus and at times sent out of the math class for his distractions. The math class observation note I quoted earlier shows Peter being sent out. Here is another example. The class barely started and Peter was the first to be told to concentrate.

> (DA pulls down the screen and turns on the transparency projector to show the home-work assignment list.) Anyone have an old assignment to turn in? (pause) Write down anything you missed to record on the green sheet on your 3-ring binder. (pause) Unclip your book and open page 58. This side come get a calculator if you need to borrow (right half rows go out to the front and get one). Now, please this side go get a calculator. (DA gives out rulers to the first students of each row to pass them back.) (pause) Any questions from homework assignment last night? (A student says, "Number 1." DA then solves the problem on a transparency. As she does it, she verbally explains the process.) (DA glances at Peter.) Peter, if you are not concen-trating, you leave. You have to focus on what you have in front of you. (DA opens her hands and holds them up and straight, perpendicularly with her body. DA con-tinues the problem and soon finishes it. Students write down or watch her solving the problem.) (Nov. 9, 1999)

During the particular class, I was not participating in the class as a student. I observed the class and took notes of teacher–student interactions at five- /ten-minute intervals. Early in the beginning phase of the class, Ms. Anderson attempted to direct Peter's attention by giving him a warning that she would send him out if he continued not to concentrate on the class task. She also showed with a clear body gesture that Peter should sit forward. Later in the mid-dle of the class, she once again said, "Peter, please [lean] your body forward and be quiet."

Lisa O'Conner, his English teacher, also remarked on Peter's distractions, but described him as "able to do the [Humanities level] work." Easily dis-tracted as he was, it didn't seem that he had serious behavior problems. But later, one day in February, I happened to see Peter having a very difficult day:

> I saw Peter going to lunch by himself. When I was finishing my lunch, I saw him again in the cafeteria. I was sitting at the end of the middle row, which was an all boys' table. But it wasn't occupied by a clique. It was a loosely mixed table of Afro and Euro boys. The next table got noisy with good laughter. As I looked at the table, Peter was standing and shouting at the rest of the boys, who were laughing hard. Peter looked very angry. He picked up an empty juice can and crushed it by hand, looking angrily at the crowd and uttering some incomprehensible words. The boys were giggling hard. I found Roy Hensel and directed him to the table. Tim Miller was coming to the table as well. As Roy and Tim went there, the boys calmed down a little bit, not

hiding their curiosity and mocking from their eyes. Peter picks up his tray, which was on top of another tray, and walks to the kitchen to put it on the trash stand. The manner he walks (stomps) tells he is still angry. He walks out with Tim. The boys' eyes chase him till he walks out of their sight, and they laugh again, some mimicking Peter's angry gesture. One of the boys came and sat in front of me. He is giggling in the same manner with the other boys, and I guessed right he came from the table. I asked him what had happened. He said somebody put broccoli in his barbecue sauce or something. According to the boy, Peter did some sort of thing first to another boy. (Feb. 7, 2000)

The administrative intern Tim Miller took Peter to his office and talked with him. Miller later said about the incident:

He would come with me and talk. But that just keeps him from having fights. He needs help. . . . He doesn't need provocation. He internalizes it and gets provoked easily if someone says like you dress funny. (Feb. 7, 2000)

According to Miller, Peter was easily provoked, because he presumably had internal reasons to be provoked. He only needed an insignificant cue to become angry and get into fights. I do not agree with Tim Miller that the cue was insignificant or that he was provoked because of his own internalized anger. Being laughed at and mocked by a crowd of his peers is not insignificant as a cause of anger, and Peter only crushed an empty can and showed his frustration through gestures. It was apparent that Peter had underdeveloped social skills, but I think his emotional display was not so much out of aggression as from frustration over being isolated.

The Rotate Eight schedule was very confusing to follow, and I myself had several occasions when I was mistaken about it. Right after the lunch room incident, I now found Peter out of his class schedule.

After lunch, I went to Ruth Edwards's class, which is in the basement. In the middle of the class, I heard someone talking aloud in the hallway. I recognized it was Peter's voice. I went out to see what was happening. Peter and two other boys were sitting on the floor near the ISD room, which is next to Dawn Anderson's classroom. Peter was talking loud probably to the boys, but I couldn't understand what he was saying and it didn't seem that the two boys were comprehending it either. I asked why they were sitting there. The two boys said that they were waiting for a hall monitor to have a quiet lunch in the ISD room. Now it is second lunch hour, and to Peter it's the fourth period class. Peter said he was waiting for Ms. Anderson. In Dawn's room, no one was there. As I was talking with Peter, Dawn came down to her room from her lunch. But Dawn said that she didn't have Peter during the hour but during the next period. Peter now realized that he was waiting for the wrong person and went upstairs. I guess after he was taken to the office by Tim and spent some time there, he was late for his class (I assume he had a pass). But he was confused about his schedule. (Feb. 7, 2000)

Yet it was not the end of his troubles on that day. My fieldnote continues:

After Ruth's class, I was going to finish class observation for the day, but I saw Peter coming to Dawn's class, this time round for a right period. So I went to the math class (Math 7) to see how Peter does in the class. Dawn always has a routine procedure. The first of it is to review homework assignments and their due dates via overhead. She stands at the projector and talks to the class about the assignment items. The class is not quite set yet. Students take their 3-ring binder out; write down assignments that they missed; open the textbook. In the meantime, I notice that Peter didn't follow any of Dawn's instructions. He looks back and asks, "Hello Mike, do you like cereal?" He asks the same question to a few others. No one responds to him, and Peter himself doesn't seem to be interested in getting a response. Some are giggling at him. Dawn already gave her attention to Peter twice. Once from where she stands, she called Peter's name and told him to keep focused. The other time, as she was passing by Peter, by lightly touching him, she corrected Peter's posture from facing aside to ahead, asking him to take out his textbook (Peter sits at the first seat of the first row from DA's desk). Now Dawn begins the day's lesson, which is a continuation of the last hour's lesson. She puts out an overhead and explains what to do in group for the assignment. Two rows become one group. As soon as the group activity starts, Peter walks around his group and picks a student out to say, "You do the overhead. I will do the talking." The student refuses to do so, and Peter then says the same thing to another boy. This boy responds to him more or less by saying, "Overhead?" Peter is not engaged in the group activity other than talking around. Now he goes to the other end row of the class and talks to some students there. Dawn calls him and says now he has to be sent out. (Dawn had already warned him that she can't give her personal attention to him one more time, when she was calling his name for the second time.) Peter comes back to his seat and packs his bag. Dawn gives him a note. As Peter was leaving the room, I followed him. I asked where he was going. He was being sent out to Ms. Davis's room. Then I asked why he was being sent out. He said he didn't know. There were two boys in Davis's room. Davis's first question to Peter was: "Which class are you kicked out of?" Davis said to Peter that he lost 100 points for getting sent out of a class. Then she said to me (I was still standing, not knowing where to sit), "Not today, Jin." I came out. (Feb. 7, 2000)

It seemed that Peter's being underdeveloped at social interaction had intensified over the course of the six months since he started junior high. Ms. Davis once commented, "He came in a happy child, but having different classes and moving around has been too much for him." She implied that the organization and pace of a school day at Lincoln, which was heavily geared toward academic achievement, had had adverse effects on Peter. With the routine structure of the school, it would be a daunting task for most students to form steady peer relationships. That task would be far more difficult for those less social, like Peter. Davis summarized Peter's problem as follows:

> He hungers for social interaction, but doesn't see things the way we do. He gets on other kids, and they don't like him. He gets "U-h-h, U-h-h" [utterances of frustration], bangs his bag down on the floor, gets into physical fights. (Jan. 28, 2000)

Dawn Anderson, his math teacher, also pointed out Peter's difficulty in relating to peers. My fieldnotes after talking to her read:

> She said she had done her best to accommodate Peter in her class. She put Peter with the nicest boys in the class, but the class had a lot more girls than boys, and when some of the girls were loud-talking girls, it was hard for Peter to get along well with them. One day, Peter said he liked a girl in the class, but the girl obviously refused him, not wanting to have anything to do with him. Peter started to cry, uttering E-h-h E-h-h (typical cry sound of a child) and beating his desk (or something) down with his hand (Dawn imitated Peter). He was showing signs of great frustration often seen in young children. He wouldn't stop, so that Dawn had to pull him out to the hallway and talk to him. (Jan. 28, 2000)

Initially Peter was one of the less seriously compromised students assigned to Ms. Davis, in terms of behavioral issues. He was not diagnosed with EBD, and although he had been suspected of having autism, he was not diagnosed for it. The only diagnosis he had was ADHD and he had come classified as an OHI (Other Health Impairment) student. At the beginning of the school year, he was assigned one resource class a day in Ms. Davis's room.

By early December, however, Peter became an active case for the Child Study Team.[5] One Friday morning at the Child Study Meeting, Peter's case was extensively discussed. The issue was that his social behavior was "seriously poor," causing trouble with other students in the cafeteria or the hallway. Both the psychologist and Ms. Davis agreed that Peter needed to spend more time in the EBD classroom. It was proposed that Peter now eat in Davis's room, because he had had "fights" in the cafeteria. From the discussion at the meeting and from my experience thus far with him, it didn't seem that Peter was aggressive toward others. According to Brenda Dixon, an assistant in the EBD program, most of his troubles started when other students teased him and he got angry. He was viewed as awkward by his peers and considerably isolated. Monday of the following week, I found that Peter had been taken out of all his mainstream classes, except music, to stay and work in Ms. Davis's room. Almost all of his school hours, including meal times (he had both breakfast and lunch at school), he was scheduled to spend with one adult, Ms. Davis. There were other students in the EBD program, but peer interaction was not encouraged in the classroom.[6]

One question that occupied me while at the Friday meeting, as I listened to suggested approaches to Peter's case, was how spending more time with the adult rather than peers would help him develop social skills in peer relationships that he presumably lacked. At one point during the meeting, Davis admitted that Peter's social relationships would be more limited that way, but asserted that in order to learn to behave appropriately, he needed "concrete plans to follow through" and had to be directed "step by step." In a brief interview after the meeting, Davis said:

> The bottom line is you can't go to the lunch room. You have to earn it back. You stop behavior. And we talk why behavior needs to be stopped. . . . He needs to walk through what to do. He has fights, near fights. He gets on others. Others stay away. They can't say "I don't want to talk to you." But they show it to him, then Peter gets angry. He will earn being with others again. One good day buys the next. He sees a social worker two days a week to talk about how to behave breakfast, lunch, and in the hallway. He fights constantly. (Dec. 10, 1999)

One day I saw him coming to the lunch room accompanied by his social worker.

> As I was going down to the cafeteria, I saw Peter and a social work intern coming together. The intern stood by Peter in line and waited till he got his lunch. Then she took him out again. After lunch I saw them returning to the cafeteria, for Peter to return the lunch tray. They were going upstairs. I guess they headed to Davis's room. (Jan. 25, 2000)

To Peter, peer relationships now became something to "earn back." Because he could not handle it well, he needed to be limited in his social life so that he could learn to behave appropriately. He needed to be walked through by adults, and thus more time had to be spent with adults. The adults, Ms. Davis and a social worker (an intern social worker assigned to him) specifically, were to "talk [to him] about how to behave." The contents of such talks were not known to me, but note that Davis said, "we talk why behavior needs to be stopped." It seems that the focus was on instilling self-discipline in Peter to keep himself from negative peer interactions, for example "fights," rather than on teaching him how to actually engage himself in positive peer interactions and to form steady peer relationships. Self-discipline being the educational goal, Ms. Davis would monitor Peter's behavior, using points to ensure rewards and sanctions, as she did with all other students in her program. With Peter, the main reward would be allowing more time with peers, and the main sanction assigning more time with adults.

I am not certain how many days exactly Peter had to spend all day in Ms. Davis's room, but the same week Peter was put back on his regular schedule. The monitoring of his behavior remained close, however. After he was back in his mainstream classes, Ms. Davis had him get an evaluation sheet signed by each of six teachers for each class period about his behavior during the class. Here is her memo to the mainstream teachers followed by the evaluation form:

> Peter Nelson is having a hard time generalizing behavior in Resource Room to mainstream classes. To help him focus on appropriate behavior I have designed a sheet for you to score at the end of class.
>
> No   Yes   Initial _____
> 1   2   3   4
>
> Just circle an appropriate number. Will add the numbers in R. Room for reward. <u>It is Peter's responsibility to give you the slip after class</u>. If he doesn't have it signed, no points. If it happens often—back to R. Room.
>
> Let's see if this works!
> Thanks, Samantha.
> -
> [Subject]   Initial _____   No   Yes
> Came in and sat down quietly   1   2   3   4
> Worked hard all hour   1   2   3   4
> Responded to teacher appropriately   1   2   3   4
> Ignored other students   1   2   3   4

Ms. Davis's memo shows the assumption that behaviors learned in the EBD class would generalize into regular settings. Based on this assumption, the EBD program functioned as a laboratory of behavior training, for which a very low teacher–student ratio was deemed necessary. And one of the most important things to learn from the laboratory was responsibility, as the underlined part of the memo shows. The student, in this case Peter, needed to learn to develop self-agency and he would be rewarded for it. He would be rewarded for his good behavior in his regular classes only if he took responsibility for getting the form graded and signed. Conversely, he would be sanctioned for not taking the responsibility, which would involve being put into the EBD program all day ("back to R. Room"). Again external rewards and sanctions were clear and used to foster inner discipline.

The evaluation form reveals what kinds of behavior specifically were expected. If Peter were to receive four points for all the four items, it would mean that he would have to be intensely focused on what the teacher did, without any peer interaction unrelated to class activity. Note that none of the four items actually were for evaluating his peer interaction. The fourth item, "Ignored other students," was to evaluate whether Peter remained focused, not distracted by or distracting other students during class. That is, the only item regarding peers was not to see whether he was engaged in positive peer interactions, but to see whether he restrained himself from negative peer interactions. Together with Ms. Davis's memo, the evaluation form shows that Peter was not being trained so much for peer relationships per se, as for the inner discipline of taking responsibility and staying focused.

The monitoring plan for the mainstream classes did not work well. Ms. Davis said Peter had brought the evaluation sheets back to her only for one day. Moreover, the overall approach proposed at the December meeting was not successful. Peter's interaction with peers did not seem to be improving, if not getting worse, and he was not responding positively to the one-on-one situation. In the meantime he was assessed for his "autistic tendencies" and was diagnosed with PDD (Pervasive Developmental Disorder). The school personnel involved in Peter's case had reached a consensus that he needed a more intensive service than the one Lincoln could offer, so that it was necessary for him to be placed in a program that could meet his needs. At the same time, Peter's continual difficulty in social adjustment was partly attributed to the fact that he had stopped taking medication (Ritalin) for his ADHD for the past seven or eight months, because his mother's current medical insurance carrier did not provide it. Ms. Davis said:

> He should be on medication. Ever since then [last summer when he stopped medication], he's been going downhill. (Jan. 27, 2000)

Subsequently, at the end of January there came a final move about Peter's case from the Child Study Team. The Team held an IEP (Individualized Education Program) meeting to consider a transfer for him, which included two special education professionals from the district office and Peter's mother.[7] I was not allowed to sit in on the meeting, but at the meeting a recommendation was made that Peter transfer to Johnson Junior High for its level 5 EBD program. Initially Peter's mother did not agree to the recommendation. The reason that the mother didn't want a transfer for Peter was not made clear, other than that she reportedly said that Peter liked Ms. Davis and Lincoln Junior High. The mother's disapproval of the recommendation seemed to come as a surprise to many. Tim Miller, the administrative intern, expressed his concern about Peter possibly affecting the school climate. He said that the whole student population should be considered and he would talk to the mother again. The social worker, Emily Robbins, was concerned that Peter was not getting "proper service" at Lincoln. In late February, the mother finally agreed to the recommendation, and Peter was transferred to Johnson Junior High to be placed in its level 5 EBD program.

The intervention work for Peter vividly shows the emphasis on the "individual" as the end goal of education and the adult–student dyad as the main pedagogical relationship. As Peter was identified as problematically lagging behind in his social and emotional maturity, he was directed into dyadic relationships with adults for more adult attention and behavior monitoring. However, observation of the intervention process raised doubts that the adult-directed effort for social development would be as effective as many educators at Lincoln appeared to believe. Peter's main problem was in routine social interaction with his peers, not with adults, yet he ended up spending more time with adults to improve his social behavior with peers. The school psychologist who had seen Peter since his elementary school years reportedly said:

> He has been taught and taught and taught, and he doesn't get it. He doesn't get it. (Jan. 28, 2000)

His "autistic tendencies" might have been a factor in the unsuccessful outcome of the adult effort. But I also posit that assumptions behind the effort were not working to the extent expected. The assumptions were that behaviors in peer relationships can be learned from an adult and that what is learned in an experimental setting can generalize into natural settings. The school social worker was in fact concerned that when Peter needed to develop social skills, keeping him with one adult was not appropriate. While the decision of transfer was still pending, she said:

> The question is, are we able to serve him? . . . He needs more attention, but we don't have staff to walk with him all day. Johnson [Junior High] has a PSD (Program for Social Development—a level 5 EBD program). He doesn't have social skills, social scripts that other kids have, to be engaged in natural interaction. He needs one-on-one coaching. He also needs social interaction. He needs both. He needs extra attention. He has not been successful here. (Feb. 3, 2000)

Emily Robbins, like many other educators, affirmed her belief in "one-on-one coaching," but she pointed out that Peter also needed social interaction with his peers to learn from. She suggested that the one-on-one approach could not be the only answer to Peter's problem. The various efforts made for Peter stemmed from the commitment to the one-on-one approach. It seemed that although adult help was much needed for Peter, the way it was given limited opportunities for his social development further. It can also be noted that many of his peers very likely knew Peter had been singled out as a problem case by adults, which could not have a positive influence on his peer relations.

The intervention work for Peter was one of many cases through which I came to reflect more specifically upon the ramifications of the emphasis on the adult–student dyad. I imagined Peter in a Korean school. Adult attention and monitoring for Peter would not be as intensely focused and goal-directed in the Korean school. But at the same time Peter would have far more opportunities for mingling with peers and thus learning social behaviors from them. Pondering "what if Peter were a student in Korea?" I came to contrast the American and Korean ethnopedagogy for social development:

> I speculate that if Peter were put in a Korean classroom, he would be less of a problem case, probably far less. Well, I am not too sure. If a problem is not named, does it mean that there is no problem? I know that there are students who exhibit problematic behaviors toward their peers as well as toward teachers in Korean schools as well. And in Korean classrooms too, there are students who get isolated or ostracized by their peers. What I can tell at this point is: If Peter were in a Korean school, still showing problematic behaviors, he would still remain among his peers, thus retaining opportunities of learning from his peers, but probably not having an opportunity of learning "step by step" under consistent and focused adult supervision. Another thing is that he would not feel as lonely in Korean schools, since he would have the same peers staying together throughout the day. I realize that to American students, the transition from elementary to junior high school may be more abrupt than it is to Korean students. (Dec. 10, 1999)

It seemed to me that having to spend many school hours with adults alone was too hard a behavior training for a seventh grader to accept and adapt to, setting aside the effectiveness of such training. Being deprived of peer interaction during lunch especially felt harsh, for lunch hour was the only time that was relatively less structured, allowing some substantial interaction with peers outside the classroom. Since I knew about Peter's case, I had been much concerned that Peter would feel very isolated and lonely.

How exactly Peter felt about being closely monitored by adults is uncertain, but some circumstantial evidence supports the interpretation that his emotional response was negative. For instance, one day when I was sitting in the main office, I heard Ms. Davis's voice calling Peter hurriedly and continuously in the hallway, and she sounded quite agitated. The hallway was crowded and noisy, for it was a passing time. Ms. Davis was almost shouting to stop Peter. I went out to see what was happening. Peter was walking fast, far ahead of Ms. Davis among the crowd, not stopping, and Ms. Davis was walking as fast to catch him. At another time, Ms. Davis herself said that when Peter was put in her room all day, he did not do his work there, but expressed his resentment through body language: for example, he banged his bag down on the floor or stomped angrily with his feet.

In the approach taken to Peter's case, both the possible pedagogical effects of and Peter's own emotional need for peer interaction were not well recognized. The importance of peer relationships was recognized only to the extent that Peter became a focus of adult attention because of his troubles in peer relations. However, Peter was not given a natural context in which to learn how to interact with peers. He was expected to learn it from adults. Yet the adult-directed training for his social development was focused on inner discipline rather than social skills to improve his peer interaction. As the intervention at Lincoln largely failed, many of his evaluators reasoned that Peter needed even more adult attention and thus a more intense program. This adherence to adult–student dyadic interaction, even for the development of peer relationships, is based on the notions of the individual and individuality as a key foundation of affective education in school. It was supposed that the adult-centered "one-on-one" approach was vital to the development of self-discipline, as the American idea of self-discipline was closely connected with internal agency and peers represented a form of external agency.

· 5 ·

EMOTIONAL CONTROL

We don't see the tears,
We don't see the feelings,
We don't see the fears,
And why don't we see.
Because it is all inside our masks.
We hold it all in, down beneath the mask.
The mask of hope and happiness.

ANON., "THE MASK," LINCOLN REALITY, JANUARY 1995[1]

A key aspect of the development of personhood concerns emotions per se. In any society, children learn to locate the boundary of the moral order in which the self is situated and to negotiate the social relations of the self in it (see Briggs 1970; H. Geertz 1961; Lutz 1988). How to display (or not to display) and communicate one's emotions is conceived fundamentally as a moral act and becomes an indispensable part of the content of affective education. I have so far discussed American personhood as grounded in the idea of internal agency, and illustrated that educators at Lincoln took internal agency as a major goal for the development of persons. Now I specifically look at the issue of emotion in relation to the American notion of personhood. What does internal agency mean regarding emotions?

In the American folk conception of emotion, particular concerns lie in negatively toned emotions, such as anger, anxiety, fear, and in their possibly adverse effects on social relations. Even positively toned emotions are guarded against in terms of the intensity of both emotional experiences and expressions (Stearns 1994). In general, emotionality is treated as a force alien to the rational self (Kovecses 2000; Lakoff 1987). In this conception, in which emotionality is thought of as antithetical to rationality, the question of internal agency directly concerns rational control over emotions or the "irrationality" of the self.

In the context of schooling, special attention was paid to negative emotions, lest they interfere with academic endeavor, which was considered a "cognitive" task. As discussed earlier regarding "learning styles," it was considered that the less emotions (not only negatively toned emotions, but positively toned emotions when too intense) were involved, the more effective learning would be. Consequently, it was not readily acknowledged that emotion is deeply involved in the learning process.[2] Emotion was seen more readily as a deterrent rather than a spur to educational performance. Nor was it well recognized that cognition mediates the process by which emotions signal messages to the individual about social circumstances. Cognitive appraisal is central to emotional experience in social settings, so that social circumstances are not only felt but also reasoned (Damasio 1994; Forgas 2000; Hochschild 1983; Lutz 1988; Rosaldo 1984; Scheper-Hughes and Lock 1987). However, in the folk conception, emotion was viewed in contrast to, rather than in connection with, cognition, and this conception of emotion undoubtedly influenced affective education at Lincoln.

In this chapter, I examine the hegemonic status of the middle-class emotional style in the school in defining personhood and setting emotional control as a developmental goal for adolescents. I discuss the characteristics of the middle-class emotional style, the relationship of ability grouping to emotional control, and emotion management training in the school. Later I highlight how the European middle-class notion of emotional control interacts with the issues of social class, race, and ethnicity. The last section touches upon the practice of medication, for which adolescents are a major target population in this society, in light of the cultural emphasis on emotional control. But first of all, I examine the folk model of emotion that seemed widely shared by educators at Lincoln, with regard to some recent developments in the study of emotion.

Emotion vs. Cognition

What undergirded much of the emotional education at Lincoln was a dualism of emotion and cognition and a folk evolutionism, in which emotion represents a lower phase in human evolution than cognition. According to the dualistic view, emotion and cognition are not connected, as emotion is a "reaction" that does not go through the "thinking" process. Yet, either of them can prevail over the other. The two faculties of mind are conceived as being in competition over the self. If emotion overrides cognition, one is "emotional" and "out of control"; if cognition wins over emotion, one is "rational" and "in control." However, the folk evolutionism gives a definite reason as to why cognition should take control of the self. Not only are emotionality and rationality coming from two disparate faculties, but more significantly they are not equal in the folk evolutionary scheme. Emotionality represents a "pre-rational" phase of both ontogenetic and phylogenetic human development, so that emotionality is lower, closer to childhood and animality, and rationality is higher, closer to adulthood and humanity.

An interesting amalgam of the dualism and evolutionism, which was particularly highlighted in the educational effort for emotional control, was the assumption that emotion could be overridden and controlled by the power of the cognitive faculty, however "uncontrollable" emotion itself might be. The notion that emotionality was inferior to rationality was grounds on which to justify "rational" control over emotion. Sam Powell, a visiting social worker who ran an anger management group for boys, articulated the folk evolutionism, along with the dualistic view of emotionality and rationality, as follows:

> I take a very biological approach to anger. There is a small walnut size part of your brain, right there in the back called the amygdala. When we were in ancient times, cave men, walking through the forest, the lion jumped out at us. We had two choices, we could run or we could fight. Those were the only two choices—fight or flight. The amygdala controls that. It is 300,000 times faster than the neocortex which controls rational thought. Now that was important back then, because you didn't have time to go "hmm, I can see by the paw size that this is approximately a three year old lion" but rather, you had to make a choice. Run or fight now. A lot of times people still get those moments where their body will just move and they don't even think about it. They just move. And that is the amygdala. *It has no connection with the higher thinking function and can move your body on its own.* It is just like an overdrive switch. (Mar. 17, 2000, emphasis added)

Sam Powell expounded a "biological view" of emotion and identified the amygdala as *the* organ of emotion, anger in this case. Produced from the amygdala, which has "no connection with the higher thinking function," emotion is a residue from the "cave man" stage of human evolution, however useful it once was. As an "overdrive switch," it is uncontrollable in itself. However, to control the uncontrollable is something that students should learn. He continued:

> What I let the kids know is that anger is ok. It is just your amygdala saying run or fight. In this culture, it tends to be an extreme emotion, it is quick. So what can you do to get the rational part of your brain, the neocortex, to catch up with the amygdala? . . . It is so much faster than how we think that by the time the neocortex catches up, we are already at anger. So if we can get the kids to realize that, to *slow themselves down enough to figure out* what is going on and then react to that. (Mar. 17,2000, emphasis added)

Supposedly, because emotion itself is uncontrollable, the only possible way to control it is through "the rational part of your brain." The difficulty is that getting to the rational part takes time, whereas emotion is an immediate response, taking almost no time. Therefore "slowing down" is an imperative for emotional control, and students are to learn to give their neocortex enough time to "catch up" with a certain emotion that has already occurred to them.

The above description of emotion is best applied to automatic emotional reactions in dangerous or otherwise emergency situations. In such situations, the potency of emotions is immense and the impulse to action is strongest, so that cognition is indeed overwhelmed by emotion. Yet emotion is a complex phenomenon, comprising a number of various kinds and different aspects. The latest studies on emotion in neuroscience show that the folk dualism of emotion and cognition do not hold true for the brain mechanism of emotion in important ways. Joseph LeDoux (1998), a leading figure in the field, worked out pathways of a basic emotion, fear, and identified the amygdala as the hub of emotional appraisal and reaction. According to him, there are two neural pathways of emotion: one is a direct road from the sensory thalamus to the amygdala, bypassing the cortex; the other is routed to the sensory cortex and then to the amygdala. The direct route to the amygdala is responsible for a quick emotional response in a possibly dangerous situation, much like Sam Powell explained in the quotation above. However, only a small portion of sensory messages take this direct circuit, while the majority take the main route through the cortex. It is the prefrontal cortex that ordinarily coordinates our emotional life, with the exception of emotional emergencies (see also Damasio 1994; Goleman 1997).

No doubt subcortically processed instantaneous reactions are part of our emotional reality, but human emotional life consists of far richer facets and finer tunings. Human beings experience emotions primarily in social contexts that require reasoning about the relationship between the social actor and his or her social environment. Some emotions that are called "higher cognitive emotions" are fundamentally social and involve much more cortical processing. Even basic emotions themselves, designed as an automatic response mechanism for the survival of an organism, can be co-opted for social functions[3] (Evans 2001: 28–29).

The folk model of emotion does accord with the theories of emotion that view emotion and cognition as separate faculties of mind (see Zajonc 1980, 1984). The problem is that the "biological view" of the model does not properly take account of the biology of human emotion. It fails to recognize as the very human quality of emotion the interconnection between the two faculties of mind or the interplay between the amygdala and neocortex. In the folk model, emotion is treated as a relic of the evolutionary past, similar to the appendix. Theorists of the evolution of emotion argue that the development of the neocortex allowed emotional dimensions of life unique to human beings (Goleman 1997: 11). Higher cognitive emotions were very likely designed by natural selection to cope with a complex social environment (Evans 2001: 30). The folk model falls short of the fact that many emotions are socially constituted and even basic emotions very often operate upon social cues.

These misunderstandings of the biology of human emotion had a serious consequence in the education of adolescents in the American school. By taking a very negative view of emotion, educators seemed to overlook positive potentials of the mental faculty, instead focusing on the control and management of it. A current conception of emotional intelligence seeks a balance between emotionality and rationality (see Goleman 1997). But the negative view of the folk model resulted in a tendency to the global control of emotion. Furthermore, by paying exclusive attention to the individual organism, not taking the social field as a larger part of the picture, the folk view construes emotion as personal property. Emotion is regarded as something inside the individual, under the skin, belonging to her/him exclusively, rather than as a socially constituted process that involves information about the relations of a person to her/his social world (see Levy 1984; Lutz 1988; Solomon 1984).[4] An implication for emotional control is that the control is to be done internally and personally. For emotion is something inside and belongs to the individual, and the individual, more precisely the rational self, is to be the agent of emotional control. Therefore the phrase "self-control" usually refers to emotional control. With this cultural conception of emotion, the educators of the school placed the ability to control one's emotions at the core of self-discipline.

The perceived high emotionality of early adolescents added an interesting dimension to the task of the socialization of adolescents for self-discipline. As the "brain on vacation" metaphor attests, early adolescents were potently characterized by their presumed emotionality. A major developmental difficulty of early adolescents was thought to be their being too "emotional" or "irrational," lacking rationality ("brain"). An urgent educational task was then to help them develop rational control over their emotions (bring their "brain" back from its "vacation"), as being able to remain controlled was considered an emotional stamp of adulthood.

Staying Cool: An Emotional Stamp of Adulthood

In his historical studies of American emotional style, Peter Stearns (1994, 1999; see also C. Stearns and P. Stearns 1986, 1988) claims that the dominant emotional style has shifted away from the Victorian combination of selective restraint on "dangerous" emotions with insistence on emotional intensity to the twentieth century's global emotion management, creating "American cool." He characterizes the middle-class emotional style of the twentieth century as a "blanket aversion to emotional intensity," compared with the nineteenth-century counterpart, in which even negative emotions such as anger were considered to have positive motivational roles and were consequently vigorously indulged in appropriate contexts (Stearns 1994: 199). According to Stearns, whereas Victorian Americans dealt with their sexuality and bodily expression with great anxiety, twentieth-century Americans have come to regard their emotions with equal suspicion and unease. They have become more constrained in their expression of emotional intensity, while they have enjoyed much freedom in other areas, like personal manners and sexuality.[5] A deep and increasingly uniform distaste for strong emotions has been developed, so that "[c]ool has become an emotional mantle, sheltering the whole personality from embarrassing excess" (ibid.: 1). To modern Americans, "the cool" became the emotional style to be desired, learned, and maintained.

A corollary of this development was that the emotional gap between childhood and adulthood widened in this process. "Childhood became more emotionally vulnerable, adulthood ideally more rational" (ibid.: 138). Adulthood was now viewed in sharp contrast with childhood, for the ability to avoid or control negative emotions. At Lincoln, the perceived emotional gap between adults and students was coupled with the ethnopsychology of early adolescence that considered junior high years as the most emotional life stage. Furthermore, the undertaking of intensive socialization for adulthood, an educational task unique to this juncture between childhood and adulthood, rendered the educators' role as "adults" only too critical. "Adults" were those who successfully met the demands of emotional control and thus could set an example for the immature.

At Lincoln, being friendly and keeping one's composure were characteristics of adult attitudes in interaction with students. I rarely saw adults "lose their temper" with students, and while they fully exercised their authority, they seemed to be careful not to let their negative emotions show. I was surprised that the teachers often remained poised and kind, even when it appeared emotionally demanding to do so. For instance, Marian Roettger, an ELL teacher, was being remarkably patient with one of her students, while I felt annoyed for her by what I perceived as "whining reluctance to work, and joking around." My field notes recorded the following:

> From the very beginning of the class, Miguel wouldn't do anything assigned. He would jokingly oppose whatever MR said. If she asks if the class understood something she said, he would say no. If she asks if there are any questions, he would say yes, correcting quickly to no. When he, like everybody, was asked to make sentences with the thirteen words given, he wouldn't even start. When Marian asked him to do it, he said he didn't have a pencil. So Marian gives him one. He doesn't like the pencil, because it's too short. I pointed to a pencil, which was longer, on the desk behind him. He wouldn't take it. Norma then takes out her pencil case and gives a completely new one. He refused to take that one too. Now he says he will use his pen. Marian sits next to him, and copies the words from the overhead for him. She gives it to him. In the meantime, she responds to him very patiently (she doesn't even seem to be trying hard to be patient; she seems just so patient). She responds to whatever he says, trying to meet his demands. Now she is back to the front, and Miguel is playing with his pen. Until everyone finished the assignment, Miguel did nothing about it. All Marian did after her effort to get him to work failed was to say that he was not going to get any points for the task. (Feb. 29, 2000)

Marian Roettger didn't seem irritated or even affected by Miguel's constant refusal. She seemed effortlessly patient with him, and cheerfully proceeded with the class afterward. Remarkable as she was, Roettger was not unusual in her way of dealing with students. When Alice Leonard described her professionalism regarding her emotional stance toward students, she in fact spoke for her colleagues as well. In her words:

> I want to conduct the classroom in a way, in a fair, equitable, friendly manner. If I am stressed, angry, if I discipline out of frustration or anger, then that is not being very

professional. I need to be effective. I need to be relaxed, directive, calm, and able to discipline a student, not out of anger. Never out of anger. (Dec. 10, 1999)

Consider the following excerpts in light of Alice Leonard's statement. These examples do not involve prolonged interactions, but they show the typical poise of teachers. The first is from Carol Knutson's GT English 8, and the second from Lisa O'Conner's Humanities English 7.

> One of them was not paying much attention most of the class hour. She didn't make noise or do anything notable, but since the class was generally quiet and hard working, her one not-so-loud laughter by herself made me notice her not doing the class work. But Carol didn't seem to be disturbed by her. She just said, "Erika, we are doing something that you are not doing." Carol didn't make a face or pause to tell that to her. It was more like a passing remark. It didn't have any sign of resentment. It was a neutral statement, and the manner Carol said that was neutral as well. However, it was not the kind of neutrality that disguises negative feelings. It was rather a concerned remark without sounding overly concerned or cold. (Feb. 4, 2000)

> Before the class, Lisa said to me that this class is loud and she tries not to be too clumsy about it. As she said, it was loud. Even after Lisa stood in front, many continued talking loud. Lisa had to say "Quiet" several times. Finally they calmed down. A few minutes later, a boy was almost sent out to the office. Lisa had told them to do their daily writing. The boy wasn't talking, but I guess he was doing something else. The boy wouldn't stop whatever he was doing right away, and then Lisa stepped forward from her desk [to get a referral form], saying "Then I'm gonna send you out." The boy stopped and started writing. Throughout the interaction, Lisa didn't lose her composure. Even right after the confrontation with the boy, albeit minor, Lisa smiled wide to the class. (May 19, 2000)

It is possible that teachers were conscious of my presence and consequently more restrained when I was in their class. My reasoning is that even without my presence, teachers' interaction style would not have been much different from what I observed, if at all. When emotional control was directly related to developmental maturity and taken as a major educational goal, it was only necessary that teachers and other adults in the school demonstrate their own emotional control. I did not miss some of the signs that showed teachers under strain from the emotional demand of their job, nor did I overlook that individual teachers varied in their degree of emotional control. However, the general level of emotional control teachers had over themselves and the professional pressure to maintain it were marked and at times astonishing. By demonstrating their own emotional control, teachers and other adults in the school set an emotional tone for students with "the cool," a reservation against emotional excess. Here is an incident when the teacher's emotional control seemed at stake no less than the student's:

At a staff meeting, Bill Meyer, the principal, reported that an eighth grade girl had "assaulted" Judy Cummings, a junior teacher. The student, Irene, was suspended and a police file was completed. According to the principal, when the girl was confronted by Judy Cummings on the hallway for her horseplay, she came nose-to-nose, threatening, and pushed Judy against a display box on the hallway. It was during a passing time after the first lunch, and many students were watching it.

After the initial report, more details of the incident were disclosed. Adults took as the most stark evidence of the severity of Irene's aggression the fact that when a hall monitor pulled Irene away, she broke from him and ran back towards Judy Cummings to "get her." Later at the Pupil's Problem Committee (PPC) meeting, Irene herself admitted that she had run to "get Ms. Cummings." However, Irene claimed that Judy Cummings pushed her first, saying "Are you mouthing at me?" and she only pushed the teacher back. No other statements of the incident, including the ones by her friends at the scene, supported Irene's claim that the teacher had pushed Irene. The PPC recommended an administrative transfer for Irene and the recommendation was accepted by all the parties concerned.

What was noteworthy during the decision making process at the PPC meeting was that despite the heaviness of Irene's misconduct, her claim that Judy Cummings pushed her first seemed to place the committee members in a dilemma. Irene's mother at the meeting asked if Judy Cummings "denied" that she had pushed Irene, strongly implying that she believed Irene's claim. The PPC committee members assured themselves of their trust in Judy Cummings's self-control among themselves (five were present), both before Irene and her mother came and after they left. When the administrative intern and chair of the meeting, Tim Miller, mentioned Irene's claim to the committee members, Don Gray, a senior teacher, said he wouldn't think Judy Cummings would've pushed her. The rest of them agreed with him. Emily Robbins (social worker) said she didn't think Judy Cummings or any other teachers wouldn't have "self-restraint" not to push a student. During the PPC meeting, Tim Miller asked Irene to describe how Judy Cummings "pushed" her and then how she pushed Judy Cummings. Irene showed it by using her right arm for Judy Cummings's push and both arms for her own push. At the end of the meeting, Emily Robbins again said, "I don't think Judy pushed her, and I know those of her friends are strong enough that they wouldn't make a statement to please teachers."

It was said that right after the incident, Judy Cummings was so shaken that she was crying hard, "crouching in a fetal position," in the principal's office. When the principal was reporting the incident to the staff, Judy looked much agitated and teary. Judy herself said she had felt so vulnerable at the moment, being "a small person." (Jan. 28– Feb. 4, 2000)

This case is very revealing of the significance of emotional control for adulthood. The incident was potentially a difficult case for the PPC, because an important part of the foundation on which the disciplinary consequence of Irene's misconduct would be based was being questioned: the emotional gap between the adult and the child. If it had been proved that the teacher had not remained "in control," that is, if she had pushed the student, the school administration would have been limited in considering disciplinary options for the student. However, the teacher supposedly did succeed in having her emotions "in check" at the crucial moment when she was confronted by an "emotional" student. In so doing, she proved herself as a mature person or "adult," and highlighted the immaturity of the student, wittingly or not. Nevertheless, the incident put considerable emotional strain on the teacher, some of which she released in the principal's office. I reason that such release was tolerated due to the fact that she was a relatively novice teacher, still on probation. In other words, she was granted an emotional release, because she occupied a lower rung of the ladder of emotional control, and thus of professionalism and ultimately personhood, than experienced teachers.

The emotional gap between adults and adolescents was a powerful ground on which educators based the task of emotional socialization of adolescents for personhood. The gap, on the one hand, enabled adults to grant emotional support and tolerance to early adolescents, who had just arrived at the threshold of adulthood. On the other hand, it marked the socialization of emotional control as a pressing educational goal for students. In order for early adolescents to develop into mature persons, educators were to guide them to fill the emotional gap by climbing the ladder of emotional control, so that they would move toward an adulthood that placed reason over emotion. This educational task involved a balancing act between tolerance and intolerance toward the "immaturity" of early adolescent students. Proactive emotional support coexisted with disciplinary lines of actions at the institutional level as well as the personal. Educators conceived both support and discipline, or tolerance and intolerance, as necessary for effective teaching of emotional control.

Ability Grouping and Emotional Control

I argue that ability grouping practiced in the school was not only about "ability" but also profoundly about "emotion." The three academic programs—GT, Humanities, and Regular—were distinguished from one another by their emotional tones as well as the composition of the student body in terms of social class, ethnic, and racial background, and teachers' pedagogical approaches. Not always clear were the differences of emotional tone, but a general trend was undoubtedly observed. Most notably, students as a group in each program were different in the degrees of emotional control while in class, and the differences influenced pedagogical practices daily and in the long term.

Classes in the GT program were a prime context in the school in which "the cool" was the normative emotional tone. In most classes, I seldom encountered feverish enthusiasm, high tension, or dramatic emotional release, but GT classes were particularly marked for their reserved atmosphere, compared with Humanities and Regular classes. The saliency of the reserved emotional tone of GT classes largely corresponded to the perception that GT students were "more idea-oriented" and thus "less emotional." Their reserve was so notable that in the beginning of the fieldwork, I wondered whether students were being engaged by their class, for I did not see visible "signs" of enthusiasm:

> Went to classes of Alice Leonard (French) and Dawn Anderson (Geometry). What was common to both classes was the fact that the students did seem to be working, but the atmosphere was low-spirited. They were not "excited." Most of the class time was for individual working. (Notably, the student seats are not in pairs. Each desk–chair set is aligned in row.) In French class, the class activities were mainly of two kinds: listen and repeat after the tape; solve the problems on the activity book. When they repeat after the tape, they didn't make a chorus-like group voice. It was rather a collection of small individual voices. It was obvious that the students were not intending to repeat in a louder voice together with others. The tape gave out the answers, so that they could check their own. When Leonard pointed to a student to answer her question, she/he remained seated and didn't become a focus of the rest of the students. While there wasn't any remarkable group activity, there seemed to exist an implicit rule in the group. When a boy interrupted Leonard by speaking out without raising a hand to wait till called, most students looked at him, a few saying "Shhh." Leonard was looking at the class, not him, without saying anything, but with the customary smile on her face, for a moment. (Oct. 20, 1998)

Although foreign-language courses were not ability-grouped, French, compared with other language classes, was more likely to be chosen by GT students, according to the French teacher Alice Leonard. Having been a foreign-language teacher myself, I was familiar with the format of the French class. Yet there was a significant difference. While I had had my students read out aloud together, the French teacher at Lincoln seemed concerned about whether each student read, rather than whether they read together. One purpose of reading together in my classes had been to let less able students practice their speaking out loud, for they were not confident in doing so if asked to do it alone. Such group activities were likely to enliven the class atmosphere. In Leonard's class, where class activities, though not so different from what I had done, were much oriented toward individual students, the class atmosphere remained at an even tone. In that atmosphere, a relatively minor breach, such as interrupting the teacher without raising a hand to be called on, drew attention from the whole class. The teacher did not respond to the student, while a few other students more overtly let him know about his transgression. My observation note continued about a Geometry class I went to after the French class. The math class was even more "unemotional," and it bewildered me:

> In Geometry class, individual working was even more remarkable. When Dawn Anderson was demonstrating solving example problems, only three to five students were looking at her and the overhead. The rest of them were working on their own worksheet. Then when Dawn asked them to show possible combinations for a quadrocubic, many volunteered one after another. Yes, they must've been working very hard. But I feel it difficult to confirm myself so, perhaps because I couldn't see the expression of enthusiasm (e.g., intensely looking at what the teacher does, responding to the teacher eagerly, interacting with peers in regard to the task, etc.). How do I know if they were enthusiastic about what they were learning? (Oct. 20, 1998)

Geometry was the most advanced math course and taken by the most "gifted and talented" students. Among the many classes I observed during my fieldwork, Geometry was one of the classes that relied on individual work most and whose atmosphere was most unemotional. It is interesting to note that students who took Geometry were the ones thought to be most "idea-oriented," and the majority of them were European American. Math being the most "rational" subject in the folk psychology was, I reason, another likely factor contributing to the tone of the class.

As a "student," I found that the even tone of GT classes required a considerable effort of emotion management on my part. My emotional experience of a seventh-grade GT English class was recorded in the following note:

> Ms. Ingold started the class with checking answers for the homework we did. First she had us ask about the problems that we found difficult. About six to eight of us raised hands and asked. I didn't. When one of us asked a question, Ingold often answered the student in the form of a question. Ingold and the student would exchange questions and answers for a brief while. I was listening to what they questioned and answered, but obviously I was not expected to participate in the exchange. Looking around, I found most of the students working on their own. When a girl in front of me asked a question, Ingold asked her back about apostrophe. The girl did seem to know what was being asked, but could not recall the exact word. Another girl in the next line quickly whispered the word toward her. She answered, and Ingold confirmed the answer, but adding with a firm (it wasn't anything negative; it was just plainly firm) voice, "But you got some help." I felt a little alarmed. I learned that I was not expected to help or get helped for that kind of class work. After checking answers for one exercise, we worked on today's assignment. Ingold walked around us to give individual assistance. I worked hard, but I felt lonely/isolated or a bit strange. I wanted to do some

activities with other students. I got to wonder why we didn't even check answers for each other, as I always had my students do. I would have felt better if I had had chances to answer in unison with other students or exchanged my answers with another student to be checked. To the end of the class, I did not have a single chance to utter a word: I checked my answers by myself and solved the problems by myself. (Dec. 1, 1998)

I perceived that the teacher strongly expected us to work diligently and independently. During that particular class, peer interaction was not needed, while the only interactions that occurred were between the teacher and individual students. It seemed that I was supposed to have "fun" from doing my assignment, that is, to have the "intrinsic reward" of the joy of learning. The students were largely performing to meet the teacher's expectation of their independent and hard work, whatever emotional state they experienced in doing so. I, however, longed to interact with my peers and to have shared fun with them. Sensing what was being expected and watching my peers meeting the expectation, I too learned to do so. But the learning was not without an emotional cost, as I felt "lonely/isolated or a bit strange."

Humanities and Regular classes were often emotionally less reserved. Take the following class observation for a comparison. It is from an eighth-grade English class in the Humanities program, where about half of the students were non-European:

This class is a lot more mixed in its racial/ethnic composition. It's very rowdy. Robert Martin proceeds with the class the same way as his Regular class I had observed just before this class. After the bell rang, RM still had to talk to Carol Knutson on the hallway. The class was loud, some still standing. As RM comes in, he says, "How come no one is doing the assignment?" The class got settled a little for a while, but as some students volunteered handing out the graded papers, they became loud again. Many of them made a paper ball with the returned paper, and threw it into the recycle box. Many, both those volunteers and others, got engaged in tumble plays. One volunteer girl was running off from a boy, and was told to stop by RM. A few others were told to stop throwing paper. During spelling test, many students raised hand, and often expressed their excitement or disappointment for their answer, openly (smiling or saying like "Ppooo," "What?"). Now, they are doing word-find. Overall, this class is louder than the other one, but they do their work. Four girls are doing their word find in a group of two each, and one boy is not working at all but only talking, till I go and tell him to work. As I watch him to start, he does his work. . . . RM said that the class would have been calmed down early if he hadn't talked to Carol Knutson after the bell. (Mar. 24, 2000)

When the teacher's attention was not directed to them, students in this class seemed to feel free to play with one another, to the point of being chaotic.

At the same time, many of these Humanities students openly showed their emotional engagement in learning, when they were presenting their answer to the teacher and their peers. One contrast in the teacher's approach was that Mr. Martin allowed more opportunities for peer interaction, both academic and non-academic. He had students volunteer to hand out graded papers to other students, and for the word-find assignment, many of them worked together with each other. In the spelling test, students were asked to present their answer to the whole class and from their peer's presentation the rest could see whether their answer was right. The presenters who openly expressed their excitement or disappointment about their answer were doing so, in part, because there was an audience for them. In other words, they were excited or disappointed for themselves partly because they knew they were being watched by their peers as well as the teacher.

If GT classes were "cooler," was it because GT students were "cooler" than students in other programs? Were GT students more "idea-oriented" and "less emotional," and students in lower-ability programs more "relational" and "emotional"? I claim that what underlay the distinctively disciplined atmosphere of GT classes was that most of the students in the GT program "knew," more or less, how to remain "cool," that is, how to manage their emotions while in class or in other places that required them to do so. Coming from middle-class families, they not only were familiar with the teacher's emotional style, but also had learned that their own feelings were meant to be managed—monitored, sanctioned, and controlled. According to the sociologist Melvin Kohn (1977, cited in Hochschild 1983: 158), middle-class parents are more likely to sanction what they later infer to be a child's feeling and intent, whereas working-class parents are more likely to sanction behavior itself. Therefore "middle-class children are more likely to be asked to shape their feelings according to the rules they are made aware of" (Hochschild 1983: 158). GT students could meet the teacher's expectation of their emotional control more readily, for they knew to "act" less emotionally.

Emotion management is then an important part of cultural capital that middle-class children acquire (see Bourdieu 1977; Bourdieu and Passeron 1977, for the discussion of cultural capital). In Lincoln, where the middle-class ideology was strongly held, emotion management functioned as a critical asset in school performance, for it readily translated into educational opportunities. A prime example involved the institution of ability grouping. Despite the seemingly egalitarian rationale of ability grouping that every student was to learn at her or his own level of ability, in reality students in the highest ability group, the GT program, were given more opportunities for more valued educational activities. It can be argued that GT students were "able" to do such activities, whereas students in lower ability groups were not. However, not all the students in the GT program were "gifted and talented," as many teachers admitted and often complained. About half the student population of the school was in the GT program. Maggie Ingold, a teacher in the GT program and advocate of GT education, said:

> Now I don't think that the GT classes that we have here, that all the kids in all of the classes are GT level kids or gifted in the sense of being able to read quickly or gifted in my area, necessarily. They might have gifts somewhere along the line or be extremely intelligent and test very high, but I think that a lot of kids here are just upper average. They are being stretched. They have parental backing because they want to be stretched. So they place them in these classes and they support the system and try to keep it at a fast and difficult pace. (Dec. 2, 1998)

According to Maggie Ingold, many GT students who were "just upper average" were "being stretched" to keep up with the demands of the GT program, with "parental backing." The parental support most often came from middle-class families, and I assert that a crucial aspect of it was emotional socialization of self-discipline, of which emotional control constituted the core. Thus when Elizabeth Riley, a teacher at Lincoln, was telling of her reaction to her daughter's being "disrespectful," she was not simply attesting to the middle-class parental concern about emotional control, but also specifically connecting emotion management as cultural capital to success in school and beyond. In her words:

> There was one day last week where I had, it was just a rough day at school, and then I had, just had been so tired of dealing with attitudes and disrespect and I went to pick up Alice, my second daughter, my sixth grader at school, and she was in her school girl mode and some boy came by and she said something really rude to him and then she sort of was rude to me at the same time and I lost it, because I thought what kind of junior high school girl she is going to be. And it is true, it was too big of a reaction and it was way strong and I know that my anxiety was such that *I don't want her to be disrespectful and to lose out on the opportunities that will shut down if she does that.* Just this simple disrespect that closes doors. And my pain was just like, you know, I am angry with you, for you. (Dec. 15, 1999, emphasis added)

As a mother and teacher, Elizabeth Riley was only too well aware of possible consequences of lack of emotional control. She had a strong reaction against her daughter's being "rude," because she knew that emotion management would translate to advancement in many aspects of middle-class life.

Carol Knutson, a strong advocate of GT education and one of the founders of the GT program at Lincoln, once pointed to the rarely mentioned, yet commonly acknowledged relationship between "behavior" and academic place-ment. She was deeply concerned that the GT program operated on "racism," particularly against African American students:

> We have very few African American boys [in the GT program] and the reason is they opt out. They opted out or people helped them opt out. And it is really hard to tell, but by the time they are in seventh and eighth grade, they are not there. They have not learned to read or they have been acting bad for so long that nobody knows what they could do if they ever possibly tried to do something. . . . We have got this whole cultural ethics that the African American boys are just kind of bad, they are just kind of out there and they are just sort of, it is really sad. I think the whole society is set up in a sort of racist way. The Jewish families in general expect high educational excel-lence from their children. And then they achieve that and the Asian parents are really after their kids. Now some of the kids try to be bad and they opt for being in gangs or whatever but the Asian kids, it is usually just the language thing but man, it is like nobody cares about those African American boys. And the girls aren't treated much better. I mean, why should so many of them be in the low classes? If it is not racism, what is it? They were not born stupid, you know, they are not. And it is a cultural thing. People say well it is because they only have a single parent family, they only have moth-ers and I grant you that that might be part of it and also they, maybe there is a lack of books in the home and all that stuff, you know, but I think it is that in general, they are looked on as not being as important as other kids. I really think that. (Feb. 29, 2000)

Carol Knutson reasoned that African American students, especially boys, had "opted out" of the GT program, or been "helped" to do so, because they were "looked on as not being as important as other kids" but "bad." While they were "not born stupid," they had been "acting bad," she contrasted. Differently put, the reason so many African American students were placed in low ability pro-grams was their "acting" rather than "ability" per se. I further argue that if many African American students were viewed as "bad," the view was largely based on the middle-class emotion management standard. Take the following case as an example:

> On the first day of the second semester, I sat in Earl Gibson's eighth grade Humanities Social Studies class. Many students were from Mr. Gibson's class last semester, but quite a few students were new to the class. The first thing Mr. Gibson did with the class was ask who hadn't had him last semester. About six raised hand. He asked one on the first row, an Afro boy, which teacher he'd had for his Social Studies last semester. The boy said he'd had Ms. Warner, and Mr. Gibson asked what level he had been in. I thought

I heard him saying, "Regular," in a small voice. In a quick moment, he lowered his upper body, looked back at an Afro girl behind him, and said something very quickly. Mr. Gibson sensed something. His face and voice got firm. He said to the boy, "You are already like that on the first day." "I don't know what you are asking," said the boy. The boy's voice was telling that he was agitated. "You have an attitude. If you don't want to be in my class, I will let you down again," said Mr. Gibson. He went to get a referral form from his back desk, returned to the front, and wrote on the form. Meanwhile the boy packed, as if he knew he was going to be sent out. When he came out to get the form, he had a thick brush in hand. Walking out of the rows, he grinned wide toward the rest of the students. Mr. Gibson proceeded asking the same questions with other new students. All of them were from Regular program, and Mr. Gibson asked them each if they were recommended up by their teacher. For instance, Mr. Gibson said to a new student, "You had Ms. Goodwin? She recommended you for Humanities?" At one point, a girl, hearing all the new students answering they came from "Regular," asked Mr. Gibson, "What is Regular?" Mr. Gibson said, "Regular is (a short pause) regular. In this school, there are different levels, Gifted and Talented, Humanities, and Regular." He did not offer any more explanation. It surprised me that the girl didn't know about the "levels."

Once students were on their assigned task, Gibson made a call to the office. He explained what had happened with the Afro boy. I could not hear all the details, but I heard him saying, "He doesn't want to be in my class, and then you can move him down." Later Mr. Gibson said to me that when asked what level he had been in last semester, Collin Harvey (the boy) had whispered to the girl behind him, "Fuck, why should I be supposed to know that?" And Gibson heard that. I suspect that Collin was embarrassed or felt humiliated by being asked for his last semester's "level." Unlike the girl who didn't know what "Regular" meant, he might have been well aware of Regular being the lowest ability program and its stigma. On the other hand, Mr. Gibson would not expect such an "attitude" from a new student on the first day of a semester. He didn't know the boy, and might have wanted to set a tone for the rest of the class by being firm to someone with an "attitude" and possibly weeding him out. When he said, "You have an attitude. If you don't want to be in my class, I'll let you down again," it was clear that what was at stake was the boy's "attitude."

After the class, Gibson went down to Alison Warner, Collin's Social Studies teacher last semester, and asked if she had recommended Collin Harvey up for Humanities program. She said she hadn't. She did not say much, but she frowned when Gibson mentioned the boy's name and said, "Oh, my gosh!" She seemed to be surprised to learn that Collin was now in Humanities, although she said his grade from her class had been a B. Gibson went to Gale Ford, a guidance counselor. He described what had happened in his class and reported that Warner had not recommended him up. He "explained" that Collin Harvey didn't want to be in his class. Gale Ford looked distressed about the boy upon hearing Gibson's report. Ford placed him back in the Regular program by doing the computer work at her desk, and said, "Done."

It seemed that it was going to happen that way, but Gwen Lundy, the assistant principal, came into the guidance office. She seemed very irritated by what was going on.

Her voice was big and up. She said that Collin Harvey had been recommended for Humanities by Dick Newman, his English teacher. Because English and Social Studies go together, he was placed in Humanities for his Social Studies as well. According to Lundy, a letter of congratulation for the "promotion" was sent to the family. She basically said that the student should not be placed back to Regular program. Gwen Lundy returned to her office. Now, Gale Ford tried to find Collin Harvey's test scores to see if he had any other supporting material for his "promotion." His folder did not have any test scores, because he had come from another state. Gwen Lundy came in again and said, "Let's deal with discipline and placement separately." She again said that she had placed him in Humanities program upon a teacher's request (so, it was not a "mistake"), which came through the guidance office. After Gwen Lundy left, Gale Ford said in a small voice, "By looking at scores, we are separating discipline and placement." Gibson whispered, "Maybe he is the discipline boy that she likes." Dana Landstrom, an English teacher, watching all these interactions in the guidance office, suggested that Gibson talk with Dick Newman, which she thought "should work." But Gibson seemed to be discouraged by the assistant principal, and said the boy would stay in his class "for now."

The next day, Collin was back in Mr. Gibson's class. He was chewing gum throughout the class period, and looked quite conscious of Mr. Gibson. But he didn't do anything noticeable. He did class work. Mr. Gibson at one point went over to him to look at how he did a class assignment, and commented "Pretty good." Collin didn't say anything or smile, but glanced at Mr. Gibson aside. Later that day, I stopped by Dick Newman to ask about Collin. He already knew that his new teacher got a "bad impression" of him on the first day, as Mr. Gibson had talked to him about it. When Mr. Newman asked Collin what he had done to Mr. Gibson, his answer was a typical one: He didn't do anything. Mr. Newman said to Collin, "You gotta shape up. Mr. Gibson is a better person for you." He said to me that Collin was able to do work, though not "brilliant," and had gotten an A for everything he had done in his class. He further commented that he had had no problem with his behavior. According to him, Collin always worked well and was quiet in class.

As I was listening to Mr. Newman, Collin was being described as a hard-working, good student. Honestly, it was a little hard for me to think of him as such. Perhaps I am deeply class-bounded as many others. That I could not easily think of him as a "good" student is coming from my impressions of him: rebellious voice, lack of assertive eye contact, holding a brush in hand, grinning while sent out, chewing gum, and half down pants. Possibly some of these things initially made Mr. Gibson feel like rejecting him at first, regardless of his "ability."

As I was walking downstairs with Mr. Newman, we met Mr. Gibson. Newman said he had talked to Collin Harvey to "shape up." Gibson told us that he had talked to Collin after his class as well and shaken hands. Mr. Gibson described his interaction with Collin: When he offered a handshaking, Collin said he had just put lotion on his hand, with a little bit of embarrassment; Gibson jokingly said, "It's ok. My hands are dry," and they shook hands. Mr. Newman again said to Mr. Gibson that Collin was able. Gibson said, "He did his work today and as far as he is able to work, I have no issue with him. If there's a discipline problem, as a teacher I have to deal with it." I was pretty sure that Gibson had thought about the case very much. He is class-bounded as he admitted once, but he is also sensitive and reflective on how he handles his students. (Jan. 31–Feb. 1, 2000)

When she said, "Let's deal with discipline and placement separately," the assistant principal rightly pointed out that in the above case a "discipline" issue was quickly being translated to the matter of academic placement. Mr. Gibson himself stated several times that it was the student's "attitude" that rendered unlikely his candidacy for a higher level program. After all, on the first day of a semester, a teacher would not have enough data to know about the "ability" of a new student. Note that Collin reported to Mr. Newman that he had done "nothing" to Mr. Gibson, while he was repeatedly told that he had an "attitude." It is true that Collin did not "do" anything to the teacher. Even the very statement that offended Mr. Gibson's feeling was not intended to be heard by him. It seems plausible to suppose that Collin negatively responded to the teacher largely out of his nervousness and confusion. It is possible that he was suspicious about the teacher's intent of asking such questions ("I don't know what you are asking"). From the teacher's perspective, however, Collin was doing something to him through his facial and bodily expressions as well as the statement he made to his friend. By not managing his emotions properly, Collin too easily showed his "attitude" to Mr. Gibson and consequently put his "promotion" in danger. Collin failed to manage his emotions, according to the Euro-American middle-class standard, which Mr. Gibson endorsed. In Mr. Gibson and several others' view, it was a problem that his level of emotional control did not correspond with the level of the academic program for which he was recommended.

Ability grouping, in the way it was practiced, was a good example of emotional control as cultural capital and the dominance of the middle-class emotional style. The middle-class hegemony was strong, but not without being questioned. I will later examine revealing critiques of it, but now I turn to look at some of the most outstanding features of the middle-class emotional style observed in emotion management training in the school.

Emotion Management Training: Rationalization of the Self

As the self was ideally the locus of control, and cognition was the inner faculty necessary for "self-control," educators endeavored to discipline students so that their cognition "prevailed" over emotion. Much of what I discussed in chapter 4 concerned this issue as well, of how the educators cultivated "rationality" in their students. Here I look at how "slowing down" of emotional response was learned, by examining two related aspects of emotional training in the school: decontextualizing and verbalizing of emotion.

Decontextualization of Emotion

One of the first things that beginning seventh-grade students learned about junior high school life was that there was a separate domain set aside for dealing with emotions. Administrators and support professionals made their class visit in the beginning of the school year to inform students about their jobs. Assistant principals provided students with disciplinary guidelines at the class visit. Counselors and social workers informed students of their services as support personnel, including individual and group counseling ("group"). After the initial introduction, students learned about the support domain on a daily basis, by being "sent out" to their administrator (assistant principal) if they misbehaved in class, or being referred to support professionals for certain kinds of help.

The main office ("office") more or less represented the support domain, hosting and connecting to offices of administrators, the school social worker, and the two guidance counselors. There were other support staff members, such as social work interns, the chemical health counselor, social workers from outside agencies, who did not reside in the main office area but were still in the world of the "office." To students in special education programs, the EBD program in particular, their special education classrooms also functioned as their support domain.

Sending students out from their classroom to the office when they were causing disruptions in class was a practice most importantly symbolic of the folk dichotomy of cognition and emotion, along with "referrals" of students of particular concern from teachers or any other adults to various support professionals. Teachers, representing the "academic" domain, were not to handle "emotions" per se. However, the goal was not just to keep the cognitive domain of the school from being interfered with by emotional issues. Students were strongly advised to bring their concerns to support personnel, even when they did not particularly involve a classroom situation. At an IEP meeting for one of her EBD students, Kurt, Ms. Davis said:

> (Speaking to Kurt) The bus, hall, lunch count. When the bus driver says "Sit down," you sit down. There's time and space you can complain in. If you think the bus driver is not fair, come to me. I can work it out. At this time of your life, this place is where

you can complain. At the sixth hour. (Now speaking to the adults at the meeting) Kurt's primary problem is making a poor decision, when he doesn't agree with adults. He needs to learn to take them to Patrick or to me, bring his problems to a right place. Kurt needs time and space daily to air concerns about fairness. (Sept. 22, 1998)

At the meeting, Kurt was being cautioned against an immediate response in an emotion-provoking situation. For example, if he had an issue with the school bus driver, he was still to talk to Ms. Davis, not the driver. It was apparently expected that the very process of bringing his concerns to Ms. Davis, without "reacting" immediately, would slow him down. Once slowed down, he would be given a chance to "air" the concerns. Moreover, now out of the immediate context, it was more likely that he would review his emotions without being too "emotional." For decontextualized emotions were easier to manage.

Another example of emotion management through decontextualizing emotions was "mediation," adult-guided conflict resolution for issues among students themselves. Mediation was routinely done by the assistant principal Gwen Lundy, social worker Emily Robbins, and chemical health counselor Tamara Johnson. Mediation was called for by either the adult or one or more students involved in a conflict situation, and the adult functioned as the mediator between the two parties of students. A typical mediation session resembles a courtroom situation: First of all, the mediator makes ground rules and procedure clear, such as "no interruption while the other party speaks." Then each of the parties takes turns to tell his or her version of the situation, against which the other party is given a chance to make his or her point right after the telling. The mediator is not to side with any one party, but to make sure that both sides are heard and each can see the issue from the other's perspective. At the end of the telling, the mediator asks them how to resolve the issue among themselves. The presence of the third party and the ground rules of the session supposedly guard against the participants being emotionally charged. That is, by being in a specially designed setting for conflict resolution, they could be "removed" from the original context in which they were "emotional" with one another. Here in a mediation session, they were expected to tell their stories and revisit the situation "without emotions."

From the educators' point of view, mediation would be an opportunity for successful practice of emotion management if students could not only decontextualize their emotions for a particular mediation session but later transfer what they had learned in the designated setting to the everyday context. De-emotionalizing or rationalizing the self was genuinely a challenging task with which educators struggled. Emily Robbins asserted that an important purpose of doing mediation was to have students "slow down" in a "real" situation:

> When I do mediation with kids, they can go through the motions, but the minute they hit the door and they had a conflict, they do it the same way. They are back in here and they go through the motions of mediation and really handle it quite well and look like intellectually they are getting it and they walk out there and they have a conflict and they react. It is just kind of like what they know, and so [doing a mediation is like] being in a situation with a kid who is going to go off like that. (June 6, 2000)

She continued to say that it would take many behavioral practice situations to learn how not to "react" but to express their feelings calmly:

> If I happen to be in a hallway and see something like that, I just kind of give them some sort of social cue, I had a relationship with them, I put my hand on their shoulder and slow them down for a minute so they think about it for three seconds before they react by saying something or swinging. And they have to have that experience a lot of times before it is going to replace responding with defense and responding with not being vulnerable and now showing, you know, that really hurt my feelings versus fuck you. I mean swearing at somebody, that is natural but it is not natural to say that really hurt my feelings. (June 6, 2000)

Along with individual counseling and mediation, group counseling was a major form of support work in the school, which also utilized and fostered decontextualizing of emotions. By taking an example of an activity called "sculpture," Emily Robbins explained what she did in her group counseling for anger management. According to her, the main purpose of the activity was to give students a chance to reflect on the emotion, anger, while they were removed from an anger-charged situation. In her words:

> If we had the right space, we could do some physical activity around those kinds of things like group sculpture, so they can identify what does anger look like in your family, and we physically do a sculpture about that and then we have a conversation about what that looks like and what it feels like to be that person in the sculpture. Who are you usually in that sculpture in your family? (I: Do they gesture what an angry person looks like?) Yeah, and do a lot of that, so that it is both physical in their body and *they get a chance to watch it and to remove themselves from it and then have a conversation about it* ((June 6, 2000, emphasis added).

The assumption underlying the decontextualization of emotions was that emotions were the property of the individual, residing in her/him, rather than emergent social products. Because they "belonged" to the individual, they could be taken from their context and held back to be addressed later and more properly (for a discussion of emotion as individual property, see Lutz 1988: 70–72). Most often, the "proper" way to process emotions was verbalizing them in a setting removed from their original setting. Having emotional distance from the situation and at the same time being able to verbalize emotions was a dual goal in the various aspects of emotional education in the school. Individual counseling, mediation, and group counseling all provided a deliberate setting in which students would have a "conversation" about their supposedly decontextualized emotions. Ultimately the goal was to rationalize the self, to which the verbalization of emotions was almost indispensable.

Verbalization of Emotions

Verbal expression of emotions was strongly encouraged as a way of emotion management in the school, for it was believed that through verbalization, one could defuse emotional tension and stay safe from getting "out of control." For instance, Diane Nash, discussing a student at the Student Support Meeting, said, "He is able to talk and he remains in control." Relating being "able to talk" to staying "in control," she meant that the situation was not too serious and intensive intervention work would not be necessary. Verbalization of emotions was fostered, however, not only because being able to verbalize was considered as a sign of emotional control on the part of the student, but also because it provided the adult with access to the student's inner feelings and thus help in managing emotions for the student, if needed. The assistant principal Gwen Lundy clearly expressed the importance of verbal expression of emotions from the adult's perspective:

> It's hard to deal with children who are not direct. To put it another way, if a child is directly angry, it's easier to deal with what their concerns are and address their anger. If a child is passive and symbolic [in showing anger], we have trouble getting into their trouble. . . . If a child is more direct, they tell you. I am angry for what. I need my father to stop [doing something]. Then you direct them how to change their behavior to acceptable social behavior. If they are only somehow demonstrating, you have no clue why they are doing it. If they don't share, you continue punishment and don't get resolution. (Nov. 16, 1999)

The double function of verbalization of emotions—relieving emotional stress of the student and facilitating adult intervention in emotion management—was well recognized and pursued in various kinds of support work, including "disciplining" by assistant principals, counseling by support staff, and intervention work involving special education programs. Most characteristically, group counseling by counselors and social workers was, in essence, a training ground for emotion management through verbal expression of emotions. Group counseling was intended to help students articulate their own emotions with social idioms of emotional expression and negotiate their social relations as "persons." At the first session of her Girls' Group, guidance counselor Cathy Brandt said:

> No one's feeling is ever wrong. . . . We learn how to talk about things. We talk about embarrassment, uncertainty. (Oct. 28, 1998)

"Talking about feeling" was a prominent theme of various groups in the school, such as the Girls' Group, Anger Management Group, Grief Group, and Family Change Group. My observations of group sessions were very limited because of concerns about the confidentiality of student participants, but I was given permission to attend sessions of three Girls' Groups led by three different adults at varying times. The following note was taken after I observed a Girls' Group led by the chemical health counselor, Tamara Johnson. The group was very mixed in terms of race/ethnicity (three Afro-, one Asian, and four Euro-Americans), and five of the eight girls present on that day were in the GT program.

> She [Tamara, the counselor] explained that they had a guest (me) today and first they'd have introduction of each other (me and the girls). So the girls took turns to intro-duce themselves. They said their name, and then told what were their "lows" and "highs" this week since last Friday. It seemed a ritualized routine. It was high-keyed atmosphere. Girls seemed to be very open to talk about themselves, and showed empathy or concerns for others, by asking further questions or commenting. Some of them looked a little shy, while talking about what had happened, but it didn't keep them from sharing it with the group. It felt that the girls were feeling secure about being in the group and trusted each other, so that having a stranger didn't seem to affect their group dynamics much. Examples of "lows" were "sick," "got into fights," "teacher called home because I talked with someone," "friend is mad," and "my parents want to send me to a private school for high school." Girls seemed to be able to more eas-ily recall their "lows," but their "highs" included "made friends with someone who I had a fight with last week," "went to a club," "got an A from math," and "got on B honor roll." . . . Now it was time for anybody who had things to discuss in the group (I figured). Not all of them spoke, but those who did competed for turns to speak. They raised their hands, shouting "I've got something." About four girls spoke this time. Three girls talked about things related to boyfriend or boys. One girl knows a boy who always "irritates" her, but today the boy was not in school, and she missed him. Tamara verbalized her feeling for her: "So, did you miss him?" She said yes. (Mar. 16, 2000)

The girls, most of the time, were very funny, playful, and cheerful with one another. Tamara Johnson did not attempt to counter the high-keyed peer interactions the girls were engaged in. A sharp contrast with a classroom situation was that when doing a "group," the peer group formed an audience for each other, an audience that was interactive. One significance of the presence of the peer audience was that it provided a social context in which they could receive responses from others about their own emotions.

The act of verbal presentation of emotions involved not simply letting emotions out, but more importantly, articulating what the girls had felt about a certain situation. The counselor helped them to name their feeling, when they had difficulty doing so. In the example above, when a girl stated that she had noticed that a boy who always "irritated" her had not come to school that day, Tamara Johnson helped her recognize that her feeling "irritated" could mean something else, by asking, "So, did you miss him?" While girls were presenting, Johnson directed them to further articulate their concerns, by asking questions such as "What is your response?," "Do you think you have a responsibility for the situation?," "Do you want some suggestions?" At the same time, she drew out other girls' comments on each other's issue. In this process, the students had an opportunity to express and scrutinize their emotions in a setting that had a peer audience.

Verbal expressions of emotions provided a basis on which the adult helped students to learn social idioms of emotions. In her Girls' Group, Tamara Johnson carefully led the girls to reflect upon the social context of their feelings in which they had a certain role and status, as described in the following:

> During the Check-In time, three girls complained about their teacher. Maria was upset with her math teacher (Lori Hogan) that she and others got a detention for not bringing the textbook on Monday, while today she didn't give a detention to those without their textbook. She only told them to bring it next time. Her point was that Ms. Hogan was not being fair. Tamara asked her what she would do about it. Maria wanted to talk to her about it. Tamara said there are appropriate ways to do so, without making the teacher feel accused. "You could say, I want to know about your policy about textbook, because I noticed that sometimes students get a detention for not bringing it, and other times they don't. Then she might say she was tired that day and forgot about it or something." Natasha complained about Ms. Riley. She said she was sent out for "nothing," and Tamara tried to hear more about the situation. It wasn't clear what happened from what Natasha said. Another girl gave her advice: "Sit there and shut up, that's what you do." Still another girl commented that Ms. Riley was "weird," and keeping shut up was the best way. Rita's advice was that she behave appropriately, even when she was upset with the teacher, but ask why she was being sent out in an appropriate manner. (May 11, 2000)

Much of the check-in time at the session was spent discussing issues regarding relationships with teachers in class. Johnson allowed the girls to freely express their feelings about particular teachers; at the same time she pointed out or guided them to talk about "appropriate" ways of dealing with the situations. She was redirecting the group's attention to the teacher's possible feeling state, by implying that it was equally important to recognize the teacher's feeling. By doing so, she was proposing to the group the very middle-class way of emotion management—staying calm and verbalizing emotions. Note that one of the girls, Rita, essentially restated what Johnson was trying to convey to Natasha and the rest of the girls. It would not be a coincidence that Rita shared with the counselor the middle-class style of emotion management and interpersonal skills. Johnson one day remarked on the socioeconomic gap among the girls. It was after Natasha complained that strawberries in the school lunch had tasted strange and it was the first time she ever had strawberries. Afterwards, Johnson said to me, "Can you believe Natasha had strawberries for the first time? She is 13 years old. Some of the girls here do horse riding, which is an expensive sport." Rita was one of the girls who did horse riding. When she was telling Natasha her opinion as to how to address the situation with Ms. Riley, Rita was very likely speaking from her own upbringing.

This section described some of the most proactive support practices for emotional socialization in the school. The socialization practices were heavily influenced by the middle-class notion of rationality and personhood. The goal was to rationalize the self, and two chief means were decontextualizing and verbalizing of emotions. Now I examine more specifically the hegemonic status of the middle-class emotional style and its critiques regarding the issues of social class, race, and ethnicity.

Emotion, Moral Order, and Social Class, Race, and Ethnicity

At Lincoln, while "emotion" was considered an "uncontrollable" physiological response, moral terms were strongly applied to "rational" control over "emotions." Partially, it was through the negation of "emotions" that emotion was connected to personhood and became a constituent of the moral order, in which the middle-class emotional style was given a hegemonic status. I stress that in the school, the basis for affective education was largely the middle-class standard for emotional management. For example, the support domain as a proactive setting for affective education was representative of the organized effort to instill in students the middle-class style of emotional management. When Emily Robbins summarized what the educational purpose of doing "groups" was, she was implicitly prioritizing the middle-class emotional style over the working-class one:

> You have a conflict, you work it out by screaming or you work it out by punching or you work it out by some physical force. That worries me. That is a lot to undo for 13 years of modeling, that is a lot to undo. . . . [I]n that ["group"] experience they have a chance to practice, again, what it is to communicate, one person at a time, what it is to kind of build community or family in a way that has some guidelines and boundaries and limits and predictability and health to it, because again they may come from a family that doesn't have any of that. It is chaotic, it is violent, it is unhealthy, it is not respectful, it is unpredictable. So it is very intentional about what we are providing for them. What we are providing for them is a practice ground for health. (June 6, 2000)

Robbins was clear that group counseling was intended to "undo" "unhealthy" ways of working out a conflict situation, for example, "screaming," "punching," or using "some physical force." It would instead impart "healthy" ways of communicating, of having "guidelines, "limits," and thus "predictability." According to her, by being in a group, students would learn how to interact with each other in a "respectful" way. In her view, the "one person at a time" rule of communication was one of the most basic ways of showing "respect." I infer that her view of "healthy" community was based mainly on the middle-class model of community, where "rational" individuals interacted within certain "boundaries" of emotional expression.

The interaction rule of "one person at a time" attests to the middle-class stance Emily Robbins was taking in her support work. The violation or neglect of this rule by some students was a frequent source of frustration experienced by educators, which often led them to discipline such students for their "disrespect" or "defiance of authority." Many African American students, whose interactional style featured "pushing," "shoving," "teasing," and "testing" of one another, drew disciplinary attention for their highly "emotional" interactional style. "One person at a time" was not likely a rule to them. When their interactional style was applied to adults, it was very often considered to be "defiant behavior." African American girls were an especially easy target, as they were called "mouthy." The labeling of African American girls as "those loud Black girls" (Evans 1988; Fordham 1993) rang true at Lincoln as well. The consequence of being "mouthy" was at times serious. In Irene's case, which I discussed earlier, it seemed that Judy Cummings's chiding her for being "mouthy" ("Are you mouthing at me?") instigated Irene's violent reaction. The social worker who had seen Irene regularly in her anger management group reported that she had listed her conflicts with teachers as a main cause of her frustration in school.

Although I did not share the Euro-American cultural background of many of the educators, I too was concerned that some African American students were not being "respectful" to adults. Many times, it troubled me as much as it seemed to affect educators in the school. Then I heard about the dinner table of a working-class African American family where "everybody is talking at the same time." Intrigued, I began asking African American adult participants how their dinner table conversation would proceed. The following is an excerpt from an interview with Harry Jackson, an African American father. As someone who grew up in a working-class African American community to be a professional in an area where people with European middle-class backgrounds dominate, he was very critical of the European middle-class standards enforced upon him in many situations, and well-versed in both worlds.

> Jackson: Now would that [everyone talking at once] happen in your family at the dinner table?
>
> I: In my family, I wouldn't think so. If my father talks, everybody has to listen to him, and it is true for everyone. So, I am not familiar with that type of interaction.
>
> Jackson: Now in my family, that is true, everybody talks. Everybody talks, there is not a protocol about who gets to talk first, who gets to listen or that you have to listen.
>
> I: You don't have to listen?
>
> Jackson: No. Particularly if my father talks, we may have heard this before, we don't necessarily want to hear it again, and as we got older, we also have our own views on these things. So we don't have to sit here and listen to yours.
>
> I: But why then do you ever talk if nobody listens?
>
> Jackson: It is not a question of not listening. It is a question of how do you challenge the views that are coming out. I mean, because if I want to challenge what he is saying, I am not going to let him say it again because he said it ten times so I am going to immediately start to tell him why I disagree with what he is saying. I know what he is saying. I know it more than you can possibly imagine, I know it, I can repeat it for him. I know it so there is this sense that one, we know each other well enough that it is not disrespectful to talk when someone else is talking. We know each other well enough, we know what is going on so we can all talk about these things, we can hear, I can talk and hear at the same time and I can trade with you. (May 24, 2000)

Mr. Jackson explained to me why "to talk when someone else is talking" was not disrespectful. According to him, it was not so much a matter of being respectful as of being able to challenge the other person's view. He pointed out that the sense of closeness with each other underlay such simultaneous verbal exchanges. The European middle-class conception of "respect" that assumed a firmer boundary between the self and non-self did not apply when the self–non-self boundary was more fluid. When the psychological regions of the self and others could overlap, instead of being clearly separated, "to talk when someone else is talking" would not be as offensive a social act. Mr. Jackson's insight into psychological closeness related to emotional interaction among working-class African Americans corresponds with a point made by Peter Stearns (1994: 248) that the preoccupation with emotional control among middle-class Americans is a sign of emotional distance among individuals.

Harry Jackson further criticized the Euro-American middle-class notion of emotional control, referring to his experience as a site council member of the school, where he was most of the time the only African American.[6] His acceptance of emotionality, such as speaking loudly and pounding on the desk, as expressions of being "passionate" contrasted sharply with the European middle-class standard of staying cool. In his words:

> When we were setting up the site council, one of the things they wanted to say was that they wanted everyone to feel comfortable coming and discussing and we want to leave the emotion out of it and I objected right away. I said, I am sorry, I don't know how to do that, how do you do that? What do you mean, leave the emotion out of it? How do you do that? So they kind of thought about it for a moment and I said, I think people can be passionate about what it is they are arguing about or have to say and it doesn't affect people's willingness to participate, it shouldn't. Now if I turn and start calling someone names, really awful names or something, that would make me not want to participate, but you know, that is not what I am talking about. I am talking about somebody who can come and speak loudly, who can wave their hands in the air or stand up or even pound on the desk. I think all of that is ok because they are just expressing themselves and you guys will have to feel comfortable with it. People are going to come in here angry sometimes. I don't want to tell them that they have to check the anger at the door and then they can come in and talk, you know, I don't want to do that and so they kind of said ok, we will back away from that but you know what I mean. We just want to be respectful of everybody and I said ok, I understand that, I just don't think that the definition you are using for respectful should mean excluding emotion and I said I don't want that kind of debate. So it was tough for them to get to that, but I said if you are also talking about respecting differences, then you got to respect the fact that some people argue with that kind of emotion, you know, and it takes a while for people to get it. They are just expressing their level of discomfort with that kind of debate. (May 24, 2000)

He then gave an example of an interaction between the school principal and a teacher, which he viewed as masked but heavily emotional:

> We have a debate that a teacher says something that Bill [the principal] disagrees with or feels like it is an attack on management/administration. He will challenge him right away and while he may not be showing any outward signs of emotion, his words are cutting and they cut that person and you can tell because the teacher will stop talking immediately, because what he has said without saying it [is] I am still the head man in charge here and I can affect your future. So they shut up. . . . But to me, all of that is emotion, all of that is emotion, except we are going to try to mask it as an unemotional, just business kind of debate. Well it is not. What you just said to that person is very emotional because it has produced an emotional response in that they shut up and put their head down. So I don't buy it. (May 24, 2000)

Harry Jackson was clear that being "respectful" could be differently defined, depending on the scope of public tolerance toward individuals' emotional expressions. In his view social interactions are necessarily emotion-incurring, however "unemotional" particular individuals would appear. To him, the insistence on being "unemotional" is nothing but a way of silencing others, especially those who have less power.

If Mr. Jackson as an influential adult could successfully articulate and defend his position regarding why he did not "buy it," it was not the case with many African American students as well as other students of color in the school. Critical as he was, even Mr. Jackson was well aware of the dominance of the Euro-American middle-class emotional style and could only seek an understanding of differences ("respecting differences"), relying on the popular discourse of multiculturalism. Needless to say, students were more subject to the socialization pressure for emotional management. A social worker, Matt Bryant, himself an African American, reflected about his internship experience at Lincoln:

> I think there wasn't very much sensitivity to how culturally kids of color are different than white children and I think they had an expectation of interacting like white kids when truly, the culture is different. The way the parents interact with their kids are different. This might be somewhat of a stereotype, but in the home, I think that, first of all, the majority of the homes are probably going to be single-parent homes . . . so that concept, having an expectation of, a middle-class expectation, the set-up is initially unrealistic. African American single-parent homes just do not act or interact as white, middle class which may have a mom at home and a dad working. The set-up is just different. . . . I think the African American kids, in terms of the way they socialize in the home or in the African American culture, come into the school different. African American kids, the majority of them, that I have been exposed to, they interact

socially loud, playing, pushing, all that type of stuff, but the school didn't really seem to have very much tolerance for it in my perception. It was kind of a set-up for kids who came into the office often, and appearing to be a problem, you know, that kind of interaction, pushing, shoving, always in the office, that type of stuff, maybe being a little mouthy, you know, creates a lot of frustration with the staff, I felt. Of course when you are dealing with 1,000 kids, you know, when you become frustrated, you might inappropriately, in my mind, inappropriately reprimand a kid. I saw staff doing that. I saw the hall monitors doing that and I don't really feel like the principal set a precedent that that was not ok to be like that, so that was part of the frustration that I had there. (Jan. 12, 2000)

Matt Bryant perceived that the school set an "unrealistic" expectation for African American students, many of whom came from working-class, single-parent homes. It was "unrealistic" because many African American students did not have the resources that "white" students had, including the "white" style of communication. He attributed the fact that many African American students were "problem" cases in the school to the interaction style that they brought from home, which was vastly different from the "white" way.

Some have argued in the case of African American students that the stereotypical interaction style of being "mouthy" was their resistance to the hegemony of the European middle-class cultural practice in the school (see Fordham 1993). Whether it is what they bring from their home environment or their expression of resistance, it seems obvious that the educational practices based on the European American middle-class ideology of individualism very often negatively affect the school experiences of students of color and from the lower class. Shortly, I bring up the case of an Asian American boy for a closer examination of the intersection of emotion, social class, and race/ethnicity.

Anger as Danger

Anger seemed to be the emotion that concerned educators in the school most deeply. Whenever there arose a case calling for either proactive or disciplinary actions, it was invariably asked whether anger was involved in the case. Much of the work by support professionals concerned anger, as controlling anger was pivotal to emotional control and thus personhood. For example, anger management groups were the most numerous in terms of "groups" that were designed for specific emotions or issues, while groups of other kinds, such as girls' and boys' groups, also dealt with anger issues to varying degrees.[7] For disciplinary cases, the presumed anger of the student was almost always seen as the main cause of the problem.

In numerous talks about and educational approaches to anger at Lincoln, I encountered the American folk model of anger described by George Lakoff and Zoltan Kovecses (Kovecses 1986, 1995; Lakoff 1987; Lakoff and Kovecses 1987). In their study of the folk model of anger through the use of metaphor, Lakoff and Kovecses uncover "Anger is heat" as the most general metaphor for anger, one version of which is the central anger metaphor: "Anger is the heat of a fluid in a container." Some examples of this principal metaphor include, in their study, "anger welled up inside," "blowing off steam," "containing anger," "blowing up," "exploding," and "hitting the ceiling" (Lakoff 1987: 384–385). Lincoln educators likewise conceived of anger as a dangerous substance contained inside the individual, something that could "blow up" or "explode." The following quotes are comments by educators on disciplinary cases.

> He is close to explosion. It [his anger] appears bottled up inside. (Oct. 30, 1998)
>
> He is easily set off. He is acting out his anger. He blew it on someone else. That can be very dangerous. (Nov. 3, 1998)
>
> I knew that he was packed up. He was so angry. (May 1, 1999)

Lakoff (1987: 386) analyzes the ontology of anger that the central metaphor reveals. Just as a hot fluid in a closed container can take only so much heat before it explodes, so the anger scale has a limit point. People can bear only so much anger before they explode, that is, lose control. Lakoff further points out that anger, conceptualized as a mass entity with heat, has its correlates in the folk theory of physiological effects of anger:

> As anger gets more intense the physiological effects increase and those increases interfere with our normal functioning. Body heat, blood pressure, agitation, and interference with perception cannot increase without limit before our ability to function normally becomes seriously impaired, and we lose control over our functioning. In the folk model of anger, loss of control is dangerous, both to the angry person and to those around him. In the central metaphor, the danger of loss of control is understood as the danger of explosion. (Lakoff 1987: 386)

The hot fluid metaphor focuses on the fact that anger can lead to a loss of control and that a loss of control can be dangerous. It is dangerous because a person "out of control" cannot function normally. That is, the physiological effects of intense anger interfere with reasoning, and actions without reasoning can be very dangerous.

The linguistic model of anger that Lakoff and Kovecses lay out fits well with the conception of anger held by Lincoln educators, especially regarding the danger of a loss of control caused by anger. However, there is an important aspect of the folk model of anger not accounted for by the metaphor but pervasive in the educators' view of anger. It is anger as a psychodynamic entity. In Lakoff and Kovecses's "prototypical cognitive model," anger is always caused by a rather immediate offending event (Lakoff 1987: 397).[8] The model does not hint at the psychodynamic process of the person who is angered. In contrast, Lincoln educators very often talked about particular cases of anger having deep, sometimes unknown, causes from the personal history of the individual student. Consider the following statements in this light:

> It is an anger issue. There's something underneath the surface. (Nov. 3, 1998)
>
> He has lots of issues internally. He is angry at the world. He is angry at authorities. (Nov. 8, 1999)
>
> She gets ballistic without provocation. I heard she was out of control. Usually people build up, but she goes off right away. (Feb. 4, 2000)

In the educators' view, not only is anger a dangerous mass entity contained inside the individual, but it also has a long residency within the person. Anger is something that is underneath. Its internal existence is rather constant. One can get ballistic even without provocation, for anger is already there.

I found that the educators at Lincoln viewed anger as profoundly psychodynamic. This is not to say that they did not count specific situations as a cause of anger. Rather it is to say that they also assumed "deeper" causes of anger and often tried to address them. At times, their emphasis on the psychodynamics of anger was such that the immediate event leading to an outburst of anger was put aside. There was abundant talk about some traumatic experiences the student was known to have had in the past. The reasoning was that the offending event was merely a catalyst to expose the anger the troubled student already had. What made anger feel dangerous was partly the conception that it can reside for a long time and be deep-seated inside the individual. I assert that together with the hot fluid metaphor, the psychodynamics of anger is an essential feature of the American cultural model of anger. I now discuss, through a case, how these two aspects of the cultural model affected the politics of anger in the school.

The Politics of Anger

Among many disciplinary cases in which "anger" was believed to be the real issue, Khoua's case revealed the politics of anger along the lines of race/ethnicity, social class, and gender most vividly as well as the two aspects of the American cultural model of anger—anger as a heated mass and anger as a psychodynamic entity. Khoua's case was considered, from the very beginning, in light of a far more serious incident the school had just experienced. The previous week, two groups of students had a fight in the neighborhood near the school building, after a Halloween dance at the school. The fight was mostly between Afro- and Asian American boys. At the fight, one Asian boy, Tou, shot a gun into the air twice, instigating a series of police investigations and disciplinary actions. The shooting incident set a heavy disciplinary tone for any possible signs of violence not only in the time span immediately following but also in the long run. Khoua's case happened less than a week after the shooting incident, when the school was still in shock.

Khoua Yee was an eighth-grade boy whose family had immigrated from Southeast Asia about five years ago, through a relocation camp. He was currently placed in the level two ELL program, the lowest level offered at Lincoln. Marian Roettger was his ELL teacher, and was in her first year teaching at Lincoln and had several years of experience in post-secondary ELL education. Thao Pang was an educational assistant (EA) in the ELL program, in his third year at Lincoln. He functioned as an interpreter between the school and many parents for the program. I did not know Khoua before his case happened, and saw him only once at the PPC meeting, when a decision was being made as to whether he could stay at Lincoln. In presenting Khoua's case, I will not attempt to condense and make it a coherent whole. Rather I intend to show who was the source of a particular portion or aspect of the case and thus highlight different perspectives on the case more readily. What was unusual about this case was that what "really" happened was not known to the decision makers, and they had to ponder upon different versions of it to make a decision concerning Khoua's future. In the following three memos, Marian Roettger recounted the beginning of the case, as it had happened during her class, Thao Pang narrated what he observed when the case was further developing in the main office, and Tim Miller described what he perceived to be the case as an administrator, as well as what he observed in the office.

Marian Roettger's Memo to Pupil Problems Committee (PPC)
Khoua Yee is a student in my Class 2, ELL 2C. On Thursday, November 4 he appeared to be quite angry in my class and was not participating in the classroom activities. Another student joked to the whole class that Tou was really cool and that he also wanted to bring a gun to school. Khoua then responded that he wanted to kill everyone. I told the two students that this is not a joking matter, it is very serious and we cannot say such things in school because there are serious consequences to such poorly chosen words. I then continued with my lesson.

During the course of the lesson, I talked individually to Khoua twice. The first time I took him outside the room, acknowledged that he seemed angry and asked if there was anything he wanted to talk about. He said there was not. Then, I told him that he had to make a choice. I would like him to stay in class, but if he did, he would have to participate in the activities. . . . He chose to return to class and participated somewhat in the lesson. Before the end of the period, he got up in front of the class and correctly named each of the planets in our solar system. He was the only student to come even close to being able to name them. I felt good about the fact that he had recovered enough to complete such a task.

The second time I talked to him was just before the bell rang. . . . He sat down with me and I told him that I understood that Tou was a good friend of his and that it must be hard to have his friend in jail. He agreed that it was. . . . [There was] a minimum of communication on his part, but I told him that I would like to help and that he was welcome to come see me if he wanted to talk or that he could write in his journal about what he was going through. He seemed to understand this. Then the bell rang and we both went on to our next classes.

After Class 3, I returned to room 209 and told Ann Herbert [the ELL head teacher] and Thao Pang what had been said about the gun and killing. They told me that it had to be reported. I hesitated because I feared that more visits to the office on this day would upset Khoua even more. They suggested seeing Emily Robins [social worker], and I agreed that this was a good idea, because I thought Khoua needed someone to talk to about everything currently going on with him. When I saw Emily, she said that this information had to be sent to administration because of the nature of the comments. I mentioned to her that Khoua had been called down nearly every day that week because of his dress and that I didn't think additional meetings with the AP would be helpful. She said she would talk to the administration about it.

Thao Pang's Memo to PPC
Ms. Roettger talked to Ms. Herbert and me after class and we both recommended that she should go down to the social worker's office and talk to Ms. Robins, so she did. Later in the afternoon, Mr. Miller [administrative intern] called me to his office and asked me to call his parents to tell them about a three-day suspension. Khoua was very angry and felt that Ms. Roettger had betrayed him. Somehow, he admitted that he and a friend did mention weapons and killing animals, but not people. He then started screaming and went out of control. Khoua was very angry, so Mr. Miller asked me to take him down to ISD. He refused to go and as soon as we got out of the main office, he started to walk toward the Glory Ave. exit. Mr. Benson [hall monitor] stopped him and took him to ISD. After that, I asked Mr. Miller to call Officer Carlson [police officer] to come and send him home, which he did.

Tim Miller's Memo to PPC
On Thursday, November 4, 1999 it was reported by Khoua's teacher Ms. Roettger and his Educational Assistant Mr. Thao Pang that he was making verbal threats in the classroom. His threat included a statement, "I don't like anything/anybody and I am going to kill everyone." When I interviewed Khoua, he was very angry about being suspended for his statement. He did agree that he made the statements. His teacher

Ms. Roettger and Mr. Pang, E. A., were also very concerned at the manner and context of his statements. These comments became very disruptive to other students in class and caused fear in them. In light of the previous gun incident, Khoua's anger grew out of control and he became reluctant to go to ISD. To insure safety of staff and students, Officer Carlson was called to pick up Khoua and take him home.

The next day I heard from Marian Roettger for the first time about Khoua's case. She started to talk to me about it by saying that she had been feeling "powerless" over a series of incidents happening to her ELL students. Khoua was adding another case, while Tou was facing an expulsion for his involvement in the racial conflict. She said she was very frustrated with the outcome of her report to the social worker, hearing from the principal that an administrative transfer was being discussed for Khoua. Her dilemma was that given the shooting incident, she couldn't just ignore his statement, but as she feared, her report was possibly resulting in a punishment. While she seemed very concerned for Khoua, it also appeared that she had been much affected by Khoua's response to suspension. She did not witness the scene, but heard that after getting a suspension, Khoua had been shouting "Ms. Roettger is a liar" repeatedly throughout his temper tantrum Thursday afternoon. Upon learning what had happened in the office, Roettger felt "shaken." She said she hadn't felt safe to be around the neighborhood of the school, although she had been planning to sit in a cafe after school. She went home directly.

From Thao Pang's memo, it appears that Khoua felt deeply betrayed by Marian Roettger, thinking that he was getting a suspension because of Ms. Roettger's telling the office on him. While talking to Khoua during the class, Roettger did not mention that she was going to report to the office what he had said (she was not sure at that point as to whether she should). On the contrary, she offered to help him, assuring him that she understood what he might have been feeling about having a friend in jail from the shooting incident. A further point of consideration was that a call from the office might have come to Khoua as a total surprise, as there was a substantial time gap between the class and the time he was called down (two classes and a lunch period). Not having anticipated what was coming might have added to his disappointment and frustration.

On Friday Marian Roettger, with Thao Pang, made a home visit to Khoua against the advice from the administration, although she still did not feel completely safe with regard to Khoua. I reason that Roettger wished to correct Khoua's misunderstanding of her intention and desired to recover her relationship with him. After the home visit, she said, "I am very glad that I made it." She further talked about the visit:

Everybody, including Bill [the principal], told me not to go. They thought it was dangerous to visit him. Even the police [Officer Carlson] came to my class to tell me not to go but to wait till he comes back to school, so that I can have my home ground to talk to him. But I was glad that I had Thao with me. It was funny to see him walking so carefully. You should've seen him. He would look back and side, and he would know what's going on in a quick second. He is very street smart. (I: Did you feel unsafe visiting him?) It crossed my mind too, but I wanted to do it.

Khoua was just a kid yesterday. On Thursday, he was very angry and he looked big (Marian puts her chest out). But yesterday, he was a small kid, watching TV. He understood the situation, and I explained that when I talked to the office, it was out of my hands. I referred him to the social worker and the social worker referred him to the administrator. He said he lost his temper. I said, with everything else happening now, he has to control his temper, especially in front of the administration, because then [if you lose your temper] you are viewed as a threat. He was mad on Thursday, because he was being reported for his clothes everyday. There are other kids who dress like that, but Ann [Ann Herbert] reported him to the office. (I: What did he exactly say? Thao said he said he wanted to kill something.) I don't know what he said. He was yelling that everybody wanted to kill him. . . . I told him not to dress like that. Matching colors, like black and black, does look good, but you have to have black and blue, something like that.

I feel bad that Bill wants to transfer him. I talked to him [Bill Meyer] on Friday. I don't think it will help him. He wants to stay and he feels safe at Lincoln. He didn't like Kennedy [Junior High]. He was transferred from Kennedy. He could get worse by being transferred to another place. I am going to talk about it at the committee meeting on Wednesday. I know him better than any other person, and I didn't feel threatened by him on Friday. He was just a kid. But Thao warned me not to talk too strongly. If anything happens to him again, I could be blamed for that. Thao is a very smart guy, and he's been around at Lincoln more than I have, so I respect his opinion. But I don't think all this situation should influence judging his case. I think his case should be seen on its own. (Nov. 6, 1999)

Note that Roettger perceived Khoua differently during the home visit from what she felt at the school. He "looked big" when he was angry during the class, but on Friday, he was "just a kid" or "a small kid." This change in Roettger's perception of Khoua, or more precisely of the "danger" of Khoua, was an element that would significantly influence the course of decision making regarding Khoua's placement, as I will discuss shortly. For now, I point out that Khoua very likely exhibited his anger substantially during the class, when he made the statement. In her effort to retain Khoua, Marian Roettger later seemed to be careful not to invoke further negative impressions of Khoua when describing the classroom situation at the PPC meeting and in other contexts. (Note that in the above quote too, when I asked about the statement, she said, "I don't know what he said.") However, during the class she did not talk "individually" to the other boy who mentioned bringing a gun but did so to Khoua twice. It is highly probable that Khoua's manner was indicating that he was very angry. If so, Roettger had a reason to feel "shaken" when she later heard about the office scene, given the conception of anger as a dangerous substance. That is, she seemed to have already suspected the "danger" of Khoua.

A PPC meeting was held the following Wednesday regarding Khoua's placement (the other boy who mentioned bringing a gun in Roettger's class was admitted to the school after his three-day suspension, without a PPC meeting). One complication was that Marian Roettger's and Thao Pang's memos to the PPC were not handed out to the committee members. Roettger and Pang had written those memos at the request of the principal. Their memos included not only detailed accounts of the incident and the home visit but also their strong appeals for Khoua's return to Lincoln. It turned out that the principal gave them to Tim Miller, chair of the PPC for Khoua, but they were not distributed to five other members of the committee (three teachers and two support professionals). The PPC members had only Tim Miller's memo about the incident before the meeting.

Khoua and his father attended the PPC meeting, while Thao Pang assisted the committee and the father with bilingual interpretation. Marian Roettger was invited to the meeting to speak about the case, although she did not have a vote. After Tim Miller reported the incident to the committee, reading from his memo, Marian Roettger objected to the way the incident was described. She stated:

> I want to make a clarification here. When he said that, I didn't feel it was threatening. The students were not afraid. He didn't yell. It sounded like more of frustration than threatening. It was a comment [rather] than directed at anybody. (Nov. 10, 1999)

As Roettger's statement partially contradicted the case as it was presented by Tim Miller (after all, she was the only person who was with Khoua when he made the statement), the committee members looked very confused as to what Khoua really said in what kind of context. Khoua himself said that he had been "joking around" when asked if he had been serious. He also said that his statement had been "I want to kill every crap" or that he meant killing "animals like squirrel." Given the confusion, one of the members expressed her frustration, wondering whether they had been spending forty-five minutes on something trivial. Another member said:

> My perception was he came very angry and said I want to kill everybody. But now it sounds he said, he wanted to kill craps. (Nov. 10, 1999)

In the meantime, Marian Roettger, Thao Pang, and the father together were making a plea for giving Khoua a chance. However, the committee members did not seem to be very convinced by Khoua himself in favor of his stay. His answer to the question about his "responsibility" was to be interpreted strongly against him. The following is an excerpt from the observation note of the meeting at a crucial moment:

> Deb Addams: I want to ask Khoua what he thinks is his responsibility for the situation.
>
> Khoua: I know other kids wear like that, but they don't get called to the office. I want to know if matching color is a problem only when you get into trouble?
>
> Tim Miller: (a pause) You are right that it's not spelled out in the [student] handbook, . . . but it's been verbally stated by teachers and administrators. (Nov. 10, 1999)

It seems apparent that Khoua interpreted "the situation" differently from the committee members. At the time, I thought that Khoua was not answering Deb Addams's question, but protesting about a different matter. The committee members thought likewise, as seen in their discussion of the case in the second part of the meeting and interviews with me later. However, no one attempted to help Khoua understand the adults' view of "the situation." Instead, Tim Miller answered his question. Miller had little to say about the clothing question, except admitting that Khoua had a point. He looked a little embarrassed to admit that the school did not have a consistent policy regarding clothing regulations.

Soon the committee dismissed Khoua and his father to make a decision, as was the usual procedure. Marian Roettger and Thao Pang were not invited to this phase of the meeting, which proceeded as follows:

> Tim Miller: The case was presented to us as a terroristic threat. What's the volume and genre? "I will kill every crap." He has a close tie with Tou. He exhibited extreme anger. He was storming out of the office, swearing, cursing. There's real fear I, even Thao, felt. He would go out and smack the wall. He was afraid of going home. He said "I will get killed [if I stay at home]." It was more than a "squirrel" conversation on Thursday.
>
> Gloria Simpson (guidance counselor): Both [Marian Roettger and Thao Pang] were extremely concerned about their safety on Thursday. Then they came back to me on Monday. If the teacher feels unsafe, we can't take it lightly. On Monday, they said they went to Khoua's home and both sincerely felt they overreacted and said, "We wanted him to stay." I'm concerned about his anger. I like to honor their opinions. But what bothers me is he is arrogant, not taking responsibility. He was saying others are not picked on, only me.

Don Gray (teacher): No remorse.

(Several repeat "No remorse," and others nod in agreement.)

Steve Hill (teacher): What did he actually say?

Tim Miller: It was reported he wanted to kill everything or everyone.

Steve Hill: Is he a gang member?

(Someone says wearing white and white could be a sign of an Asian gang.)

Pam Larson (intern social worker): If he was afraid of going home, that leads me to
    believe he's a gang member.

Steve Hill: After the meeting [this morning], Marian said, "I am really upset now."

Gloria Simpson: They were extremely emotional on Thursday. On Monday, they
    both came and said, "I want him to stay." I don't know why they turned 180
    degrees.

(Someone said that it was possible that Marian wanted Khoua to stay because she
    feared retaliation from him, and several agreed.)

Tim Miller: Marian wrote a 3 page long report to Bill, detailed about the incident and
    how poorly we handled it.

Steve Hill: He's been in the office for his clothes. . . . He didn't apologize [for his state-
    ment]. If he were involved in gang, would he be a leader?

Tim Miller: I'd see him as a supporter.

Don Gray: It's confusing. Sounded like serious. We acted on that, and now it's not
    serious.

Gloria Simpson: They were fearful on Thursday. She'd not enter her room. Thao was
    fearful too.

Tim Miller: Marian requested her phone number unlisted. And she called me at home
    after school and asked, "Do you think I am safe at home?" . . .

(Tim Miller asks for the committee's recommendation. No one raised a hand for staying. All of them raised their hands for administrative transfer. Miller concluded that
it was a "unanimous vote.") (Nov. 10, 1999)

Once the exact nature of the statement, previously perceived as a "terror-
istic threat," was open to question, the committee members could not ground
their decision solely on the statement. For other signs of his transgression, Tim
Miller listed Khoua's tie with Tou, his "extreme anger," and the fear that
Roettger and Pang had expressed regarding Khoua's anger. Many others pointed
out Khoua's showing "no remorse" and not taking "responsibility" as clear
indications of his unwillingness to improve his behavior. They also shared
Miller's concern that his anger had caused strong fear in the two staff members.
The last piece of information from Tim Miller on Marian Roettger's initial
response seemed to convince everyone on the committee that she was indeed

fearful and that Khoua was dangerously angry, regardless of the seriousness (or lightness) of Khoua's statement and of Roettger's present sincerity and willingness to retain him. For that reason solely, they could not but favor an administrative transfer for Khoua, I speculate.

Talking individually to the committee members after the meeting, I was assured that the conception of anger as a dangerous substance profoundly affected the PPC's decision, whether or not each of the decision makers attached much weight to Khoua's initial statement. Don Gray and Gloria Simpson did not seem to be entirely certain about the seriousness of the statement, but to them, Khoua's reaction warranted seeing him as a "danger." To them, Khoua's violent reaction loomed larger than anything else:

> If he wasn't reacting that way, if he admitted and said I didn't really mean it, and was calmed down, it might've been different. Or if it happened last year, it would've been different too. If he stays here and something happens later, we may say, something could've been done in November. (Don Gray, Nov. 10, 1999)

> Maybe he was fooling [during the class], but afterwards he was totally irrational and out of control. If he hadn't reacted like that, he would have stayed here. None of us thought we'd vote for administrative transfer, but his behavior didn't help at all. He showed no remorse about what he did, which is scary. We can't take any threat lightly. It [Khoua's statement about Marian Roettger being a "liar"] was a threat of harm to staff. . . . I've seen him in white and white. The other day, he was wearing white and white with a red belt. That's serious. The Asian gang, the Tiger gang, wears white and white. He may be a gang member or a wannabe. A wannabe is more dangerous. Because they want to have recognition from the gang, they do stupid things. (Gloria Simpson, Nov. 10, 1999)

By acknowledging that the decision making about the case was influenced by the shooting incident, Don Gray also acknowledged, in my view, that he perceived Khoua's reaction as dangerous enough to be associated with the incident. To Gloria Simpson, it seemed that his showing "no remorse," making a "threat" to the staff, and wearing matching-colored clothing were good reasons to believe that Khoua had serious anger issues and thus could be "totally irrational and out of control" anytime again, just as he was upon learning about his suspension.

By exhibiting an "explosion" of anger, Khoua himself came to be thought of as an "explosive." And it was most obvious in Marian Roettger's initial response. As described earlier, Roettger felt "shaken" when she found out that Khoua had gone out of control, accusing her of being a "liar." According to Tim Miller, her feeling "shaken" was so strong that she asked Miller, "Do you think they will drive by and shoot at home?" when she called him that day to request unlisting of her phone number to prevent possible threatening phone calls. It seemed that Miller was puzzled and irritated by Roettger's later effort to have Khoua stay, after he had seen her frantically afraid of the boy. "I can't act on one thing and change," said Miller. Even after he saw Roettger trying hard to retain Khoua, Miller still believed that she remained in fear of Khoua. To him, "she changed her story because she was even more afraid." Only after I found out that Roettger had reacted upon her worry that she might be the victim of a gang attack, could I understand that the committee members were greatly confused about Roettger's "changing story." Maggie Ingold, having heard of the case and the PPC's decision, also remarked on Roettger's seemingly inconsistent stance:

> Marian was so afraid of the student that she cried in the teacher's lounge on Thursday. Then she flipped over (Ingold flips her hand). Now she wants him to stay. . . . She was emotional and irrational. (Nov. 10, 1999)

Ingold pointed out an important factor that set a direction for decision makers early in the process: Marian Roettger's "emotionality." In two ways it worked against her wish to retain Khoua. One, Roettger's initial reaction confirmed the possible danger of Khoua as an "explosive," which had already been attested to by his own behavior. When a staff member felt her safety threatened, whether projected or real, it was a serious matter to the administration. Roettger's "fear" provided the PPC members a basis on which to justify their decision, despite all the confusions. Two, by getting too "emotional," Marian Roettger had lost her credibility with the administrators and PPC members, so that her effort to retain Khoua, which I felt was sincere and genuine, was not received as such. Rather, it was dismissed as an act of "changing the story," coming not from "reasoning" but from "fear," an emotion. Just like Khoua, Marian Roettger was "irrational." Differently put, she was not viewed as fully a "person" regarding the case, and her opinion thus would not be considered seriously.

Interestingly, Marian Roettger's memo to the PPC as well as Thao Pang's was not passed out to the committee members. She was "astonished" that "false" infor-mation had been passed on to the committee members by Tim Miller, and very disappointed and frustrated that her three-page letter, which she had written at the request of the principal, was not handed out to them. At the PPC meeting, Tim Miller mentioned her memo to point out her inconsistency, while referring to it as a "report to Bill [principal]" (see the observation note of the meeting quoted above). After school that day, I happened to observe a short interaction between Roettger and Miller when Roettger confronted him about her memo not having been read by the committee members. He said to her that Bill Meyer had given him the letter without saying anything about passing it out to the committee. He then added, "Maybe he just assumed I would pass it out, but I don't know." When I asked him, two days later, why Roettger's memo was not distributed, he said, "The letter wasn't for the PPC. It was addressed to me and Bill." The first line at the head of Roettger's memo read "To: Bill Meyer and PPC" in block print. It is not certain whether Tim Miller did not notice the addressees correctly. In a talk with me, the principal Bill Meyer admitted the issue regarding Roettger's memo as "the only flaw" of the decision-making process, but he did not consider that flaw for very long. He emphasized that it was a unanimous vote, so that he wouldn't reconsider the case. He expressed his trust in the decision-making process by saying, "The Committee looks at the whole picture," adding that he himself had seen some "warning signs" from Khoua. Marian Roettger's sympathy for Khoua had to give way to consideration of a "whole picture."

I pointed out earlier that anger as a psychodynamic and thus rather constant entity is one important dimension of the American conception of emotion, along with anger as a dangerous substance. In Khoua's case, the folk notion of anger as a psychological constant was marked, heavily influencing the decision-making process. The initial statement and his "acting out," and his lack of "remorse" for that matter, were perceived to be instances of the deep anger Khoua had. The anger was treated as a constant that was already there inside him, independent of those instances. The question of what offending event led him to make the statement was never asked during the decision-making process. Khoua himself was considered to be the cause of his own anger. It was perceived that he had "inner" causes of his anger, which were not known to the adults. Gwen Lundy, the assistant principal, had been dealing with Khoua when he was sent to the office for his clothing. Although she didn't seem to think of Khoua's "acting out" as serious, she viewed it as an indication of anger that was "larger" than single instances of acting out might indicate:

> That week, he was being angry, but he was not direct. . . . On the day when he was acting out, he lost control. He was being angry. It was a temper tantrum, profanity, "I hate everybody," storming up and down, that a younger child would do. . . . I don't know what's going on with this child. He was pulling other kids into whatever he does, wearing matching color clothes, disrespectful, threat, organized fight. He was not doing them clearly, but he talked about all of them. He'd keep the situation going. When he was sent down to the office for his clothing, I got few answers. I said, "You can't do that. It appears to be a gang symbolism." [But] I didn't get to how and why.

He did lots of distancing (e.g., shrugging the shoulder, laughing away—Roettger also observed this from him), "I'm not engaging you" kind of attitude. He didn't demonstrate [being] angry at that point. The anger was larger. . . . He was unwilling to address the real issues. (Nov. 16, 1999)

Whether Khoua expressed it or not, Gwen Lundy considered that there were "real issues," of which wearing matching-colored clothing, being disrespectful, and talking about fights were manifestations. The difficulty Gwen Lundy felt when dealing with Khoua was that he was not "direct." In other words, Khoua was not verbalizing his motivations and feelings. As discussed earlier, verbalization of emotions was strongly associated with the ability to remain in control and encouraged by adults as an appropriate intervention. While Gwen Lundy attempted but failed to solicit verbal expressions of "the real issues" from Khoua, in her view they remained in Khoua, and he eventually "lost control" and acted them out.

Deb Addams's comment on the case shows more specifically how the conception of anger as a psychological constant influenced the PPC's decision:

The statement of killing is serious. It shows anger on the boy's part. He didn't show remorse. He wasn't sorry. He changed the subject. We decided to go with the report [of Tim Miller], because possibly it is more accurate. (Nov. 10, 1999)

Note that Addams remarked that Khoua had "changed the subject." This refers to the fact that Khoua pointed out the school's inconsistent policy practice regarding matching-color clothing, when she asked about his "responsibility" for his statement. Tim Miller shared Addams's view, as shown in the following interview excerpt:

I: What do you think was the main factor that led to his transfer?

Miller: Main factors were, based on the report, the statement he made, "I want to kill everybody or everything," the people around him, when he said that, heard it, and the fact that he had a close relationship with the people who were involved in the [shooting] incident. Secondary factors were he showed no remorse or apology. If he said I shouldn't have said that, it might have been different. It was almost a denial, changing "everything" to "animal." He didn't seem to be sincere. He didn't admit what happened. He skirted the issue by bringing up a side issue. After the second session [of the PPC meeting], I was very happy about the decision.

I: Do you think his acting out influenced the committee's decision?

Miller: Oh, yeah. There's a lot of anger. It's out of the environment he is in, maybe not from the immediate family. He hit the wall, cursing, smacking the wall. (Nov. 16, 1999)

Miller viewed the clothing issue as a "side issue," while counting as important factors the statement, his relationship with Tou, lack of remorse, and insincerity. To him, Khoua only showed his insincerity further when he "skirted the issue" by bringing up a matter not directly related to the case under discussion.

Among the PPC members, the clothing issue was considered a sign of Khoua possibly being a gang member and thus of his being dangerous, but not as a source of his anger. At the meeting, I myself was much puzzled by Khoua bringing up the issue, when he must have known that he had been suspended and was now being considered for a transfer for the statement he had made. Listening to him asking about the school policy for clothing, I felt very frustrated for Marian Roettger, Thao Pang, and Khoua himself. From the situation it appeared that he was talking about something else, and I thought that it would work against Roettger's and Pang's effort to retain him. However, I began to suspect that it might have been a direct cause of his anger after an interview with Thao Pang regarding the PPC's decision. I noted that Pang spent considerable time talking about the clothing issue, when he apparently understood I was interested in hearing about the case, not so much about something vaguely related to it. My interview with Pang seemed to somewhat replicate the interaction between Khoua and the PPC members at the meeting. One difference was that Thao Pang was more explicit than Khoua and explained that Khoua had been angry all that week because he had been disciplined for his clothing.

I had heard from Marian Roettger, when first learning about the case, that Khoua had been sent to the office for his matching-color clothing. Although she was concerned that more visits to the office would upset Khoua and for that reason hesitated to report it, Roettger did not then seem to relate the clothing issue to his statement. From her memo to the PPC quoted earlier, she initially seemed to infer that Khoua's anger had much to do with having a friend in jail and circumstances related to the shooting incident. When she talked to Khoua individually at the end of the class, regarding his statement, she mentioned Tou and the incident to acknowledge what she thought Khoua was "going through." When she labeled Khoua's statement as an "expression of anger and frustration," she did not list the treatment he received regarding his clothing as a cause of the anger, but seemed to assume a deeper cause. However, it appears that she began to take the clothing issue more seriously after her home visit to Khoua. The following is part of her memo to the PPC that described the visit:

> Thao and I spent nearly an hour with Khoua on Friday afternoon. While we were there, I did not see any anger. He said that he understood why he had been suspended. . . .

I told him that he was in danger of being transferred from Lincoln and explained that his dress and actions are making people believe that he should not continue at the school. He admitted that he lost his temper and that he needed to work on this. He also understood that his clothing is making people nervous and agreed that he needs to mix the colors. He seemed sincere when he told me that he really wanted to stay and that he would make an effort to change his dress and behavior.

In his memo to the PPC, Thao Pang presented the clothing issue as the cause of Khoua's frustration and as leading to the statement:

> He felt that he had been picked on all week. He saw other students who wore the same type of clothes to school and didn't get sent to the office, but he did. Therefore, he was frustrated and joked about killing everything.

According to Thao Pang, on Thursday the previous week Khoua was sent down to the office by the other ELL teacher Ann Herbert for wearing a red top matching with a red pair of pants. Pang did not recall what Khoua wore on Friday, but on Monday he wore white–white, for which he was again called to the office. That Monday was the day when the police came and questioned in the office many students about the shooting incident. Pang said that Khoua was not questioned because of the shooting incident but was in the office for his clothing, which was confirmed by the principal later. On Tuesday, he wore green–green, and on Wednesday another set of matching-color clothing, the color of which Pang could not recall. For two days, the office did not take any action about Khoua. On Thursday, he wore black–black. This time, Bill Meyer, the principal, came to his homeroom class in the morning and talked to him about his clothing. The statement was made in the second hour that day.

It seems plausible to infer that Khoua was indeed angry for having been singled out for his choice of clothing, and that this led him to make the statement "I want to kill everybody," when an opportunity was given (another boy was talking about Tou having brought a gun to the Friday incident). Especially considering that he was visited by the principal that morning for his clothing, after a series of calls to the office, it is easy to imagine that he became very angry with the school administration.[9] Marian Roettger later more clearly connected the clothing issue to the statement:

> His friend was in jail, . . . and he was called down [to the office] every single day from Thursday the previous week. There were reasons to be angry by Thursday. And there's

a rebellious piece coming in (Roettger refers to the fact that Khoua continued match-ing colors despite the administrator's overt concern). He was feeling powerless, frus-trated. It was really like he was being singled out. I could easily point to other kids who were doing the same thing. When you think about it, *it's all connected.* He was angry for getting picked on, that morning too, he was called down,[10] and that's probably why he said that in the classroom. But the committee didn't see it. (Nov. 16, 1999, emphasis added)

If this inference about the clothing issue is correct, there appear to be several gaps between Khoua's and the decision makers' understanding of the sit-uation. To Khoua, his clothing issue and his making the statement were directly related, so that when he was asked about his "responsibility" for the statement at the PPC meeting, he brought up the clothing issue. He did not "change the subject," nor did he "skirt the issue" by bringing up a "side issue." To him, it was the main issue. By bringing up the issue, he did convey why he was angry, and asked about the "responsibility" of the school for the situation. He presented the concrete context of the particular anger he felt on the day, whereas the adults looked at the clothing issue in terms of his general presumed anger. Furthermore, to Khoua, how he felt about being disciplined for his clothing was central, while to the adults, the fact that he wore matching-color clothes was highlighted, rather than the fact that he was disciplined for that matter.

Another decisive gap concerned each party's understanding of the case in regard to the Friday shooting incident. To Khoua, it is highly likely that his case was perceived independently of the incident. He first drew disciplinary atten-tion for his matching-color clothing on Thursday, that is, before the shooting incident shook the school. On Monday, when the police investigation was pro-ceeding in the main office for the incident, Khoua was called to the office, not for the shooting incident but for his clothing again. From Khoua's perspective, the only connection between his case and the Friday incident, if he ever related the two, would be that he took the occasion of someone's comment on the incident to make his angry statement. To the adults, however, Khoua's case was clearly connected with the incident. He not only implicitly referred to the incident while making the statement, but also had befriended the main per-petrator of the incident, Tou.

In the adults' view, a more important connection between Khoua's case and the incident was the anger that both cases presumably expressed. Khoua's anger could be ultimately as dangerous, in the decision makers' view. That Khoua's case was dealt with by the school as part of the Friday incident was indicative of the view; therefore, although the police did not see him as related to the incident, he was administratively transferred out to another school, along with other students directly involved in the incident.

Another point I want to make about Khoua's case concerns his "lack of apology." All the committee members agreed that he did not show "remorse," and most of them alluded to this as an important factor in their decision. At the meeting, Khoua didn't look discouraged, but looked quite resentful when he mentioned the inconsistency of school policy regarding matching-color clothes. Steve Hill, a PPC member, reflected that if Khoua had apologized, the decision might have been different:

> I don't think we handled it very well. . . . There were lots of misunderstanding. We were frustrated, fed up by the [shooting] incident. It set up the severe tone. . . . Even with all his anger, if he said I am sorry, it would've been different. (Nov. 16, 1999)

Marian Roettger was critical of the expectation of an apology, however, on the ground that Khoua did not have the "cultural and linguistic background" to understand what was being asked for, that is, an apology. In her words:

> He was on level 2, which is the lowest at Lincoln. He can't use subtle language that could make a difference when you have to defend yourself. He doesn't have the background to understand the question culturally and linguistically. . . . It was not fair that that he didn't have the cultural and linguistic background wasn't taken into account. You can't eloquently express your apology if your language ability is limited. . . . The family has been here for about 5 years, through a relocation camp. (Nov. 16, 1999)

Regarding Roettger's concern that Khoua's ability to express himself in English might have affected his communication with the committee members at the PPC meeting, Gloria Simpson remarked that Khoua's English was better than Roettger thought, meaning that he spoke English well enough to be able to make an apology. Most likely, the committee did not need an "eloquently" expressed apology from Khoua. All they needed to see, perhaps, was a clear sign of his being sorry for causing such a situation. Yet a question arises whether Khoua's "linguistic ability" could be separated out from his "cultural ability." It does not seem that Khoua had the cultural understanding of what was being asked of him at the crucial moment. In that case, it was not so much the "linguistic" skill per se that Khoua lacked as the "cultural" background to understand that he was expected to take "responsibility" for his "own" action. Again I see a significant gap between the decision makers, who were middle-class "American" adults, and Khoua, who had lived the American life, mostly through schooling, for only five years. From Khoua's perspective, the situation might not have been all his "own" doing; the school played an important part in creating it. However, "responsibility," as the adults used the term, assumes the self-agency of the individual. The individual, in this case Khoua, was viewed as the sole agent of his own actions and thus asked to take "responsibility."

As an ELL speaker myself, I could not but reflect on my experience regarding Khoua's sociolinguistic ability. Like Khoua, I had been about five years in the United States when I was following his case. I could easily recall instances of my miscommunication with native speakers. Many of these instances I came to realize only later. Aside from minor ones, I did have a few cases, especially earlier in my stay, in which my limited understanding of American culture, American conceptions of emotion and person in particular (e.g., how close I could/should be with someone I had met a few times), was marked. Many times, it seemed that my apparent fluency in English led native speakers to assume that I had a comparable level of understanding of their culture. But I learned that cultural competency is not just linguistic competency, for culture is "embodied" in the person. Five years of U.S. life might have been long enough for Khoua to speak fluent English, however foreign it may sound. But it may be an overestimation of his competency in the dominant American culture to assume that he understood the situation as the American adults would. His English itself was not easy for me to follow, after all, because he had a different intonation from the native one, which was telling of his status as a new immigrant.

Throughout the development of the case, Khoua's unwillingness to verbalize his feelings and thoughts was perceived as a clear sign of his inner anger as well as of his immaturity. I point out that this perception is very much based on the middle-class Euro-American concept of the self and emotion and the corresponding childrearing practices. As I discussed earlier, middle-class adults expect negative emotions to be vented through verbal expressions of them, and utilize the verbalization of feelings as a major means of accessing and thus directing the child's emotional state. Yet from the child's point of view, he or she is not allowed to remain silent about his or her own inner states of mind. Joseph Tobin and his colleagues (1989), in their cross-cultural studies of preschool in China, Japan, and United States, showed that the American emphasis on verbalizing could be very restraining to the child. It is highly probable that Khoua was not familiar with the American childrearing practice and its implications. Further, recent evidence shows that the verbal expression of emotion can be harmful rather than helpful to a person with traumatic experiences (Evans 2001: 83). Even if Khoua had some emotional trauma from having lived in a relocation camp, as suspected by many adults in the school, the verbal expression of the trauma might not have been as effective for treating it as was desired. Instead of subjecting him to direct adult control, providing him with a social environment in which he could learn from his peers would have been more effective, I speculate.

Control via Medication

The last issue I want to examine in relation to the cultural emphasis on emotional control concerns the use of prescribed medication for "psychophysiological" symptoms among adolescents, such as ADHD (attention deficit hyperactivity disorder) and depression. In the American cultural model of emotion, when an emotion, whether it be "impulse" or "depression," cannot be controlled by oneself, it still needs to be controlled by some means, for uncontrolled emotions are potentially dangerous. In other words, when "self-control" is not in effect, external control is in order. Medication, a form of external yet poignantly personal control, comes as an alternative to self-control of emotions. I argue that the use of medication, as an external control that is intended to have "internal" effects on the body and self, fits well with the conception of emotion as personal property rather than socially emergent. Through the use of medication, the individual achieves at least a personal control, if not "self-control."

When discussing behavioral training for developing self-discipline in the previous chapter, I pointed out that in the school, a psychophysiological view of emotion coexisted with a behaviorist stance on emotional control. Whereas the behaviorism underscored the idea that emotional control can be learned, the psychophysiological view of emotion suggested that emotions are ultimately "uncontrollable," as they are the outcome of physiological processes.[11] The conception of emotion as "uncontrollable" was a distinct aspect of the ethnopsychology of early adolescence (see chapter 3). The following excerpt from a conversation with an EBD teacher shows the psychophysiological view of emotion, directly concerning the practice of medication:

> Davis: Paul is ADHD. . . . He can't focus. He is on medication. The goal is for kids to
> take responsibility to know how their body feels. They raise their hand quietly and
> respectfully; they ask for medication.

I: How do they know how their body feels?

Davis: Diabetic persons know how their body feels. They know the sugar level in their blood. You need to know how you feel. You come to know how it feels. Paul knows. It [medication] calms them. (Oct. 23, 1998)

According to Samantha Davis, ADHD is a bodily process like diabetes: a certain "feeling" arises from it. Just as a diabetic person cannot control the sugar level in the body, an ADHD student cannot control the lack of focus. The uncontrollable bodily process gives a signal, upon which medication is to be taken, and it thus becomes controlled.

ADHD and depression were the two conditions for which "medication" was most often applied, yet in different manners.[12] Discussions of medication by school personnel were more likely to involve ADHD cases than depression, to the extent that the term "medication," when used without further qualifications, usually meant medication for ADHD. The school showed more active concerns about ADHD, sometimes even recommending medication for ADHD, while medication for depression seemed to be left more to family decision making. In Child Study Team and Student Support Meetings, behavioral problems were readily associated with ADHD, a condition that customarily accompanied the question of whether the particular student under discussion was "on medication."

In the case of ADHD, a folk connection was made between "behavior" and "medication," as it was believed that "impulsiveness" as a primary characteristic of ADHD was likely to cause behavioral problems. According to Sarah Cooper, the school nurse, the effects of psycho-stimulants used for treatment of ADHD, such as Ritalin, included "following the rules" as well as "concentration" and "focus" on a given academic activity. Medications for ADHD were thought to help students who were "impulsive and reactive" to "have a second to stop and think." The view was that as medication "calms" impulsivity, the student becomes able to "think before acting." That is, if excessive emotionality is suppressed, rationality emerges and gains control. Surprisingly, the desired effect of ADHD medication was much the same as the goal of emotional management training in that both aim to have students "slow down" their emotional response so that they can take a second to think. As my earlier discussion of the rationalization of the self in emotion management training illustrated, it was thought that processes involving emotions were faster than reasoning. Owing to medication, the rational self is achieved, ideally producing the same effects as when self-control is exercised.

I refer back to the case of an eighth-grade Afro-American girl, Irene, examined earlier in this chapter to elicit the folk connection between behavioral problems and medication.[13] In regard to Irene's "assault" attempt on a teacher, many educators mentioned the fact that she had stopped medication for ADHD several months prior to the incident, and attributed Irene's aggressiveness, at least partially, to this fact. For example, when the principal first reported the incident at a staff meeting, one of Irene's teachers said, "She is supposed to be on medication, but she refused to," strongly implying that had Irene been on medication, she would not have caused such a serious problem. At the PPC meeting about Irene's case, the administrative intern Tim Miller explicitly said, "She needs medication." I had known Irene since she was a seventh grader. I was in the same group as her for an activity that lasted for about four class hours in Maggie Ingold's GT English class. She was absent for two days, and I did not get to develop even a nodding acquaintance with her. However, my impression of her was as anything but someone who would "assault" a teacher. When I expressed my surprise to Ingold, she said to me:

> You know why? She was on medication for one and a half years, but she stopped it, because their insurance didn't want to pay for her medication and the family couldn't afford it. (Feb. 7, 2000)

Ingold also credited Irene's mother's teaching her to "hold her head high" for her frequent confrontations with adults in the school, which had just culminated in the incident discussed. But it was apparent that she regarded a physiological disturbance, ADHD in this case, as a major cause of Irene's aggression. Irene's mother seemed to share this psychophysiological view of emotion. At the PPC meeting for her daughter, she said:

> She does have a problem. She has ADHD. She sets off very easily. Everything escalates very fast. Lots of stuff is going on. Lots of activities are going on around her. I was disappointed that she didn't slow down. . . . Outside of this incident, she is a pretty good student. She works hard. (Don Gray [a teacher] asks about ADHD and if she's on medication for that.) She's not on medication now. That's why you see a difference between last year and this year. (She explains that her medical insurance refused to pay for the medication, but lately it decided to do so, so that Irene will be on medication again.) (Feb. 4, 2000)

Like Maggie Ingold, Irene's mother specifically related the "difference between last year and this year" to the discontinuation of medication for ADHD. She implied that "setting off easily" and "not slowing down" were direct symptoms of ADHD, which Irene supposedly did not exhibit last year while on medication.

In many accounts of Irene's case, including her mother's, her ADHD (or the lack of medical treatment of it) was taken as a main cause of her aggressive behavior and medication was presented as a necessary treatment for the cause. It was perceived that Irene needed medication to control her emotions and be "rational." However, I think it is questionable that aggression was directly connected with ADHD in the way the adults assumed. The condition of ADHD may influence the attention span and activity level, but not necessarily aggression. In my view, what the discourses on ADHD readily revealed was not only the cultural emphasis on rationality and emotional control, but also the primacy of the psychophysiological model of mind and body. I do not claim to know whether ADHD has any influence over aggressive behavior or not. But in Irene's case, it would be plausible to consider her growing self-esteem and sensitivity to her surroundings as a source of the aggression, given that Irene reportedly had spoken of her frustrations with teachers in her anger management group. The school social worker described Irene as "very talented" and as having "incredible ownership of her action." Granted that her ADHD had a role in her aggressive behavior, what would have been other factors contributing to the seemingly sudden rage from one of the very few Afro-American students in the GT program at the school? Unfortunately, this kind of question was not asked, at least not openly, and Irene was transferred out to another school.

Not only in Irene's case, but in many other cases that demanded serious disciplinary attention, ADHD and medication for it were very often mentioned. In contrast, depression seemed to draw less overt attention from the school, partly because students with depression were less likely to "act out." For example, compared with ADHD cases, depression cases were less frequently brought up at Child Study Team or Student Support Meetings, two primary contexts for discussions of particular cases. The Health Condition Report of the school indicates this tendency well. In spring 2000, the report showed only four cases of depression, while cases of ADHD numbered thirty-six. Among ADHD cases, there were twice as many boys as girls (twenty-four boys vs. twelve girls). The four depression cases in the report were divided equally, but the two boys with depression were also diagnosed for ADHD or EBD, whereas for the two girls, depression did not accompany any other diagnosis. Moreover, the Daily Medication folder had no one for depression, but fifteen for ADHD. Among the fifteen students with ADHD taking their medication during school, twelve were boys.

The report listed only those cases that had been reported to the school, so it is most likely that there were more cases of both ADHD and depression. Yet it seems at least that the gender imbalance in the numbers in the report is congruent with the research findings that ADHD cases are diagnosed predominantly for boys, while girls are more likely to be diagnosed for depression.[14] Regarding the small number of reported cases of depression, the school nurse said that there would be more depression cases than the number the Report showed. She went on to say:

> People tend to personalize depression more than they do ADHD. For ADHD, there are genetic elements. But depression is more environmental[, they believe]. Families don't want to say their child is clinically depressed, because they may be viewed as a cause. (May 12, 2000)

Through interviews with students, I also came to suspect that the diagnosis and medication of depression were more widespread than they appeared, particularly among girls. Depression was dealt with more as a clinical issue than ADHD; thus it was handled more on the personal level, and less likely reported to the school. It is true that unlike with ADHD cases, with depression cases the environment was taken into account more readily, as the nurse remarked. However, environmental factors referred to in depression cases were often past life events, such as childhood abuse, rather than the immediate social environment the student was in. Or depression was attributed to the student's "personal" issues. For example, low self-esteem, anxiety, and ultimately "hormones" were counted as causes of depression, whereas family relationships, friendships, or aspects of school life were not scrutinized as much.

I was not the only person to take a serious look at the social context of depression. The school nurse pointed out that the transition from elementary to junior high school was so abrupt that many students experienced some depression. In her words:

> A lot of kids get into depression in junior high. They have new feelings about their body, parents, and self-esteem. I remember my junior high. It was horrible. It got a little better at the ninth grade, but it was very hard. It's so different from elementary school. (May 12, 2000)

It was indeed puzzling to me that what causes such anxiety, low self-esteem, or even hormones could as well come from the social environment, yet attention was not properly paid to it. Because it was conceived to be a personal problem, depression was treated individually, most often through medication.

My argument is not that all depression cases are socially derived or that the social context is more important than the individual's psychophysiology. I rather argue that the present tendency does not view the sociocultural environment as an equally significant factor in the condition. Beth, an eighth-grade girl at Lincoln, attested potently to the role of social context in depression and the powerful influence of the psychophysiological model of body and emotion in U.S. society at the same time. Beth was a Euro-American from a middle-class family and enrolled in the GT program. I came to know her through my observation of her History Day drama project. In an interview, when I asked her to talk about her junior high school experience, she mentioned that she had been on antidepressant medication, and later shared an essay with me. The essay, titled "A Memoir of a True Story," is an account of Beth's transition from the elementary to junior high school, which caused severe anxiety in her. Here is Beth's memoir in its entirety:

A Memoir of a True Story
Beth Turner, English GT Class 4

I really like my life, but there are some drawbacks. One is anxiety. When I started seventh grade, I was so anxious about getting homework, not being with a lot of people that I know, and going into a whole new atmosphere.

The elementary school that I went to was a montessori called "C. C. Young." First, second, and third graders shared a room and learned from the same teacher. This was the same for fourth, fifth, and sixth graders.

In my class, we had a work plan that we had to follow during the week. Sometimes I tried hard to get my work done, other times I didn't. However, I always got my homework done.

My teacher wanted to prepare the sixth graders for jr. high by giving us homework (which included math, spelling, sometimes logic problems, and an essay). The homework was given every week on a Friday. We got a whole week to do it, but I felt that I had to get it done on the weekend. This way, I wouldn't have any homework to do in the week. I would sometimes feel guilty if I didn't work on it before doing something fun.

When I entered seventh grade, I was really scared. I thought that it would be fun starting off somewhere else. After 8 years at C. C. Young (pre-K–sixth grade) I felt like I wasn't going to school, [but now] I was going to a different one. I had to get up earlier, which I eventually got used to, but I was very sad and unhappy because I didn't want to go to school, and I had to.

I had gone through a big transition moving on to jr. high. After the first few days of school, I realized how much homework I got, and how little time I had for myself. I was determined to do well in school and in my studies. I pushed myself to get all my homework in by the day it was due. However, there were a few exceptions, because I had no clue about things; I needed detailed directions, and a lot of answers. I asked teachers many questions.

Every day I knew I would get homework. I felt anxious because I got about four hours a night or more. Maybe it was that I wasn't used to the work, or maybe it was hard for me, or maybe that's just how much it was supposed to add up to. A lot of times I would cry on my mom's shoulder. I really hated going away from home, my family, and going off to school where I would get homework. I worked my buns off after school. I really didn't ever want to go. I knew I would get hours of homework, and I really disliked it. It may sound pathetic, but I hated going to school. Sometimes I held my pain in so long at school that I cracked in one of my classes, or perhaps more than one.

My mom and I decided this year that I should go to counseling. I did and I got a wonderful medication to calm my problems. I am no longer full of anxiety. I love the new schedule, and my homework seems to be not half as bad as it had been for seventh grade. This school year has gone by so fast. I'm usually tired, but school is okay, and sometimes fun.

The essay shows that despite her initial hope and expectation, Beth found junior high school to be overwhelmingly challenging. Beth articulated that the sudden changes she faced in the beginning of her junior high school life were the main causes of her anxiety. She listed getting up earlier, having too much homework, and not being given enough directions for homework as major difficulties. She also suggested that the difference in the organization of daily school life between the elementary and junior high schools was a comprehensive factor contributing to her anxiety. Unlike the elementary school, at Lincoln she did not have a designated room with her own teacher. She was instead expected to be an "independent" social actor in organizing and maneuvering in the daily school life. For a starting seventh grader, this change would come as very sudden and arduous. The story tells how she, however, found a solution in a "wonderful medication." Although the demands of junior high school life remained the same, school now became "okay and sometimes fun."

In my observation, Beth was a cheerful and dedicated student, but it can be argued that she was also prone to anxiety and depression. Even so, it seems that the cultural emphasis on independence and autonomy faithfully reflected in Lincoln's curriculum and schedule played a significant role in initiating the anxiety. Although Beth herself clearly pointed out challenges in the school life as a main source of her anxiety, the anxiety was treated ultimately as her own ("my problems") that needed personal counseling and medication. Beth's essay vividly conveys the sense of being burdened by school at the same time that it expresses the folk belief that emotion is personal property and physiological substance, and can be managed by the use of medication.

In this chapter, I have discussed the educational focus on emotional control based on the American cultural conception of emotion, in which emotionality is seen as in opposition to rationality. The central place that emotional control took in American personhood led to a preoccupation with the so-called negative emotions. There were abundant social discourses in the school about negative emotions, anger in particular, and their control. However, positive emotional experiences (e.g., joy and excitement), or possible positive effects of some negative emotions (e.g., the effect of tension on focusing), were not given as much attention. In the next chapter, on creativity, I show that positive emotions, nonetheless, were actively utilized by teachers for engaging students in learning and cultivating creativity as an important aspect of American personhood. The education for creativity at Lincoln also implies that some emotions that are usually designated as negative ones are involved and used in effective learning.

· 6 ·

CREATIVITY

At Lincoln, self-discipline and self-expression constituted a dual educational goal, both closely tied to the ethnopsychology of self in American individualism. In the previous two chapters, I focused on one side of the goal, self-discipline, with emotional control being a major aspect of self-discipline. In this chapter, I examine the other side of the dual goal, self-expression. Self-discipline and self-expression were interrelated in that self-discipline was perceived to be the ground on which to cultivate the creativity of the self. In the educators' view, "individuality" presumed a high degree of self-discipline, the ideal end point being the development of the self-disciplined individual with "inner freedom." With this end point in mind, they worked simultaneously for self-discipline and the development of creativity in their students. This dual educational goal paralleled the contrast between constraints and freedom observed in everyday school life at Lincoln.

As much as I was astonished by the routine behavior control aimed at fostering self-discipline in students, I was genuinely impressed by creativity education at Lincoln. The school, taking a strong pride in its program for gifted and talented students, placed a heavy emphasis on academic excellence, but did not limit itself to "academics." My observation was that creative expression and artistic appreciation were wholeheartedly promoted by many teachers and permeated different areas of academics. There were classes that were specifically designed for creativity development, such as Art, Creative Writing, Theater

Arts, and Orchestra, but they were by no means the only classes in which students were guided to develop self-expression and creativity. Elements of creativity and art were abundant and prominent in classroom activities in the "core" subjects as well. Core subject classes often involved interdisciplinary projects for which students were asked to exercise artistic and intellectual creativity. Even math, a subject that is not usually associated with art, was not an exception. Dawn Anderson, a math teacher, incorporated creativity into her math class through research projects and artistic activities such as tessellation drawing, paper folding, and optical illusion. Her classroom looked much like an art room, with the drawings and shapes her students made displayed on the walls.

The emphasis on creativity in education was the aspect of Lincoln that I enjoyed most during my stay there. Watching students absorbed in an expressive activity was one of the most positive emotional experiences of my fieldwork. The excitement and intensity students showed were contagious, and I missed my students in Korea, who, like Lincoln students, shone beautifully in their moments of creative endeavor. While some of the behavior training for self-discipline at Lincoln felt rigid and constraining, creativity education was inspiring. I rather painfully envied the fact that American students were less pressured for college entrance exams and teachers had far more freedom in designing their curricula, so that both students and teachers had more room for creativity.[1] But it was not just that American classes were less subject to standardized tests. A more crucial foundation of creativity education, I think, was the paramount cultural value attached to self-expression. I am not suggesting that self-expression is the only manifestation of creativity, but in American education as observed at Lincoln, creativity was closely associated with self-expression. The "individual" being an end goal of education, the creative expression of the self was viewed as a key to this goal. In the following sections, I first examine teachers' conceptions of creativity and their approach to developing creativity in students. Then I describe my cultural learning experience from two class activities for which "self-expression" was required. Last, by presenting my observation of students during their most intensive engagement in creative projects, I argue that a rich learning experience occurs at the junction between cognition and emotion.

Creativity as a Higher Level of Learning

To Lincoln teachers, creative activities represented a higher level of education, compared with "fundamentals," "basics," or "textbooks." They greatly valued creativity as a "step beyond." In the teachers' view, "fundamentals" were needed in order to exercise creativity, but they were not the end goal of education. Rather, the expression of creativity was regarded as an ultimate goal, for which the lower level of learning served as a means. Elaine Ferguson, a science teacher, and Carol Knutson, an English teacher, talked about creativity as follows:

> My idea of creativity is to take what you are learning and move it a step beyond what you are learning. To me that is creativity. . . . Creativity to me is taking whatever you are learning . . . as a means [and] taking the idea a step further. . . . It is to get out of the mold of this is what I have learned, and that is the end of that. To me, you take what you have learned and you do something different with it. And it doesn't have to be brand new, but it is just different from what you would expect. (Elaine Ferguson, June 2, 2000)

> We give choices in GT English and we try to incorporate creative things, but we sure didn't do it much this year. We were just way too busy doing what we had to do. But creativity involves choice and it involves going beyond the book. . . . [For example], for a book report we would say write a sequel or a prequel. So there was this straight-forward analysis of the theme, but there was also the creative writing that went with it. You could say that creativity is messy and it takes extra time, and it does and it is hard to grade, but it is valuable. (Carol Knutson, June 9, 2000)

Ms. Ferguson and Ms. Knutson shared the view that creativity involved taking a step further and doing "something different" with what was being learned. For instance, writing a sequel to a book was such a step, and the analysis of the theme of the book was an activity for "fundamentals," which had to be done before taking the further step. "Fundamentals" were by no means devalued by teachers. Most of all, teachers could not afford not to focus on "fundamentals." In fact, sometimes, something that took "extra time" and was "messy" and "hard to grade" had to be sacrificed when demands for the "accountability" of public education were ever increasing and the accountability, in the popular discourse, amounted to scores in standardized exams that tested students on "fundamentals." Frequent complaints by teachers about pressures for "test scores" often directly concerned not having enough time for nurturing creativity, as indicated above by Carol Knutson. I observed that Lincoln teachers struggled between the demand for high test scores and what they perceived to be the most valued kind of education. Nevertheless, they took creativity development as part of the essence of education and attempted to incorporate various "step further" projects, such as poster making, dramatic presentation, and research paper writing, in their classroom teaching. In their perspective, "fundamentals" became more meaningful when applied to creative projects.

Note in the above quote that Carol Knutson stated that creativity involved "choice." The concept of "choice" embodies a value that is close to sacred to Americans (Beeman 1986: 59). It points to the free individual as the locus of power and control. Furthermore, through the exercise of free choice, it is believed, the uniqueness of the individual is demonstrated. To Lincoln teachers, creativity involved free choice at two levels. First, in many cases, doing creative activities was given as an option—students could choose either to do or not to do such activities. Second, and more significantly, students could make their own choices in doing a creative project. They were the decision makers regarding many aspects of their chosen project, so that they would "feel more ownership of it." Teachers strongly maintained that allowing students to choose was crucial to any creative expression and therefore trained students to exercise their free choice. Elaine Ferguson told me about her mother's insistence on a certain way of cleaning the house to point out that "rigidity fights creativity." She stated thus:

> There are some families where you absolutely must do it this way, absolutely, absolutely, and you try to do it a different way and somebody says that is so stupid, you know, that is going to stifle creativity, you know, right off the bat. I think that I have a fairly creative side. I don't necessarily think I am always creative, but I remember when I was growing up . . . that there was a way that my mother wanted me to clean the house and you cleaned from the top to the bottom and if you didn't do it that way, even if everything was clean, you had to do it over again . . . because her theory was that the dirt falls down. . . . If my whole life had been that, if I had been raised to do everything as I was raised to clean the house, you know, I would have been stifled big time. And I think there are students who, because their parents are insecure, can't allow their kids to do anything except in a very rigid manner, and rigidity fights creativity. (June 2, 2000)

However, having "choices" did not mean having unfettered freedom. Choices were allowed only "within certain parameters." That is, free choice had to be exercised in a structured way. One reason was that structuring choices made creative projects more readily gradable. But more importantly, in the teachers' conception, creativity required structure. Ferguson continued to elaborate this point:

> I think there are also people who believe that letting it all hang out brings creativity, and I think that chaos also can stifle creativity. If you have never been given any guidelines, if you have never been given any background . . . it's not going to happen. Creativity is really a very orderly way of doing things. You have to get some basic information. You have to get some ways of thinking of things, and then you can bloom. . . . Some people say I want my kid to be really creative, so I am not teaching him anything. That child will never be creative at all, because they have no basis and also they are very insecure. They are fighting forever to find out who they are and what they are and everything else. (June 2, 2000)

For creativity to bloom, guidelines are necessary, according to Ferguson. Allowing free choices was not the same as allowing "chaos," which was as detrimental to creativity development as rigidity. Not providing guidelines for making choices very likely caused learners to feel insecure, for they would be lost among unlimited choices, not knowing what to choose. Creativity thus required both freedom of choice and structure of guidance. In other words, freedom was to be constrained. I commented earlier that the dual educational goal of self-discipline and creativity paralleled the coexistence of freedom and constraints as a salient aspect of the everyday school life at Lincoln. It is interesting to find the theme of freedom and constraints in the conception of creativity itself.

Ferguson, in the same interview, argued that emotional security of the learner was a prerequisite for creativity development. Being creative was risk-taking; hence if students didn't feel secure about themselves and their environment, they would not be willing to take risks to be creative, she reasoned. In other words, if they lacked confidence, students would not be motivated to be creative. This issue of self-confidence and motivation speaks to another important aspect of the teachers' idea of creativity: creativity involves "self-motivation" and "intrinsic reward." The two concepts, "self-motivation" and "intrinsic reward," are intertwined and in turn they are connected with the concept of "choice." It was reasoned that creativity required high self-motivation, because choosing to do something in a creative way involved taking risks of failing. Being "self-motivated," by corollary, meant seeking "intrinsic rewards." Again, I quote Elaine Ferguson:

> I encourage in the classroom, like when I see them taking risks, saying, and at this age, you can't give them candy, but usually you go, "Right on," and all of a sudden you can see these kids just going, "Oh," you know, "I think I would like to have that happen again." They have to feel that feeling inside because that is what will take them out of here. I can't be forever patting them on the back. They have to, kind of, like that little voice that says "That was a good thought." And then, when that happens again, they will feel it again and that will keep them going. . . . Once you feel the reward of that, nobody can take that away from you and it is an internal thing, not external. (June 2, 2000)

Ferguson contrasted "candy," an external reward, with the "internal" reward of feeling good about oneself, and asserted that students needed to learn to rely on the internal reward. In order for them to succeed beyond school, where they wouldn't have "candy" or the teacher's pat on the back, having the internal reward would be necessary. Further, Ferguson implied that the internal reward was superior to external rewards, for "nobody can take that away." The internal reward witnesses the self as the locus of power and control, which is crucial to American personhood.

It is remarkable that creativity embodies central American values, such as "choice," "self-motivation," and "intrinsic reward." The significance of these values speaks to the meaning that Lincoln teachers attached to developing creativity in their students. Just as persons with internal agency were ranked higher in the ethnopsychological hierarchy of personhood, learning experiences that involved internal agency were placed on a higher level. In the teachers' view, creative activities required internal agency more than any other learning experiences, challenging learners to go beyond what they knew.

Education for creativity presented no fewer challenges to teachers. In promoting creativity in their students, teachers were also taking risks to go further than what was asked of them. Curtis Howell, a science teacher, talked about challenges teachers faced in creativity education:

> You are continually on the front line. You are continually presenting yourself. And how much you want to risk as a teacher. I mean you can be a very boxed-in teacher. Give assignments, do this and this and not really risk much of who you are or your own creativity. If you create something and you are going to bring it in, you are going to have the students do it and it falls flat on its face. You have to be able to deal with that and if you feel badly or if they don't like it, these are things that you deal with. (Mar. 9, 2000)

Howell perceived creativity education to involve "presenting yourself" on the teacher's part. Guiding students for creativity development meant to "risk much of who you are," as it required the teacher's own creativity. Much like the learner, the teacher also needed to have emotional security and self-confidence to be able to try creative teaching and not to be defeated when it didn't yield the desired outcomes. Lincoln teachers drew considerably on peer support for the emotional security and self-confidence to try out creative teaching. As a "team," the teachers held their morale high for creativity education. Not all of the teachers were committed to creativity development to the same degree. Yet the kind of community they built among themselves boosted the professionalism and enthusiasm for creativity development at a general level, which certain teachers took further. I learned from my field experience at Lincoln that creativity comes out of a community of learning at its best, a "community" for all those involved.

Ethnopedagogy of Creativity: Structuring of Choices

Then, how did the teachers actually foster creativity in their classroom? The balancing act between choice and structure, or "structuring of choices," was at the core of the pedagogy of creativity education at Lincoln. Lincoln teachers strongly believed that the development of creativity required both choice and structure, and that providing a balance between the two was a crucial part of teaching. They provided a structure on which students could develop their creativity, by giving very detailed instructions for requirements, evaluations, and feedback. Each of the requirements became a criterion for evaluation, and thus evaluations were finely itemized. Long-term projects were divided into several phases. Directions were given and evaluations were made at every phase of the projects. Students were graded and received feedback on their intermediate products as well as the final ones. For instance, when students in Jennifer Kramer's beginning art class did a mask-making project, they went through a series of steps before working with clay, for example drawing a mask in a small size, drawing parts, incorporating the parts in a big drawing of a mask, and painting the mask drawing. In this project, mask drawing was a finished product in itself, in addition to the clay mask. I was often amazed at how detailed the instructions that teachers employed were and could easily see that they attempted to structure their assignments in certain directions.

On the other hand, as remarkable as the teachers' meticulous attention to process was their seeming indifference to the end product. They deliberately designed creative projects to be open-ended, not specifying what form a project was to take. They left many important decisions to students themselves, so that students had much freedom in the course of a given assignment. Such freedom could be very demanding, for students constantly faced choices that would affect the quality of their project. In what follows, I examine in detail a class assignment in seventh-grade English, to illuminate the open-endedness of the final product and structuredness of the process in creativity education at Lincoln.

American Artist Project

The American Artist Project was a major research project in the seventh-grade GT English course in the second semester. The Artist Project consisted of two parts: writing a 1,000-word research paper about an American artist and becoming the artist. The term "artist" in this project was used very broadly, so that students could choose their subject from a variety of genres (e.g., architecture, film making, fine art, music, photography, writing). The final stage of the project was to present their own art piece to the class with a speech about the artist.

In the Artist Project, students had freedom in choosing their subject and subsequently developing the project. At the same time, there was a set of requirements students were to meet throughout the process. That is, a guiding pedagogical principle of this project lay in the "structuring of choices." A hand-out for the assignment detailed the requirements for the content of the paper and the art product. For the paper, students were asked to write about three things: the artist, the art of the artist, and what the art says about America and/or what the art is about. Therefore, students needed to include biographical information about the artist, a critical examination of the art of the artist (e.g., the particular style of the artist, her/his influence on other artists in the field), and accounts of what the art conveys about American society or human life. For becoming the artist, they were asked to make an art work of the genre their artist worked in, taking on the style of the artist. For example, they were required to produce a collection of poems for a poet, a 500-word or longer writing sample for a writer, or a painting for a painter, suggesting the artist's theme or style. For the art work, taking on the style of the artist was to be the boundary within which the students were going to express their own artistic creativity.

Not only were there requirements for the content of a paper, the writing process also had directions to follow. The whole process of writing a paper was divided into many steps, each one leading to the next. In fact, in the course of two years, GT students were required to do four major research projects for their English course, one each semester, of which substantial writing was part. This step-by-step approach was used for all of the four projects, with variations depending on the type of the project and grade of the students. General steps and requirements of writing a research paper were as follows, though some of these had further detailed instructions:

I. Researching[2]
   1. Sign up your topic;
   2. Visit the school library and/or a public library and decide on ten references;
   3. Take fifty notecards from ten references (notecards are written in phrases only, not sentences); and
   4. Find five good quotes and record them with the author name and page number of the reference.

II. Outlining
   1. Make a rough thesis of your paper;
   2. Organize notecards into categories and make an outline of your paper;
   3. Revise your thesis; and
   4. Think up a title and subtitles.

III. Writing
   1. Write an introduction to present your thesis;
   2. Write the body according to your outline;
   3. Incorporate five quotes into the body; and
   4. Write a conclusion.
IV. Finishing
   1. Put ten references in alphabetical order by author's last name;
   2. Annotate each of the references as to how you used it; and
   3. Write a title page with name, class, and date.

At the beginning of the project, the teacher distributed a calendar that indicated due dates and grade points of the assignments for given stages. Students were usually given four weeks for completing a rough draft, and two more for revising and submitting the final draft, after their rough draft was returned. During the process, they were monitored for their progress by being checked and graded at each step, as almost all the above steps resulted in grading. For the final evaluation, teachers used a very detailed evaluation form, which reflected the requirements of the middle steps. For example, Maggie Ingold graded seventh-grade GT English research papers for twenty items on a scale of one to five points:

I. Form
   1. Timeliness
   2. Readability
   3. Title Page
   4. Thesis Statement
   5. Outline
   6. Parenthetical Notations
   7. Annotated Bibliography (Format)
   8. Mechanical Errors/Spelling and Grammar
   9. Paragraph Structure
   10. Opening/Introduction
   11. Closing/Conclusion
   12. Transitions/Carrying the Reader
II. Content
   1. Information
   2. Organization/Logical Order
   3. Length
   4. Variety of Sources/Bibliography

5. Sentence Variety
6. Use of Attachments/Visuals
7. No Use of "Your" or "I"

An important aspect of creative education at Lincoln was that it engaged students in multiple mediums of expression through a series of carefully designed tasks. For the American Artist Project, students were first asked to write about the genre or style of the art employed by the artist. Then they were expected to express in a different medium what they had examined in their writing. After that, they were to present their research and artwork in a still different medium in the class, this time through a speech.

One day when I was observing Carol Knutson's class, three students made their speeches for the Artist Project, respectively on Georgia O'Keefe, Duke Ellington, and Maya Angelou. For the speech on Georgia O'Keefe, the girl showed her own painting done after the painter's style. Like O'Keefe, she painted a flower big, occupying most of the canvas. Her speech covered what abstract painting is, what kind of abstract painting O'Keefe made, and what kind of things she painted. The girl who presented on Maya Angelou read her autobiographical writing sample about a camping trip, after her speech about the writer. And the speech about Duke Ellington drew my attention. My field-note recorded it as follows:

> The second presentation was very impressive. A boy (Euro) did his research and made a creative product on Duke Ellington. . . . The boy had good eye contact overall, and looked pretty relaxed. He followed through Ellington's life by decade, taking into account historical contexts, including WWII and racism, around the particular times, and commented on the significance of the artist. For "creative product," he composed a jazz piece, titled "A Night in Harlem." He showed the note and began to play the violin. It wasn't a sophisticated jazz piece, but it sounded like having some jazz beats in it. After he finished playing, he passed the note around. It was an A4 size single page note. Along with his name (Brian Needham), his father's name was there as well ("Arranged by Jeffrey Needham"). I guess his father helped him composing the piece. Carol asked how jazz is differentiated from other forms of music. Several (mostly boys) spoke up. One said it has a certain beat. Another boy said jazz has a lot of improvisation. True. It seems everybody was impressed by Brian, the presenter. (Mar. 27, 2000)

Brian's paper, titled "Duke Ellington: Musical Mastermind," traced the musical life history of Duke Ellington, taking into account the development of jazz as a music genre, and the social and political context of the world the artist lived in. For the paper, Brian received an A+. One of the comments on the paper from Carol Knutson read: "I'm super impressed with the depth of knowledge and excellent writing in your paper."

Despite the excellence of his work, Brian initially claimed, in an interview, that he did not enjoy doing the Artist Project. As his parents were musicians and he himself played the violin, he said he was very interested in Duke Ellington and had learned much about him by doing the project. He asserted, however, that he "didn't like that kind of work." I asked him why:

I: Why? What was the difficult part?

Brian: They gave you directions, but they weren't specific. So you didn't really know what to do. Sometimes you were kind of searching for something, but you didn't know what you were searching for.

I: At first, Ms. Knutson would give you . . .

Brian: A sheet of what we need to have.

I: Assignments, right? Bibliography by? Note cards by? So, was that hard to follow? Or?

Brian: That was easier, but like what we need to do was very specific. We had to have five to seven pages, we need to have ten to fifteen note cards, that was specific, and I knew that, because I had done that before. What was hard is like you didn't really know what you were going to put on those note cards, and there was a lot of information. I had to pick and choose the right things, and I didn't know if what I chose was going to be right, and sometimes what I chose could be wrong. And so, how would I know that?

I: What do you mean by wrong? Not fitting?

Brian: Not fitting for the topic idea and so then I would have to go back and get back what was right. But she can't tell every single person what to get. So I can't really blame anyone, but it was just like, I guess, that is kind of good for learning, because, you know. (June 8, 2000)

Later in the interview, when I assured him that I thought his paper was very well written (I said I had seen college papers no better than his), Brian hurried to say that he did not mean that he did not like the project, but that it was "a lot of work." Brian's reflection states that the Artist Project was very demanding work, especially the writing part of it. To follow the teacher's direction was "easier," according to Brian, but "to pick and choose the right things" from an array of information was hard. Although the teacher provided him with detailed instructions about the writing process, it was he who had to search for proper sources, and organize and make sense of them, to write about his subject in a coherent and convincing manner. The project was, undoubtedly, a hard training for students.

Research projects seemed as demanding to teachers themselves, for they meant an overwhelming workload to the teachers. Maggie Ingold said that she had to spend many hours grading research paper assignments after school and during weekends. I often saw her, as well as many other teachers, staying long after school with piles of students' papers to grade. Nevertheless, many teachers remained committed to such activities, which they strongly believed fostered creativity in students. My fieldnote below hints at the enthusiasm the teachers had for their work and students. It was recorded after the Artist Project speech presentation in Carol Knutson's class:

> While a presentation is going on, Carol writes down diligently on an evaluation sheet. She is always a good listener for her students. After one presentation, she clapped hard, as she always does, but then she also looked around as if asking for claps. With the Maya Angelo presentation, it wasn't clear whether or not the presentation was over, so that the audience remained quiet. With Carol's nonverbal but strong request, they clapped. It was funny to see Carol asking for applause, holding her clapping hands up high. (Mar. 27, 2000)

The Artist Project engaged students in richly interdisciplinary and multidimensional learning, challenging them to bring out and enhance their intellectual and artistic capacity. Regarding the ethnopedagogy of creativity, it was a prominent case in point. The whole process was divided into smaller steps in order to make the task more feasible. The English teachers attempted to make explicit every aspect of the writing process, at least in terms of its procedure. It was intended that each step should lead to the next, and the smaller steps be incorporated and make a whole, that is, a research paper. At the same time that they laid out smaller steps, they closely monitored the process by checking and grading the assignments at each step. However, the project required far more than merely following the teacher's instructions. Teachers tried to give students a balance between choice and structure, but eventually the balancing act itself was to be learned by the student. Just as students were expected to learn self-discipline modeled on external discipline, they were to learn to be creative with the help of an external model. Teachers took it as their job to provide a well-structured boundary. The boundary had an internal structure like a maze in which students themselves were expected to find a way through various conditions to reach a goal. The ultimate goal behind immediate ones was "self-expression." A seeming paradox was of course that between the freedom of and structure for expression.

Self-Expression

"Self-expression" was a recurring theme in the education of creativity at Lincoln. It was supposed that students would express their own "self," or "who they are," by being engaged in creative endeavor. Students would ideally "choose" a topic that reflected their interest, be "self-motivated" to work on the topic, and seek "intrinsic rewards" for their work. Some class activities involved "self-expression" more directly than others, but in general, creativity seemed inconceivable without its association with the notions of self and self-expression. The idea of originality, in Western individualism, presumes the autonomous individual as the creator and self-expression as the paradigmatic form of creativity (Montuori and Purser 1995). Creative expression becomes a practice of "being oneself," so that a final product would reveal part of the self, at the same time standing as a proof of the self as the creator. Differently put, the self is both the subject and object of expression.

In this section, I examine two class activities, one in English and the other in social studies, in which I participated as a "student." The English class assignment, writing a "bio-poem," was explicitly designed for "self-expression," in which the self was the object of creative expression. The "Personal Geography" activity in a social studies class gave me much insight into the pervasiveness of "self-expression" in American education, although it was less explicitly about self-expression per se.

The Visual Bio-Poem in Motion

The bio-poem was the earliest major project that Maggie Ingold assigned to the incoming seventh graders in her GT English course. It was to write an autobiographical poem and present it in a visual art work. Two preparatory steps preceded the main activity of writing a poem about oneself: free writing and a bio-map. We students were asked first to do a one-page free writing exercise about "who I am" as a homework assignment. In the next class, based on our free writing, we made a bio-map. We were instructed to circle important words or phrases that described "me" in the free writing and to draw a web-like outline of how to represent the self. In the bio-map, the self ("I am") was placed in the center, surrounded by each of the constituting elements (circled words). This process led me to construct my self in a certain way, a way that corresponded with the cultural psychology of individualism. The self was to be an independent entity with a repertoire of distinct features (see Markus and Kitayama 1991;

Sampson 1988). To discover and express the features, an imperative in American personhood, was a key goal of the activity.

As we now had an outline of our self-representation, writing a poem and making its visual presentation were given as a homework assignment. Maggie Ingold requested that not only the poem but also its presentation reflect "who you are." While explaining the assignment, she said to her students:

> "I need to know who you are visually as well as in a written form." She showed an example from a past year. It was a work by a girl. She used an old file folder, but decorated it in such a way that we didn't realize it was a folder. She drew smiling faces and put glittering stars around her poem. Her handwriting was very neat. With the example, she asked us what we can tell about her personality from the art piece ("How does her personality feel?"). Students said, "She is happy" (Maggie: Yes, she has these smiling faces here), "She is neat" (Yes, her handwriting is very neat), and "She likes to draw." Maggie told us about many other examples, which were artistically expressing oneself. She again stressed, "I need to see visibly who you are." (Sept. 17, 1999)

For the poem, we could choose either to write it on our own or to use the formula given by the teacher. We could differ from or add to the formula as well. The formula was as follows:

Name
Renaming yourself two times
Three adjectives describing yourself
Four adverbs
Three verbs
Any two phrases

I fully participated in the project, going through the middle steps to presenting my autobiographical poem in a visual work. It was through this participation that a revelation about myself in regard to "self-expression" came. It was astonishing to realize that I was not familiar with the kind of self-expression that was asked for in the assignment. The following fieldnote of a class session of the project shows the dilemma I faced in the assignment:

> We had to draw a map of ourselves with four or five significant things. Maggie took an example of her and drew a map on the board. As I wrote a free writing and drew a map of myself, I realized that the work required me to open up myself, about which I felt a little embarrassed. Perhaps Maggie wasn't asking "opening up" so much as "expressing" myself. I am not sure how much the assignment was about what kind of person I "am" versus what kind of person I want to "present" as myself. Here I find that I seem to differentiate the persona, which is more social, from the self, which is more inner and reflective. Would the students feel any conflict or embarrassment,

thinking of a gap between the two modes of the being? What is the "I" when Maggie asks us to write about it? I found that my free writing on myself was telling the way that I don't usually use, which felt to me a bit like boasting. In short, I am not used to claim about myself in such plain, thus powerful, words. For instance, I've never said to anyone or even to myself that I am an organized person. It was said to me by others, but whenever it was said to me, I was automatically thinking like "Oh, I am not." . . . Or, I have never, indeed never, even thought that I am generous. But I wrote down, "I am generous to people who need help." It felt awkward much, but that kind of line was asked by Maggie, I think. It felt like I was boasting. (Sept. 17, 1999)

My dilemma about the assignment was twofold. First, I felt that I needed to "open up" myself for the assignment and I was not comfortable with it. It seemed that my inner self, which was not easily accessible to others, was being asked to make an appearance to the public. Not accustomed to such appearances, I could not easily decide how much I should reveal of my "self" and in what ways. I was not sure in the least whether I took the assignment too seriously. The other discomfort came with the descriptive terms that were expected to be used in the poem. As I labored to find words to "express who I am," I felt as if I was transgressing the virtue of modesty. I managed to write a poem in the manner that many other students wrote theirs, and my work, though simple, was displayed in Ingold's room, along with other visual works. My feeling of me "boasting" lingered, however.

Yet students did not seem to have the same dilemma. Or at least they did not seem to feel as much difficulty as I did, if any. The tones of their poems seemed very confident and assertive. Some of the words repeatedly found in many poems included "bright," "creative," "funny," "honest," "intelligent," "outgoing," "shy," and "sports person." Favorite things or activities, pets, and sports, being the most popular items, were presented in the poem, as part of the self. Many students wrote after the formula with different degrees of variation, while quite a few took the freedom of writing an unstructured poem. Their visual works were remarkably diverse, some being superbly original. For example, a girl made a big piece of cookie (a pizza size) for her bio-poem titled as "If I Were Food . . . ." She represented herself as a cookie and wrote about her ingredients. Each verse of her poem was written on a small paper flag, hung onto a decorative toothpick, and put on the surface of the cookie. Some students made a montage of visual images that spoke about themselves. Some others used objects that represented important things to them, such as a ballet slipper or a cat doll. Notwithstanding my own difficulty, I enjoyed the students' works, many of which were apparently products of many hours, much effort, and creative spirit.

Following are two of the bio-poems I collected. The one by Olivia Tate was presented in an artistic booklet with her self-portrait on the front. In the pages of the booklet, the poetry lines were accompanied by cute yet elegant images made of color paper. The poem by Nick Voigt, titled "In My Room," was written on a palm-size paper with a cover, painted as a room door. For their bio-poem projects, both Olivia and Nick received a full score, Olivia getting extra credit for her visual presentation. These poems were judged good examples of "self-expression," in that each revealed the poet's "personality" in a unique, not necessarily boastful, way. Olivia followed the suggested formula, and Nick did not use it.

[Bio-poem]
by Olivia Tate

Olivia Tate
Owner of a hyperactive dog
Painter of puppets and pictures
Artistic
Organized
Always adventurous
Quietly reading,
Happily skiing,
Neatly drawing,
Slowly eating,
When I'm not acting or dancing about,
I'm not opposed to fishing for trout
Quiet as a mouse
Cool as a cucumber
O.T.

In My Room
by Nick Voigt

In my room, a cut a bump,
Upon my head a giant lump!
Could my brothers wish for more?
The answer is a locked door.
But o what a bloody fight,
A kick, a scratch, a punch, a bite!
To whom is the punishment stuck like a burr?
Daddy's little angels oh no sir!
To my [room] is where I go,
The door is locked, I scream oh no!

In my room I sit alone,
A bruise, a cut, an aching bone.
All seems lost and then I hear,
The sound of words inside my ear.
I take a step and then a look,
Upon my bed there lays a book!
I open up the cover, black,
All the anger I now lack!
My mom says, "Nick!" with a sigh.
"Five more minutes!" I reply.

Personal Geography

"Personal geography" was another class assignment requiring self-expression, where I felt a contrast between myself and other students. The assignment was given in an eighth-grade Humanities social studies class, which was for a survey course of world geography and culture, taught by Earl Gibson. "Personal geography" was the very first class activity of the course, and as the semester proceeded, the class advanced to the geography of the state, and to world geography. One of the later class assignments was to choose an ethnic group living in the state and research its country of origin for its geographical and cultural features. The course was designed in such a way that students would move from their self progressively out to the world and look at it from their own vantage point.

In the first week of the semester, Earl Gibson introduced the course by stating what he thought geography was about. He said:

> You are born geographers. (He starts from when we were in mother's womb; when we were just born; when we began walking, to say that we always try to figure out "where we are.") As we grow up, we expand the horizon. All we are gonna do this year is learn way around. You're gonna feel power. Geography gets you power. The more you know about the world, the more confident you feel. . . . We want to push the boundary further. (Sept. 8, 1999)

He then went on to illustrate how he himself had "expanded the horizon" and "pushed the boundary further," by telling students his life history in terms of world geography. Through the stories of his growing up, he led students to reflect on their own life history and its relation to geography. He again stressed, "We have been a geographer since we were born. That's why we start with

ourselves." Gibson also pointed out the importance of the sense of space, physical and psychological, in our everyday life, by doing a simple experiment
about spatial distance among people in the class. He remarked that how people
locate themselves in the world can vary across societies, each with a different
sense of personal space. I was soon to experience a cultural difference in geographical conception between me and the rest of the class.

The assignment of "personal geography" involved two parts: first, presenting to the class our own personal history in terms of geography and our
interests in other places, and second, drawing a map of where our house was
located. We were given questions on a worksheet for the first part. For the map
drawing, we were instructed to use our "mental map" and draw a map "around
our house" on a blank sheet of paper. Gibson told us to draw "as far as" we could
go, so that I drew my house and many other places that I frequented. My
drawing covered about six miles in total, in three directions from my house.
Next class, Gibson showed our maps, most of which were still in progress, using
an overhead projector. My reaction after I saw other students' drawings was
recorded in my notes:

> It was interesting to see each of the drawings. Some were very detailed and quite artis-
> tically expressing the area around their house. What struck me was the difference
> between the students' drawings and mine. Everyone, except me, drew the nearby area
> in detail. That is, they didn't draw an outline or skeletal sketch of a wide area, as I did.
> Most of them covered about three or four blocks at most. EG showed mine too, and
> commented that it can be used to tell people directions to get to my place. Students
> recognized mine (They said "It's hers," looking back at me), because it was too neatly
> written and drawn to be one of theirs. I felt a little embarrassed, not because mine was
> shown, but because it was too different from other drawings. I was reminded of a com-
> parison made between Korean children's drawing and American/Western (I am not
> clear about this) children's drawing of "rockets." Typically Korean children drew
> many rockets located in a vast space. Those rockets are small and inside is not shown.
> All you can tell is the shapes and colors of the rockets, looked at from outside. On the
> contrary, Western children typically drew a rocket, big enough to occupy almost all
> the drawing space. The rocket shows a very detailed inside structure, which may show
> the operational mechanism of the machine. . . . I recalled that EG said, "Draw the area
> around your house as far as you can go." . . . It's surprising why I didn't take EG's
> instruction the way the students did. I automatically assumed that I was doing exactly
> what was expected. And Earl said "Good" after all. Now I realize that his "Good" was-
> n't really about my work but about my willingness to work. (Sept. 14, 1999)

After the drawings were returned for completion, I started a new map, instead of
finishing my first map. This time I drew in much more detail the surrounding area

of my place, covering two or three blocks. Earl Gibson looked at my second drawing and said, "It's better. That's closer to what I expected."

It struck me hard that I had not had the faintest idea of what the teacher had really expected. At the same time, it was astounding to find that no other students had drawn their map in the same fashion as I did, that is, that they had known what had been asked for. In my initial understanding, the purpose of the activity was to show where my house was located in relation to other places, so that in my drawing, directions to get to my house were made obvious, as Mr. Gibson pointed out. Yet what was being asked for was, rather, to show what the area my house was in looked like. I realized that I was to treat my neighborhood as a unit of geographical perception and represent it in my drawing. Earl Gibson, therefore, commented that the farther we moved out in our drawing, the less detailed the picture would be, as we were less familiar with the farther area. It seemed as though the neighborhood was to be treated as an extended self and the self was to be represented in detail. The counterpart in my first drawing would be my house. Interestingly, my "self" was not extended (or expanded) as much, nor was it shown in detail. However, my drawing clearly showed the positioning of the self against others. I did not "express" my extended "self" but located it in regard to other places.

When I listened to the teacher inform the class that we would start with "ourselves" and "expand" out, I sensed and was surprised that even for a world geography course, the starting point was "I." Yet I did not exactly understand what he meant. For I did not share the cultural conception of the self, which could be "expressed" and "expanded." As an operational premise of the assignment "personal geography," the concept was shared by the teacher and other students, without being questioned. I, as a cultural learner, however, needed to make a conscious effort to reveal the premise in order to learn it. And it was revealed only through my trial and error.

"Self-expression" not only concerns creativity per se, but points to the stance of the self to be taken toward other people and the world more broadly. It presumes the autonomous individual with unique internal attributes. The individual is to express the attributes, rather than his/her social positioning, for example, as they are thought to lead him/her to be and behave in a certain way. The attributes of the self become the objects of expression, while the self is the agency of apprehending its own attributes. Therefore we have "self-expression" as a prevailing form of creative expression.

Creativity: Going beyond the Dualism of Cognition and Emotion

In the previous chapters, I argued that the dualistic notion of rationality and emotionality underlay personhood in American individualism—emotion being conceived as antithetical to the ideal of the rational self. The Euro-American, middle-class idea of personhood, which emphasized rational control over emotions, was a dominant influence in the socialization of personhood at Lincoln. When the dualism was applied to the conception of schooling, a particular association was made between "academics" and "cognition." "Emotion" was thought of mainly as a deterrent to educational performance as well as personhood development, a view that was pointedly illustrated in the metaphor of "brains on vacation." Yet one of the most important features of the "academics" at Lincoln was its active involvement of the "emotion" of the learner. Lincoln teachers fostered in their routine activities the expression of feelings and emotions as a prime example of "self-expression" and thus creativity, some of the most creative projects invoking strong emotions in students.

In many classes different subjects, I observed that "journal writing" was a regular part of the class. For example, Lisa O'Conner, an English teacher, started her class with daily writing. She gave the students several topics they could choose from, which one day were "What is the hardest thing about growing up? When was the last time you told your parents you loved them? What things have adults told you that you suspect are not really true? Do you think they actually believe these things? What tricks do your friends use to get you to do things they know you really don't want to do?" Similarly, Diane Nash, an LD (Learning Disorder) teacher, started her class with "journaling" for the topics of "depression and sadness" when I was visiting her team teaching class for seventh-grade science.

Teachers encouraged students to express their feelings through more complex assignments as well. The Weather Journal assignment in Curtis Howell's seventh-grade GT science is illustrative in this regard. The assignment was to record for four weeks "what you see, smell, and feel" about changes in daily weather. The following fieldnote further recorded the requirements of the assignment:

> Students need to record general weather observation for each day; record changes in the observed weather; give some explanations for the observations; identify thoughts and feelings for themselves related to the weather; present five different types of clouds through photographs, video tape or sketches; take time to relax and note what

thoughts come to them about three sun sets, three sun rises, and a full moon, and aspects of their life; and write or draw either a poem, sketch, or short story about sun set, sun rise, and full moon. (Apr. 14, 2000)

Through this assignment, Curtis Howell intended students to explicitly recognize and reflect on their subjective experiences of natural phenomena. The Weather Journal shows a typical design of a class assignment that was clearly aimed at creativity development. It asked students to apply what they had learned in class to different or real-life contexts, draw on their own experiences, synthesize, and express their understanding in an artistic medium.

The dramatic performance for History Day best exemplified a high level of intellectual work that required an intense emotional involvement.[3] In this case, emotional involvement was multiple, in that students were to enact their engagement in their topic and characters, and at the same time to show their own self-confidence regarding presenting themselves in public through a performance. The performance project consisted of a research part and a dramatic presentation of the research. The research part was much like the one I described for the American Artist Project, except that writing an abstract of their research with annotated bibliography and a script was required, instead of a research paper. Students could do either an individual or group performance, and were responsible for directing the play as well as supplying costumes and props.

In the theatrical performance part, students' emotional engagement in their project was heightened, which of course was transferred to the audience. The following fieldnote describes a History Day play at the school-wide competition that strongly affected the audience. The play was about the Vietnamese War, performed by five Asian American students, including one boy who had recently immigrated from Vietnam to the United States at the age of ten:

> There were three parties—South Vietnam, North, and Hmong. And later, the United States, as a place to migrate to after the war. The play shows that the Vietnamese who are now living in the United States are still haunted by the war (a flashback is a dream of a Vietnamese student in class in a school in the United States). The tragedy is also revealed by the Hmong woman who accidentally "kills" her baby by giving it too much opium to soothe not to have its crying sound, while escaping in the mountain. The actors say a once beautiful land became a bloody battlefield during the war, of which the impact is still felt. I got very emotional at several scenes. Especially battle scenes made me almost frightened and sad. (Mar. 24, 2000)

The following is from the observation of an individual performance at the state-level competition by Molly, a seventh-grade student at Lincoln. The play was about a labor strike in the 1930s in the metropolitan area, a local historical event:

> Molly's father and sister, who came with her, didn't get to see her performance, because she thought she'd be more nervous if they were watching her. There were two judges (1 F, 1 M) sitting in the front middle of the room. . . . As Molly was ready to start, the male judge told her to take a deep breath to be relaxed, and then the two introduced themselves to Molly. Molly started. . . . Molly didn't look nervous during her play. She didn't forget any line of the script, and acted very well. . . . When she was changing from a reporter to a newspaper editor at the hanger, with her back against the audience, she took a deep breath, which I felt was of relief and determination at the same time, as she finished the first character without any mistake and had two more characters to act. I imagined that performing a one-person play in front of judges and audience would need, and train them to have, self-confidence. (Apr. 29, 2000)

Both drama projects illustrate that engaged learning involves an array of emotions, not just positively toned emotions or good moods. In the case of the Vietnamese War drama, the actors played out their experience, though indirect, of the violence of the war in a theatrical form. It was as though the students were reliving a phase of their parents' life history and thus tracing the process of their becoming "American." The note on Molly's presentation highlights that tension and nervousness, as well as confidence and eagerness, were part of her emotional experience in the competition. While a high level of anxiety most likely undermines the intellect, a modicum of anxiety (a mildly elated state) enhances mental performance (Goleman 1997: 78–85). It seemed that a successful public presentation of History Day projects depended on the optimal relationship between anxiety and intellect. The emotional intensity, from enthusiasm and anxiety at once, was characteristic of students' experience of the History Day project. Two eighth-grade girls, Cathy and Beth, talked about their participation in a state-level competition as follows:

> I: How did you like doing the actual play in front of the judges?
>
> Cathy: It was kind of intense but it was fun after a few minutes of being on. You kind of got a little less intense.
>
> Beth: At first. Oh gee. At first, during the rehearsal when we got there, our stomachs were in knots and butterflies and we were so nervous and scared.
>
> Cathy: Then Alissa [another student] gave me a few shoulder rubs and that helped me relax a little more.
>
> Beth: When we started we were really scared and then once we got into it like our second or third line, we were fine. (May 16, 2000)

Students who played in performances regularly stated that they took their drama project at a deeply emotional level. Unquestionably, the emotional involvement was a major directive force of the remarkably challenging task. Without enthusiasm and perseverance, it would not be possible to spend extra hours daily on researching, writing, practicing acting, and searching for props, for at least seven weeks. Seven weeks was the time from the beginning of the project in class until the school-wide competition.[4] Many students spent far more time than the minimally required time, spending hours and days in searching through academic literature, collecting primary data, or interviewing. In the process, teachers and many parents helped them in various aspects, ranging from giving a ride to suggesting ideas to finding props. Even with all the support, the task could not be completed without the zeal and persistence students themselves had. Cathy, who performed a play about the women's suffrage movement with Beth and two others, pointed to the righteous anger about male chauvinism as a critical force behind her emotional involvement:

> I would say *acting out what you feel is so right*. Like, I really got into this part, as we were writing the play. I felt or got upset with a quote that Napoleon Bonaparte said. He said that nature intended women to be our slaves and it continues on and then the last line is like women are only machines for producing children. That upsets me. I can't believe that men would actually think that. That is just wrong. (May 16, 2000, emphasis added)

Another important source of emotional involvement came from working with peers. Making and maintaining friends was a paramount concern of early adolescents. In most cases, students preferred to work with other students in class, and some teachers even used working with peers as a reward. Doing group work for the History Day definitely gave an opportunity for developing solid friendship with other students. Cathy and Beth told me that they and two other girls were more or less on a "hi" basis before the project, but as they worked together for a prolonged period of time with a common goal, encouraging one another, they became very close. Cathy said that one important reason to choose to do the drama project was the opportunity to work as a group:

> I knew that it would seem better for me to do history day, because I felt that it seems more fun to work with a group and make a play. I like to act. I think that doing a performance for history day was turning like research and writing into fun, something really fun. . . . I kind of miss it, because now we don't spend as much time together. (May 16, 2000)

According to the students, in the case of group work, the two most important factors of engaged learning were personal interest in the topic and peer interaction. Both factors speak clearly to the significance of affect in learning. It seems that those students who were able to form a viable community of learning enjoyed the intellectual challenge the most, thus preparing themselves for further challenge. Needless to say, the kind of community is the one that allows and encourages learners to incorporate their emotion and cognition in personally relevant and creative ways. I will return to the issue of the community of learning in the concluding chapter, as part of the cultural critique I attempt to present.

I have repeatedly pointed out that learning is fundamentally an affective process as well as a cognitive one, and this critical feature of humanity cannot be adequately explained by the commonly held Western dichotomy between rationality and emotionality. This could not be argued more effectively than in these simple words. Beth stated:

> I think stuff should be fun. . . . If it is more fun, it would probably encourage students
> to really get into it and learn it and take it into their brain more. (May 16, 2000)

The "brain" of early adolescents was metaphorically supposed to be "on vacation," due to excessive emotionality. The metaphor is an expression of a deep concern about emotional self-discipline, but it is also related to the cultural assumption that learning is about cognition, set apart from emotion. However, the experiences of learning and teaching in reality do not match with the assumption. It was indeed very fulfilling to observe that the dualism of emotion and cognition was not an omnipresent force in schooling. Teachers actively sought to engage students emotionally in their learning, and students were sensitively tuned to express their emotional, rational, and social self all at once. The cultural emphasis on "self-expression" as a principal form and foundation of creativity was a main factor in the incorporation of emotion into classroom learning. I assert that this is one of the main strengths of American education. To strengthen it further, it needs to be applied to a broader range of students, not just the "gifted and talented."

· 7 ·

CULTURAL CRITIQUE

I have so far discussed how individualism influences the socialization of personhood during early adolescence in a school setting, heavily focusing on the workings of the American cultural conceptions of human development, emotion, self, and person in adolescent education. Examining the influences of individualism demanded special attention to the role of the middle-class model of personhood in affective education, for this social class is noted for its allegiance to the core values of American individualism.

In the Prologue, I pointed out that my own subjective experiences of two societies were a critical tool in this ethnographic study of American schooling, and alluded to some important cultural differences in education between Korea and America. Now I wish to present more clearly "anthropology as a cultural critique" for American schools, through my comparative perspective.

My critiques of emotional socialization in American schooling can be summarized in three points. First, the socialization of personhood was largely based on the negative view of emotion, in which emotions were regarded as obstacles to intelligent action. Second, the socialization process was heavily adult-centered, with every individual student ideally becoming the focus of the educational attention of the adult, as the middle-class model of the parent–child dyad would grant. An unfortunate corollary was that a negative view prevailed over the peer group orientation of adolescents, leaving much to be desired for fostering positive peer influence in school. Third, one of the most significant strengths of American schooling was the education of creativity, its powerful motivation coming from the cultural emphasis on individuality. All three aspects of American education, observed at Lincoln Junior High, are related, and each speaks to the potent influence of individualism.

The negative view of emotion was a strong backdrop to the cultural model of emotion, self, person, and adolescence. The Enlightenment legacy of individualism extols rationality. Emotion is to be controlled by the faculty of reason, so that the rational self reigns over the emotional one. Emotion is regarded as damaging, rather than vital, to reasoning. This negative view of emotion is blended to the biological model of adolescent development, resulting in the popular notion of the storm and stress of adolescence. In the biological model, emotionality is regarded and highlighted as an effect of the biological process of sexual maturation. Just as maturation during early adolescence is dramatic, its effect on the psychophysiology of the adolescent body and mind is thought to be correspondingly dramatic. Early adolescence is therefore characterized by a remarkably vulnerable emotional state, due to "hormones." The primacy of the biological model of adolescent development has consequences. The problem of the biological model is not in conceptualizing adolescence as a biological process, but in its tendency to separate the biological process from the social and cultural context. The model does not seem to allow room for considering cultural influence on biological development. The impact of the ideology of individualism on adolescent life is tremendous but has not been explored as such. In fact, individualism promotes the biological model, by keeping the individual apart from the environment and prioritizing the former in modeling human development. In this sense, the biological model itself is part of the cultural context in which American adolescents grow up. The biological model of human development and the cultural psychology of individualism together contribute to adolescent socialization in a way that puts an excessive emphasis on the control of emotions.

Adolescence is perhaps the most poetic of the human life stages, being at the threshold betwixt and between the two distinct worlds of childhood and adulthood. Yet the emotional richness and sensitivity of this period is not well understood, much less welcomed. Even more worrisome is that adolescence itself is conceptualized as a pathological condition in need of treatment. I am afraid that this view provides a rationale for the expansion of the treatment market targeted at adolescents, ranging from medication to hospitalization.

The emphasis on emotional control is directly related to my second point, adult-centeredness. In the middle-class household, where a nuclear family is a standard form of family composition, the dyadic relationship between the parent and child is given a greater weight. In an extended-family household, where the child can form multiple relationships with more adults and siblings, the attention and affection are more diffused. The child is positioned in a wider kin network of adults, who assume parental roles for the child. In contrast, in the nuclear family, the child receives focal attention from the parent, and parental roles are rather exclusively reserved for the parent.

An American addition to the family dynamics is the cultural stress on emotional management and independence. Given that emotional control is an important aspect of the cultural capital of the American middle class, it becomes a main concern in child rearing. The parent–child dyad is fully utilized to train the child in the art of impulse control. Upon puberty, the parental concern for emotional control is accentuated, and so is the child's urge for independence from the parent. On the one hand, perceiving early adolescence as a critical time (final before adulthood) for inculcating emotional control, the American parent directs the adolescent development of moral sentiment through a strong dyadic relationship. On the other hand, another cultural message given to the adolescents themselves is of being independent. Adolescence everywhere is a time to intensify the separation process from the parent. Yet in the United States, where independence is a cardinal cultural value, the separation process seems to involve particularly intense psychological and behavioral responses. As the stress on the dyadic relationship results in a stronger attachment between the parent and child, the child may need greater effort to individuate from the parent. A cultural drama seems to be unfolding in that in early adolescence, the parent attempts to retain the child within the framework of the dyadic relationship, while the child vigorously begins a journey to independence. The view that early adolescents still need focused attention from the adult is buttressed by the American cultural model of human development, which takes early adolescence as the most emotional period. Consequently, in early adolescence the parental ambivalence about the child's independence is most heightened.

I observed that the importance given to the adult–child dyad and its dynamics was a salient structural feature of the American school. The school was conceived of as an enlarged version of the nuclear family. However many children there were, the relationship between the adult and student was given a primary focus, leaving the peer dimension among students themselves largely incidental. This constituted both the strength and weakness of American education in school.

The emphasis on the dyad is an important source of strength, in that it strongly promotes individual attention to the student and thus fosters creativity, working together with the cultural ideas about self and individuality. At Lincoln, a "one-on-one" relationship with each student was persistently pursued by educators, though to varying degrees. The dyadic or one-on-one relationship was a pedagogical enactment of the ethnophilosophy of education that took the "individual" as the ultimate goal of education. Because individuals were "unique," composed of different innate abilities and motivations ("every kid is different"), there ought to be individualized teaching ("different ways of doing it"). In other words, the adult–student dyad was emblematic of the shared commitment to the "individual." The careful guidance of the adult in charge was noted in virtually all aspects of schooling, including the emotional socialization of self-discipline and creativity.

I presented self-discipline and creativity as a pair of pedagogical goals for personhood. Despite acting as a dual set of educational goals for every student, self-discipline and creativity were positioned at opposite ends of a spectrum of educational focus. With those students who were thought to need the training of self-discipline most, creativity development was least pursued. With those who presumably needed self-discipline training least, creativity development was most actively pursued. And the farther toward either end of the spectrum, the more faithfully the dyadic relationship was adhered to. This means that in the school, both "gifted and talented" and "emotional and behavioral disorder" students received more focused educational attention, making two poles of special education. At one end of the continuum, students in the EBD program were monitored closely to learn to behave, on the basis of a one-on-one relationship with the adult.[1] At the other end, students in the GT program were led carefully by the adult, through variously structured, intermediate steps, to express their creative self. The fact that the GT program was big and strong at Lincoln was very encouraging for its emphasis on creativity. Yet students in the Regular program, which was as big, generally were not given a tailored educational program for creativity development, but more disciplinary attention. That is, about half of the students in the school were not being as much benefited from one-on-one relationships and the emphasis on individuality, one of the most promising aspects of American education.

On the other hand, there were trade-offs of the emphasis on the dyadic relationship between the adult and student. These included under-recognition of the importance of learning from peers, including emulation, and under-appreciation of adolescents' social and emotional needs for peer relationships. In early adolescence, when the child begins to move farther out from the parent–child dyad, the peer group provides a social world in which adolescents try out quasi-adult roles in preparation for adulthood. It gives adolescents comradely support in a rapid individuation process from the parent. Further, an important dimension of learning, cognitive and otherwise, involves peers. However, the American fascination with individuality goes hand in hand with the anxiety about group conformity. The peer group is regarded as an archetypical source of group conformity. At Lincoln, many parents and educators were wary of the influence of the peer group, all the while ardent to develop self-agency and self-reliance. Interestingly, it seems that conformity to authority is taken as far less a problem than conformity to peers.

What is most troubling to me until this day is that the school day of the American junior high did not have any substantial time for meaningful peer interaction. It is not only that classmates change every hour, but also that there was no recess time for unstructured play. Concerns about control outweighed the adolescent need for casual yet significant interaction or just some rest from class work. Anyone in school notices the roughness of the hallway scenes during the passing time or lunch. Adults easily take it as a sign of "junior high being crazy." It may well be. But just imagine how adults would behave during a passing time with the schedule of the junior high. It seems that adults structure the life of adolescents in a way that such emotional reactions are inevitable, and then reproach them for their emotionality.

While there was a constant worry at Lincoln about "not enough individuation," positive peer influence on learning received a far less cultural articulation. Simply, there was no comparable concern about peer learning. If individuation was a global concern, though not always realized, peer learning was activated in limited circumstances. In many curricular and extracurricular activities, students participated in a pair or in small groups, and peer influence was effectively used for learning by many teachers. But doing a common project with peers was a privilege to be earned, along with opportunities for such projects themselves. Students in GT tended to be given more opportunities to work with peers for creative "fun" projects. The rationale was that they were self-disciplined enough and thus able to work together with peers for a common goal, without distracting one another. While group work in GT classes often involved more than two students, working in pairs was a more common form of group work in lower-ability classes. It was believed not only that students in lower-ability classes performed better when paired than alone, but also that they could not handle larger group work. Opportunities for the kind of work that necessitates a long-term engagement in peer interaction, in which work and play merge, were rather exclusively given to students in higher-ability groups, or students with middle-class backgrounds in the present politics of social class and academic ability grouping in school.

Other than the effects of peer cooperation on specific goals, peer influence in a broader and more inclusive sense was not well recognized by educators at Lincoln; it was recognized to a far lesser degree in comparison with the institutionalization of peer influence in Korean schools. I will take the example of the school concert to highlight the difference in cultural emphasis. When I was observing a concert at Lincoln one evening, I came to naturally compare the event with a similar one in Korean junior high schools. A marked difference lay in which kind of relationship, dyadic or peer, was given the organizing role of the event: the dyadic relationship in American schools and the peer relationship in Korean schools.

In American schools, the concert is an event primarily intended as a presentation to the parents. It is usually held in the evening, so that parents can come to see it. At the evening concert at Lincoln, the music teacher would compliment each band or choir for its achievements, asking applause for recognition from parents and other family members. There the significance of the adult–child dyad is theatrically presented: the teacher as the delegate of the parent now pays his due respect to the primordial dyad of the parent and child, by presenting what has been accomplished through the entrusted guidance of the child. By comparison, group contests are more common in Korean junior high schools than individual band or choir presentations. In the contests, the homeroom class usually becomes a unit of presentation and every student participates, competing with other homeroom classes. All homeroom classes practically do the same kind of presentation with a different repertoire, and the rest of the students watch their peers perform, for which homeroom does better. Peers comprise the main audience, and it is indeed perceived that the event is to show off to one's peers. If there is a special event, it is often the case that the entire student body is involved or targeted at least as an audience.

I observed that American schools provided parents with more opportunities for their involvement in school, evening concerts being one example, whereas in Korean schools, parents are not routinely invited to school events.[2] Accordingly, American parents seemed to feel it easier to visit their child's school. The level of parental involvement was one of the many aspects of American schooling that I appreciated. I posit that because in the United

States, the school is conceived of as doing what is traditionally done by the family (more precisely, the parent), communication between the educator and the parent is given a greater significance. This is certainly a strength of American schooling. Yet the relative lack of attention to peer learning concerned me very much. To the evening concert, other students are not invited. At Lincoln, students were allowed to come only if they were accompanied by their parents or other adults. In my observation, there were few activities that were designed for presenting to peers. Even the most exciting works by students, such as History Day projects, passed unobserved by many other students.

The fact that other students were not part of those special events felt so bothersome to me that the otherwise excellent events seemed to lack something very important. Most of all, I missed seeing student faces amused by and attuned to the rhythms and tempos from the stage, at times playfully responding to the peer performers. Simply put, what I missed for students was "having fun with friends" in a school activity. If they had been invited, they would have had not only enjoyment but a great opportunity for learning from their peers. This kind of learning may not have immediate or concrete outcomes, but is likely to have long-term and diffused effects on student performance.

In the American conception, peers are mainly associated with social and emotional dimensions of adolescent life, which are, by implication, non-academic and thus non-school. This perception is yet another example of the dichotomy between cognition and emotion. With regard to peers, the dichotomy is expressed as "work" vs. "play." Interactions with peers are aligned somewhat exclusively with play, while work is to be done for the most part under adult guidance. As pointed out earlier, peer interactions are also closely associated with group conformity, which certainly evokes negative feelings in the American mind, as in the phrasing "peer pressure." I understand that in this society, there are ample sources of negative peer influence, against which adults are right to be cautious. Yet to bestow upon peer influence an overall suspicion is not helpful; it has much too great a potential for enhancing healthy adolescent development.

For a school to be a community of learning, the peer dimension needs to be given more attention. From the student's point of view, peers may give more reasons to go to school than, say, teachers. I do not claim that American schools need to foster or institutionalize peer relations in the way Korean schools do. In my observation, American junior high school had its own ways of encouraging positive peer relationships. I will review two examples in this light, one from support work and the other from classroom teaching. Of many kinds of support work, group counseling was the one that explicitly relied on and promoted peer learning. The adult purposefully organized and coordinated peer interactions, clearly recognizing that not only the relationship between the counselor and students, but also the ones among students were crucial to building a healthy community of learning. It was not that he or she did not take an active role as an adult and counselor. Rather, part of his or her role as an adult in the setting was to connect students with each other as well as to himself or herself. Students were relaxed, lively, supportive, and responsive to others. The group sessions induced the kind of social atmosphere and learning opportunities for students not possible in one-on-one sessions.

The other example that showed the effects of positive peer influence is group projects in GT classes. Many students who participated in a long-term and challenging group project indicated that peer involvement was a crucial factor in their motivation and thus achievement. In the course of the project, they could build a community of learning in which work and play did not separate. Despite the cultural myth of the creative lone individual, these students attested to the importance of peer learning for creativity.

A constant source of resentment among American teachers was that they could not pay enough individual attention due to more than optimal numbers of students. Yet the adult and student dyad may not always be effective. Or if the classroom reality does not match the cultural ideal of a one-on-one relationship, it may give opportunities for creativity in organizing instructions in alternative ways. I reason that American classrooms would benefit from taking peer learning more seriously. To make a school or classroom a community of learning, a community in its genuine sense, the peer relationship is to be included, not as a subsidiary but as an indispensable element of it. I repeatedly point out that the peer relationship is a building block of the learning community, as critical as the adult–student relationship. The dichotomy between emotion and cognition, play and work, socialization and education is misleading and futile for the development of the whole person.

My take on the question of adolescent emotionality in this book was what would be its possible cultural factors in American society. The psychophysiology of adolescent development is undoubtedly a key factor in the emotional and behavioral characteristics of adolescents. Yet the psychophysiology itself is a biocultural outcome. The bodily and psychological process takes place only within a specific social and cultural process, so that it is pointless to assume either one as separated from the other. In present-day America, the biological model is prevailing and powerful. This can mean less insight into the cultural context of adolescent development.

In the two-year span of my fieldwork at Lincoln, there was a particular period of time that seemed to perfectly fit the image of crazy junior high students. It was several days until the end of the school year for the eighth graders. Dramatic emotional displays seemed to be the currency in the school during the final days. In particular, the passing times in the hallways were chaotic, with loud laughter, shouting, rough play, or hugging. Then on the last day of school, the emotional drama would culminate in a curiously sad tone. That day, it seemed that a translucent curtain of the blues draped over them. They still showed signature hyperactivity, but did not hide tracks of melancholy. Some girls were tearful, saying bye to friends. Boys looked tired, either alone or hanging around in groups.

This emotional exhibition came as little surprise to me after I learned that there would be no graduation ceremony for the outgoing eighth graders. I deeply resented the fact that no ritual was given to the graduates of junior high. It was as if junior high was too insignificant to conclude in a ritual. Rituals structure an otherwise undistinguished flow of time into distinctive segments and give a sense of significance to each one (Leach 1966). They allow participants to reflect on the course of a given event or life stage, and to have a closure to move on. A critical function of ritual concerns emotion. The dramaturgical convention of a ritual provides an affective channel through which subjective feelings about the event are reviewed and expressed (Turner 1974). I wished that the eighth graders were given a ritual, so that they could look back at their experiences of junior high, at a reflective distance and in relation to other members of the school community, peers and adults.

This absence of a graduation ceremony and the unstructured emotional displays by students were telling of both the marginality and emotionality of early adolescents. I think that the junior high school period represents a lapse in public consciousness about adolescence. Adults seem to act more as spectators of presumably the most dramatic stage of human life, while they pay serious and active attention to the high school years. It is as though because early adolescents are overridden by emotions, it is better to wait until they recover their rationality or return from their "brain vacation." Adults do not seem to feel capable of dealing with emotions. In the meantime, they work hard to reinstall the "brain" in those emotional adolescents.

My suspicion is that the adults' own ambivalence toward emotion is strongly reflected in their attitude toward adolescent emotionality. To instill rationality, as argued earlier, the adult–child dyad is upheld, and the child's peer relation-ship remains largely subordinated to the dyadic relationship. I wonder whether some features of peer culture in early adolescence may indicate that adolescents need more structural attention for peer relationships. By structural attention, I do not mean more adult control over peer interactions, but providing more settings in which the adult role is inconspicuous and children take initiatives in building their own community of peers. Adolescents certainly need to try out community-building skills without unnecessary intervention from adults. And that is the skill that is most needed in adulthood.

The dyadic relationship is essentially hierarchical, so that when it accom-panies close and institutionalized supervision over children, as it often does in schools, negative emotional and behavioral responses may result. The cliquish-ness of peer groups in the junior high years may speak to adolescents' need for intimacy among themselves. Yet even the school, where opportunities for friendship are most abundant, does not provide a stable setting for a long-term peer relationship. The worry about not making friends easily comes true. In this cultural environment, it would still take the most social child much effort to make and maintain friends, not to mention the less social.

I argue that the observed emotionality of early adolescents may be in part a response to the intensive, adult-centered socialization for rationality. In gen-eral, the adolescent peer group may represent an anti-structure against the struc-ture of the adult–child dyad. The stronger the structure is, the more rebellious the anti-structure gets. Just as the lack of a proper structure (e.g., graduation ceremony) can bring about unstructured displays of emotions, the lack of a secure and general structure for peer relationships may lead some adolescents to be more readily drawn to destructive aspects of peer culture. Granted that early adolescents are emotionally vulnerable, it should mean that they need more caring than controlling. The societal cries about the emotionality of early adolescents, I am afraid, come from the concern for managing, rather than listening to, the adolescent heart. To listen better, we need to realize that emotion also constitutes our cherished reason. To control emotion is good. But to appreciate the blessings of emotion is even better.

Finally, I want to address the issue of multicultural education in regards to emotional style. I make a strong case that in urban schools, multicultural education needs to be strengthened, and without seriously considering the impacts of emotion and emotional style on schooling, it cannot be a success. Much of the difficulty urban schools are facing centers on the issues of emo-tion. There are important differences in the display rules of emotion and thus rules of interpersonal interaction between educators with largely European middle-class backgrounds and students of different racial, ethnic, and social class backgrounds. At Lincoln, the educators' heavy emphasis on emotional control showed the hegemonic status of the Euro-American middle-class emotional style in the school. Students who received disciplinary attention were often from working-class, minority families. Those with a different emotional style became subject to intensive socialization into the middle-class style of emotion management, often without much success.

Throughout my fieldwork, I was particularly concerned about pointed disciplinary attention toward many Afro-American students. In general, Afro-American students with working-class backgrounds showed a much higher degree of emotional expression, both positive and negative. Because their emotional exhibition was perceived to be "loud," that is, uncontrolled, even positive expressions were not well received. When the "loud" exhibition was possibly a sign of negative emotions, such as anger, it evoked deep concern, if not fear, in adults, as to whether it was going to result in violence. In contemporary America, a connection seems to be made too easily between being Afro-American and being violent. But what about the positive aspects of their emotionality? Many proud features of American culture, such as music and literature, are owed to the richness of the Afro-American community in their experiences and expressions of emotion.

I do not advocate the kind of multicultural education that, by exaggerating cultural differences, seems to widen a social and cultural distance and thus further strengthen the present hierarchy in the politics of class, race, and ethnicity. Nor do I argue that minority students do not need the socialization of the middle-class emotional style altogether. To be able to succeed in mainstream American society, where becoming American equals becoming middle class, students of any background ought to learn to be versed in or familiar with the middle-class norms of interpersonal relations. Yet skills and loving care are in order here, for at stake is the psychological integrity of the learner. I will speak from my own learning experiences of American society. As I revealed in the Prologue, because of my own personal orientation toward certain aspects of individualism, I was rapidly socialized into the middle-class world of individualism. However, it took me some time and painful reflection that my own emotional sensitivity was not being accounted for by the middle-class model of emotion. And it took much courage to finally recognize and affirm my own emotions. For minority students, especially Afro-American students growing up in poverty, a critical task of educators is to guide them to face the duality of their social reality and learn to live in both worlds, without compromising their integrity. This challenging task calls simultaneously for tolerance for different emotional styles and education of common human values. Most of all, we need to recognize that a foundation of education comes from positive and creative potentials of emotion.

NOTES

Chapter 1

1   Mary Pipher (1995).

2   Distinguishing among the concepts of individual, self, and person, Grace Harris (1989) viewed the individual as a member of humankind, the self as the locus of experience, and the person as the agent-in-society (see also Morris 1994). However, the three concepts are much related and thus often result in conceptual confusions (see Spiro 1993 in his response to Markus and Kitayama 1991; for fuller discussions of the concept of person, see Carrithers et al. 1985). Much of the difficulty comes from the fact that "individual" is a cultural category of person in the West. J. S. La Fontaine therefore observed, "for Western Europeans the distinction between the individual and person is hard to make" (1985: 125). Likewise "self," as culturally constructed in the West, refers to more than a human being's self-awareness, which is universal. In this book, I show that the concepts of self and individual are deeply interrelated with the notion of person in the American discourse of individualism.

3   The phrase comes from the French reformer Alexis de Tocqueville, who observed early nineteenth-century American society and identified American "habits of the heart" as individualism (Tocqueville 1945 [1835–1840]). He saw that in the new republic, individualism prevailed as a main effect of the equality of democratic conditions (for other historical observations of early American society, see Chevalier 1961 [1838]; Crevecoeur 1981 [1782]). Many later writers have also singled out individualism as a key element of the American ethos (e.g., Bellah et al 1996 [1985]; Du Bois 1955; Gorer 1964 [1948]; Hsu 1972; Kluckhohn 1951; Lipset 1963, 1997; Mead 1965 [1942]; Potter 1967 [1962]; Riesman et al. 1950; Spindler and Spindler 1983; Varenne 1977; Wolfe 1998).

4   I look at the junction of social class, race, and ethnicity, primarily focusing on social class. I agree with Sherry Ortner (1991: 164) that "class is central to American social life, but it is rarely spoken [about] in its own right." According to her, the class category is represented through or displaced by other categories of social difference, most often race and ethnicity. In this book, which examines the role of the middle-class ideology in education, the class dimension, in its crisscrossing with race and ethnicity, is given more emphasis.

5   "United States." *Encyclopedia Britannica*, 2005.

Chapter 2

1.   The Humanities specialty was intended to offer an interdisciplinary approach to English and social studies. But in practice it served a different ability group, the one between the GT and Regular programs (for a discussion of the three programs at Lincoln, see the section on 'Ability Grouping and Emotional Control' in chapter 5).

2.   During my fieldwork, Lincoln was hiring an administrative intern for its second assistant principalship as a means of saving the personnel cost, as the salary for an intern was considerably lower than the one for an assistant principal. However, in the school, the administrative intern had authority as an administrator, if not fully as an assistant principal.

3.   In addition to the regular staff, there were four educational assistants (three in the special education department and one in the English Language Learner [ELL] department), two hall monitors, and one security guard. Several others routinely visited the school, including intern social workers, a psychologist, a speech therapist, and a police officer.

Chapter 3

1.   For a similar observation of the American classroom in comparison with the German one, see Spindler and Spindler 1987.

2.   Some educators were critical of the popular view of early adolescents as emotional and potentially dangerous. For example, Ms. Ingold, an English teacher in her fifties, commented, "There is prejudice against teens. People are afraid that they don't understand teenagers. They think my job is terrible, because teens are difficult. No, they are not. They are wonderful."

3.   In South Korea, junior high schools run seventh through ninth, high schools tenth through twelvth grades.

4.   By "fashion judge," she meant someone who was critical of how others dress.

5.   When examining the nature of the relationship between folk and expert theories of emotion, the linguist Zoltan Kovecses asks "whether and how the people who create our expert theories of emotion can free themselves from the folk theories that they obviously share with other members of their culture (in their 'role' as lay people)" (Kovecses 2000: 114). According to him, there can be three kinds of relationship: first, expert theories derive directly from the folk model. That is, the folk model gives rise to the expert theory. Second, the existence of particular metaphors in the folk model lends intuitive appeal to or motivates the corresponding scientific theories. Third, the expert theory gives rise to a pervasive metaphor in the ordinary conceptual system. In the case of the American conception of the psychology of early adolescence, the folk model and expert theory are closely linked with and influencing each other, making it difficult to discern the exact nature of the relationship between them.

Chapter 4

1.   I suspect that she could not recall the fourth set correctly because the two poles in the fourth set were not as readily contrasted in terms of whether or not internal agency was involved.

Although she was attempting to explain what MBTI could mean regarding learning, her own perspective distorted her presentation.

2   It was considered that the level of abstract thinking mattered most in math, so that math classes were "the one[s] really tracked" through placement exams at the beginning of seventh grade.

3   Students at risk are those who were academically and/or socially at the margin of the school, often experiencing truancy, depression, or chemical health issues.

4   At the other end of the continuum, there were "gifted and talented" students for whom the adult–student dyad was deemed most necessary and desirable.

5   The Child Study Team consists of the assistant principal and professionals for special education, including special education teachers, psychologist, speech therapist, and nurse. On special occasions regarding important decision making, the team included district personnel.

6   That EBD had the lowest teacher–student ratio among the different programs at Lincoln was revealing of the emphasis on the adult–student dyad in the program.

7   IEP is designed for each student in the special education program.

Chapter 5

1   *Lincoln Reality* was the monthly newspaper of the school put out by students in the journalism class. The poem quoted from an old issue was written by an anonymous writer.

2   Here I am referring only to the ethnopsychological conception of emotion shared by educators at Lincoln. The educators, teachers especially, did not de facto hold firmly to the conception. They actively utilized emotion in their educational practices, perhaps intuitively and from their teaching experiences, aware that learning fundamentally involved emotion. Chapter 6 shows that some of the most creative pedagogical routines in the school were the ones relying on deep emotional experience.

3   "Basic emotions" refer to those emotions that are universal and innate. Researchers do not agree on how many basic emotions there are, but a consensus is that they include joy, distress, anger, fear, surprise, and disgust (Evans 2001: 6; for more on basic emotions, see Ekman 1992). "Higher cognitive emotions" are thought to have evolved later than "basic emotions," upon the expansion of the neocortex, and include love, guilt, shame, embarrassment, pride, envy, and jealousy (for discussions of higher cognitive emotions, see Frank 1988; Griffiths 1997).

4   For critiques of the folk view of emotion, see Levy 1984; Lutz 1988; Solomon 1984.

5   Stearns maintains that not only emotional expression but also subjective experience itself has been affected by the emphasis on emotional control. Arlie Hochschild, in her study on flight attendants to whom emotional management is a central job skill, also argues that continuous effort for emotional control affects the very capacity to feel (1983: 21).

6   The school district newly mandated that every school have a site council consisting of school staff, parents, and students, to provide a communication channel for all the parties concerned for the goal of school improvement.

[7] In the year of 1999–2000, for generic groups, there were seven girls groups and one boys group. For purpose-specific groups, there were five anger management groups, one family change group, one grief group, one concerned teens group, and two chemical health groups. The family change group was for students whose parents had gone or were going through divorce, the concerned teens group for those whose parents or other family members were dealing with chemical health issues, and the grief group for those who experienced a death of someone close to them.

[8] Lakoff and Kovecses find that various metaphors of anger converge on a certain prototypical cognitive model of anger, which can be conceived of as a scenario with a number of stages. The prototypical scenario consists of five stages: Offending Event, Anger, Attempt at Control, Loss of Control, and Act of Retribution (Lakoff 1987: 397–398).

[9] What the principal said to Khoua that morning is not known, but it would have been a warning against such clothing.

[10] According to Thao Pang, that morning Bill Meyer came up to the classroom to talk to Khoua about his clothing. It's more likely that Khoua was not sent down but was visited by the principal.

[11] Behind these two conflicting views of emotion lies a folk opposition between agency (or free will) and the psychophysiology of the body. Needless to say, the opposition is also between reason and emotion, which is deeply rooted in the dualism of mind and body.

[12] My interest here is in the folk conception of emotion expressed in the medication of ADHD and depression, not in the physiological nature of them as medical conditions. The discussion of the effects of medication for ADHD and depression is also beyond the scope of my inquiry.

[13] It may be recalled that in Peter's case too, his EBD teacher related his behavioral problems to his having stopped medication for ADHD (see chapter 4).

[14] For the gender difference in depression, see, for example, Petersen et al. 1991, and for the one in ADHD, see Sciutto et al. 2004.

Chapter 6

[1] The standardized college entrance exam in South Korea was very competitive, and a national curriculum was followed in schools when I was teaching in junior high during the early 1990s. Educational reforms have been underway to improve the situation, especially to foster creativity in students. But the competition for college entrance makes any substantial changes difficult.

[2] These titles were not used by the teachers, but the writing process was organized according to the four stages.

[3] The History Day contest had four divisions (paper, performance, poster, video/slide show) at many levels of competition, from the schoolwide contest up to the nationwide final, following the national standards and yearly theme. Participation in the History Day was an elective for English in the GT program, so that students who chose not to do a History Day project were assigned alternative projects. The American Artist Project was the seventh-grade alternative, while for eighth graders, science or world geography projects were given

as alternatives. Both the History Day and alternative projects were profoundly interdisciplinary, for which artistic and intellectual creativity were essential.

[4] Those who won at the school level spent more time in preparation for the next level competition. For students who were selected to compete at the national level in Washington, D.C., the entire second semester was devoted to the project.

Chapter 7

[1] The Learning Disability (LD) program also utilized focused dyadic attention to a similar degree.

[2] At present, Korean schools seem to be in an unproductive competition with after-school cram programs. Multiple factors are creating the overheated educational marketplace in Korea, but I speculate that mistrust of schools by middle-class parents is a significant one. In my view, the mistrust has come in part from the lack of communication channels with the school, while their desire for involvement has been greatly increasing.

BIBLIOGRAPHY

Bateson, Gregory. 1965 [1958]. *Naven*. Stanford, CA: Stanford University Press.

———. 1976. *Steps to an Ecology of Mind: Collected Essays in Anthropology, Psychiatry, Evolution, and Epistemology*. San Francisco: Chandler Publishing Company.

Beeman, William I. 1986. Freedom to Choose: Symbols and Values in American Advertising. In *Symbolizing America*, ed. Herve Varenne, 52–65. Lincoln: University of Nebraska Press.

Bellah, Robert N., R. Madsen, W. Sullivan, A. Swidler, and S. Tipton. 1996 [1985]. *Habits of the Heart: Individualism and Commitment in American Life*. Updated Edition. Berkeley: University of California Press.

Blos, Peter. 1962. *On Adolescence: A Psychoanalytic Interpretation*. New York: Free Press.

———. 1967. The Second Individuation Process of Adolescence. *The Psychoanalytic Study of the Child* 22: 162–186.

———. 1979. *The Adolescent Passage: Developmental Issues*. New York: International Universities Press.

Bourdieu, Pierre. 1977. *Outline of a Theory of Practice*. Cambridge: Cambridge University Press.

Bourdieu, Pierre and J. C. Passeron. 1977. *Reproduction in Education, Society and Culture*. London: Sage.

Briggs, Jean L. 1970. *Never in Anger: Portrait of an Eskimo Family*. Cambridge, MA: Harvard University Press.

Carrithers, Michael, Steven Collins, and Steven Lukes, eds. 1985. *The Category of the Person: Anthropology, Philosophy, History*. New York: Cambridge University Press.

Chevalier, Michael. 1961 [1838]. *Society, Manners, and Politics in the United States: Letters on North America*. New York: Anchor Books.

Cremin, Lawrence A. 1964. *The Transformation of the School: Progressivism in American Education 1876–1957*. New York: Vintage Books.

Crevecoeur, J. Hector St. John de. 1981 [1782]. *Letters from an American Farmer*. New York: Penguin Books.

Damasio, Antonio R. 1994. *Descartes' Error: Emotion, Reason, and the Human Brain*. New York: Putnam.

Devereux, George. 1979. Fantasy and Symbol as Dimension of Reality. In *Fantasy and Symbol*, ed. R. H. Hook, 19–31. New York: Academic Press.

Diamond, Stanley. 1971. Epilogue. In *Anthropological Perspectives on Education*, ed. M. Wax, S. Diamond, and F. Gearing, 300–306. New York: Basic Books.

Doise, Willem and Gabriel Mugny. 1984. *The Social Development of the Intellect*. Oxford: Pergamon Press.

Du Bois, Cora A. 1955. The Dominant Value Profile of American Culture. *American Anthropologist* 57: 1232–1239.

Dumont, Louis. 1985. Modified View of Our Origins: The Christian Beginnings of Modern Individualism. In *Category of the Person*, ed. Michael Carrithers, Steven Collins, and Steven Lukes, 93–122. Cambridge: Cambridge University Press.

———. 1986. *Essays on Individualism: Modern Ideology in Anthropological Perspective*. Chicago: University of Chicago Press.

Ekman, Paul. 1992. An Argument for Basic Emotions. *Cognition and Emotion* 6: 169–200.

Erikson, Erik H. 1993 [1950]. *Childhood and Society*. New York: Norton.

Evans, Dylan. 2001. *Emotion: The Science of Sentiment*. New York: Oxford University Press.

Evans, Grace. 1988. Those Loud Black Girls. In *Learning to Lose: Sexism and Education*, ed. Dale Spender and Elizabeth Sarah, 183–190. London: Women's Press.

Finn, Janet L. 2001. Text and Turbulence: Representing Adolescence as Pathology in the Human Services. *Childhood* 8 (2): 167–191.

Fordham, Signithia. 1993. "Those Loud Black Girls": (Black) Women, Silence, and Gender "Passing" in the Academy. *Anthropology and Education Quarterly* 24 (1): 3–32.

Forgas, Joseph P. 2000. *Feeling and Thinking: The Role of Affect in Social Cognition*. New York: Cambridge University Press.

Frank, Robert. 1988. *Passions within Reason: The Strategic Role of the Emotions*. New York: Norton.

Freud, Anna. 1946. *The Ego and the Mechanisms of Defense*. New York: International Universities Press.

———. 1958. Adolescence. *The Psychoanalytic Study of the Child* 13: 255–278.

———. 1965. *Normality and Pathology in Childhood*. New York: International Universities Press.

Geertz, Clifford. 1975. On the Nature of Anthropological Understanding. *American Scientist* 63: 47–53.

Geertz, Hildred. 1961. *The Javanese Family: A Study of Kinship and Socialization*. New York: Free Press.

Goleman, Daniel. 1997. *Emotional Intelligence*. New York: Bantam Books.

Gorer, Geoffrey. 1964 [1948]. *The American People: A Study in National Character*. Revised Edition. New York: W. W. Norton.

Greenfield, Patricia and Jean Lave. 1982. Cognitive Aspects of Informal Education. In *Cultural Perspectives on Child Development*, ed. Daniel Wagner and Harold W. Stevenson, 181–207. New York: W. H. Freeman & Co.

Griffiths, Paul. 1997. *What Emotions Really Are: The Problem of Psychological Categories*. Chicago: University of Chicago Press.

Hall, G. Stanley. 1916 [1904]. *Adolescence: Its Psychology and Its Relation to Physiology, Anthropology, Sociology, Sex, Crime, Religion, and Education*. New York: Appleton.

Handler, Richard and Daniel A. Segal. 1985. Hierarchies of Choice: The Social Construction of Rank in Jane Austen. *American Ethnologist* 12 (4): 691–706.

Harkness, Sara, Charles M. Super, and Constance H. Keefer. 1992. Learning to Be an American Parent: How Cultural Models Gain Directive Force. In *Human Motives and Cultural Models*, ed. Roy D'Andrade and Claudia Strauss, 163–178. New York: Cambridge University Press.

Harris, Grace G. 1989. Concepts of Individual, Self, and Person in Description and Analysis. *American Anthropologist* 91: 599–612.

Hart, C. W. M. 1987 [1955]. Contrasts between Prepubertal and Postpubertal Education. In *Education and Cultural Process*, Second Edition, ed. George Spindler, 359–377. Illinois: Waveland Press.

Heelas, Paul and Andrew Lock, eds. 1981. *Indigenous Psychologies: The Anthropology of the Self*. New York: Academic.

Herdt, Gilbert H. 1982. Sambia Nosebleeding Rites and Male Proximity to Women. *Ethos* 10: 189–231.

Hinde, Robert, Anne-Nelly Perret-Clermont, and Joan Stevenson-Hinde, eds. 1985. *Social Relationships and Cognitive Development*. Oxford: Clarendon Press.

Hochschild, Arlie Russell. 1983. *The Managed Heart: Commercialization of Human Feeling*. California: University of California Press.

Hollan, Douglas. 2000. Constructivist Models of Mind, Contemporary Psychoanalysis, and the Development of Culture Theory. *American Anthropologist* 102 (3): 538–550.

Hsu, Francis L. K. 1972. American Core Values and National Character. In *Psychological Anthropology*, ed. Francis L. K. Hsu. Cambridge, MA: Schenkman.

Kett, Joseph F. 1977. *Rites of Passage: Adolescence in America 1970 to the Present*. New York: Basic Books.

Kluckhohn, Clyde. 1951. Values and Value-Orientations in the Theory of Action. In *Toward a General Theory of Action*, ed. Talcott Parsons and Edward Shils, 388–433. Cambridge, MA: Harvard University Press.

Kovecses, Zoltan. 1986. *Metaphors of Anger, Pride, and Love: A Lexical Approach to the Structure of Concepts*. Amsterdam: John Benjamins.

———. 1995. Metaphor and the Folk Understanding of Anger. In *Everyday Conceptions of Emotion*, ed. J. A. Russell, J.-M. Fernandez-Dols, A. S. R. Manstead, and J. C. Wellenkamp, 49–72. Dordrecht: Kluwer.

———. 2000. *Metaphor and Emotion: Language, Culture, and Body in Human Feeling*. New York: Cambridge University Press.

La Fontaine, Jean S. 1985. Person and Individual: Some Anthropological Reflections. In *The Category of the Person: Anthropology, Philosophy, History*, ed. M. Carrithers, S. Collins, and S. Lukes, 123–140. New York: Cambridge University Press.

Lakoff, George. 1987. *Women, Fire, and Dangerous Things: What Categories Reveal about the Mind*. Chicago: University of Chicago Press.

Lakoff, George and Zoltan Kovecses. 1987. The Cognitive Model of Anger Inherent in American English. In *Cultural Models in Language and Thought*, ed. D. Holland and N. Quinn, 195–221. New York: Cambridge University Press.

Leach, Edmund. 1966. Two Essays concerning the Symbolic Representation of Time. In *Rethinking Anthropology*, 124–136. London: Athlone.

LeDoux, Joseph. 1998. *The Emotional Brain: The Mysterious Underpinnings of Emotional Life*. New York: Touchstone Book.

Levy, Robert I. 1984. Emotion, Knowing and Culture. In *Culture Theory: Essays on Mind, Self, and Emotion*, ed. R. A. Shweder and R. A. LeVine, 214–237. Cambridge: Cambridge University Press.

Lipset, Seymour Martin. 1963. *The First New Nation*. New York: Basic Books.

——. 1997. *American Exceptionalism: A Double Edged Sword*. New York: W. W. Norton.

Lukes, Steven. 1973. *Individualism*. Oxford: Basil Blackwell.

Lutz, Catherine A. 1983. Parental Goals, Ethnopsychology, and the Development of Emotional Meaning. *Ethos* 11: 246–262.

——. 1988. *Unnatural Emotions: Everyday Sentiments on a Micronesian Atoll and Their Challenge to Western Theory*. Chicago: University of Chicago Press.

Markus, Hazel Rose and Shinobu Kitayama. 1991. Culture and the Self: Implications for Cognition, Emotion, and Motivation. *Psychological Review* 98 (2): 224–253.

Mauss, Marcel. 1985 [1950]. A Category of the Human Mind: The Notion of Person; The Notion of Self. In *The Category of the Person: Anthropology, Philosophy, History*, ed. M. Carrithers, S. Collins, and S. Lukes, 1–25. Cambridge: Cambridge University Press.

Mead, Margaret. 1961 [1928]. *Coming of Age in Samoa: A Psychological Study of Primitive Youth for Western Civilization*. New York: William Morrow.

——. 1965 [1942]. *And Keep Your Powder Dry: An Anthropologist Looks at America*. New York: William Morrow and Company.

Montuori, Alfonso and Ronald E. Purser. 1995. Deconstructing the Lone Genius Myth: Toward a Contextual View of Creativity. *Journal of Humanistic Psychology* 35 (3): 69–112.

Morris, Brian. 1994. *Anthropology of Self: The Individual in Cultural Perspective*. London: Pluto.

Myers, Isabel Briggs and Mary H. McCaulley. 1985 [1962]. *Manual: A Guide to the Development and Use of the Myers-Briggs Type Indicator*. Palo Alto, CA: Consulting Psychologists Press.

Offer, Daniel and Judith Offer. 1975. *From Teenage to Young Manhood: A Psychological Study*. New York: Basic Books.

Offer, Daniel, Eric Ostrov, and Kenneth Howard. 1981. *The Adolescent: A Psychological Self-Portrait*. New York: Basic Books.

Offer, D. and M. Sabshin. 1984. Adolescence: Empirical Perspectives. In *Normality and the Life Cycle*, ed. D. Offer and M. Sabshin, 76–107. New York: Basic Books.

Ortner, Sherry B. 1991. Reading America: Preliminary Notes on Class and Culture. In *Recapturing Anthropology: Working in the Present*, ed. Richard Fox, 163–189. Santa Fe: School of American Research Press.

Petersen, A. C., P. A. Sarigiani, and R. E. Kennedy. 1991. Adolescent Depression: Why More Girls? *Journal of Youth and Adolescence* 20: 247–271.

Pipher, Mary. 1995. *Reviving Ophelia: Saving the Selves of Adolescent Girls*. New York: Ballantine Books.

Potter, David M. 1967 [1962]. The Quest for the National Character. In *Individualism and Conformity in the American Character*, ed. Richard Rapson, 59–73. Boston: D. C. Heath & Company.

Rabichow, H. G. and M. D. Sklansky. 1980. *Effective Counseling of Adolescents*. Chicago: Follett Publishing Co.

Riesman, David, Nathan Glazer, and Reuel Denney. 1950. *The Lonely Crowd: A Study of the Changing American Character*. New Haven, CT: Yale University Press.

Rosaldo, Michelle Z. 1984. Toward an Anthropology of Self and Feeling. In *Culture Theory: Essays on Mind, Self, and Emotion*, ed. Richard A. Shweder and Robert A. LeVine, 137–157. Cambridge: Cambridge University Press.

Sampson, Edward E. 1988. The Debate on Individualism: Indigenous Psychologies of the Individual and Their Role in Personal and Societal Functioning. *American Psychologist* 43 (1): 15–22.

Sanjek, Roger, ed. 1990. *Fieldnotes: The Makings of Anthropology*. Ithaca, NY: Cornell University Press.

Schachter, Stanley and Jerome E. Singer. 1962. Cognitive, Social and Physiological Determinents of Emotional State. *Psychological Review* 69 (5): 379–399.

Scheper-Hughes, Nancy and Margaret Lock. 1987. The Mindful Body: A Prolegomenon to Future Work in Medical Anthropology. *Medical Anthropology Quarterly* 1: 1–36.

Schlegel, Alice. 1973. The Adolescent Socialization of the Hopi Girl. *Ethnology* 12 (4): 449–462.

Schneider, David M. and Raymond T. Smith. 1978. *Class Differences in American Kinship*. Ann Arbor: University of Michigan Press.

Sciutto, Mark J., Cara J. Nolfi, and Carla Bluhm. 2004. Effects of Child Gender and Symptom Type on Referrals for ADHD by Elementary School Teachers. *Journal of Emotional and Behavioral Disorders* 12 (4): 247–253.

Shweder, Richard A. and Edmund J. Bourne. 1984. Does the Concept of Person Vary Cross-Culturally? In *Culture Theory: Essays on Mind, Self, and Emotion*, ed. R. Shweder and R. LeVine, 158–199. New York: Cambridge University Press.

Solomon, Robert C. 1984. Getting Angry: The Jamesian Theory of Emotion in Anthropology. In *Culture Theory: Essays on Mind, Self, and Emotion*, ed. R. Shweder and R. LeVine, 238–254. New York: Cambridge University Press.

Sommer, Barbara Baker. 1978. *Puberty and Adolescence*. New York: Oxford University Press.

Spindler, George D. and Louise Spindler. 1983. Anthropologists View American Culture. *Annual Review of Anthropology* 12: 49–78. Palo Alto, CA: Annual Reviews.

———. 1987. Cultural Dialogue and Schooling in Schoenhausen and Roseville: A Comparative Analysis. *Anthropology and Education Quarterly* 18 (1): 3–16.

Spiro, Melford. 1993. Is the Western Conception of the Self "Peculiar" within the Context of the World Cultures? *Ethos* 21 (2): 107–153.

Stearns, Carol Z. and Peter N. Stearns. 1986. *Anger: The Struggle for Emotional Control in America's History*. Chicago: University of Chicago Press.

———. eds. 1988. *Emotion and Social Change: Toward a New Psychohistory*. New York: Holmes & Meier.

Stearns, Peter N. 1994. *American Cool: Constructing a Twentieth-Century Emotional Style*. New York: New York University Press.

————. 1999. *Battleground of Desire: The Struggle for Self-Control in Modern America*. New York: New York University Press.

Strauss, Claudia. 1984. Beyond "Formal" versus "Informal" Education: Uses of Psychological Theory in Anthropological Research. *Ethos* 12 (3): 195–222.

Tobin, Joseph, David Wu, and Dana Davidson. 1989. *Preschool in Three Countries: Japan, China and the United States*. New Haven, CT: Yale University Press.

Tocqueville, Alexis de. 1945 [1835–1840]. Democracy in America (Vols. I and II). New York: Alfred A. Knopf.

Turner, Victor. 1974. *The Ritual Process: Structure and Anti-Structure*. Harmondsworth, UK: Penguin.

Varenne, Herve. 1977. *Americans Together: Structured Diversity in a Midwestern Town*. New York: Teachers College Press.

Vygotsky, L. S. 1962. *Thought and Language*. Cambridge, MA: MIT Press.

Wellenkamp, Jane C. 1988. Notions of Grief and Catharsis among the Toraja. *American Ethnologist* 15: 486–500.

Wolfe, Alan. 1998. *One Nation After All: What Middle-Class Americans Really Think About*. New York: Viking.

Zajonc, Robert. 1980. Feeling and Thinking: Preferences Need No Inferences. *American Psychologist* 35: 151–175.

————. 1984. On the Primacy of Affect. *American Psychologist* 39: 117–123.

INDEX

AC SS Adolescent Cultures, School & Society

Joseph L. DeVitis & Linda Irwin-DeVitis
GENERAL EDITORS

As schools struggle to redefine and restructure themselves, they need to be cognizant of the new realities of adolescents. Thus, this series of monographs and textbooks is committed to depicting the variety of adolescent cultures that exist in today's post-industrial societies. It is intended to be a primarily qualitative research, practice, and policy series devoted to contextual interpretation and analysis that encompasses a broad range of interdisciplinary critique. In addition, this series will seek to provide a pragmatic, pro-active response to the current backlash of conservatism that continues to dominate political discourse, practice, and policy. This series seeks to address issues of curriculum theory and practice; multicultural education; aggression and violence; the media and arts; school dropouts; homeless and runaway youth; alienated youth; at-risk adolescent populations; family structures and parental involvement; and race, ethnicity, class, and gender studies.

Send proposals and manuscripts to the general editors at:

Joseph L. DeVitis & Linda Irwin-DeVitis
The John H. Lounsbury School of Education
Georgia College & State University
Campus Box 70
Milledgeville, GA 31061-0490

To order other books in this series, please contact our Customer Service Department at:

(800) 770-LANG (within the U.S.)
(212) 647-7706 (outside the U.S.)
(212) 647-7707 FAX

or browse online by series at:

WWW.PETERLANG.COM